Praise for *The Woman in the Mirror*

"Dr. Cynthia Bulik shows us the absurdities by which we live—worrying about body image, trying to match unrealistic standards, and beating ourselves up because we cannot achieve what we do not see as ludicrous and impossible. With her keen scientific intellect, comedic wit, and remarkable prose, she not only outlines the forces that helped us internalize these images but provides us with the skil needed to defeat those negative self-images and embrace the wor erful reality of who we are. For every woman who ever thought 'If c y I were . . .' And really, isn't that all of us?"

—**Deborah C. Beidel, Ph.D.,**
director of the doctoral program in
clinical psychology, University of Central Florida

"Bu practical advice—grounded in evidence-based research and cou d with the experience and wisdom of a woman, mother, teacher, and ician—give the reader an untethered look at the reality of hov h our biology and environment contribute to devastating eating ders and other problems with self-image. Brava!"

—**Chevese Turner, CEO, Binge Eating**
Disorder Association (BEDA)

"A erful book, written in a language that speaks to all . . . a seri nust read"

—**Lynn S. Grefe, president and CEO of the**
National Eating Disorders Association

The Woman in The Mirror

How to Stop Confusing What You *Look* Like with Who You *Are*

CYNTHIA M. BULIK, Ph.D.

BLOOMSBURY

LONDON · BERLIN · NEW YORK · SYDNEY

First published in Great Britain 2012

Bloomsbury Publishing, London, Berlin, New York and Sydney

50 Bedford Square, London WC1B 3DP

A CIP catalogue record for this book is available from the British Library

ISBN 978 1 4088 2804 5
10 9 8 7 6 5 4 3 2 1

Typeset by Westchester Book Group

Printed in Great Britain by Clays

MIX
Paper from
responsible sources
FSC® C018072
FSC
www.fsc.org

www.bloomsbury.com

If you are a woman, this book is dedicated to you.

Contents

DISCLAIMER

All matters regarding your health require medical supervision. This book applies my decades of experience as a psychologist, a woman, and a mother to the topic of self-esteem and body esteem in women. It is neither intended nor designed to replace the opinions of your health-care professional.

I have used my own clinical experience and have incorporated the personal stories of many patients, acquaintances, and family members to illustrate the principles outlined in this book. To protect their privacy I have used pseudonyms and, in some cases for clarity or convenience, combined experiences or commentaries into one character.

Introduction

We're never good enough, smart enough, pretty enough, tall enough, thin enough. If our skin is dark, we lighten it; if our hair is curly, we straighten it. We look in the mirror and say things to ourselves that we would never say to other people. We wound ourselves with our own words. Our self-insults aren't just about looks, although appearance might be the number-one target. Women are experiencing a self-esteem crisis. Even the ones who seem self-assured on the surface are often paralyzed by self-doubt in the privacy of their own thoughts. We doubt ourselves, undervalue ourselves, and second-guess ourselves, and much of this devaluation gets played out on the weight and physical-appearance battlefield. We think that if we were thinner, fitter, taller, less wrinkled, or more put together, we'd feel better about ourselves, be more powerful, be more lovable, and be more successful. So we try to fix what's ailing us on the inside with a diet, a nose job, implants, Botox, expensive antiwrinkle creams, and new shoes. We go to great lengths and expense to change our bodies and dress them up to fit some external notion of what's ideal. Yet for all the diets, cosmetics, and procedures, we are no happier with our bodies or ourselves.

Why does our inner struggle with identity and self-esteem translate directly to weight and appearance concerns? The primary reason is that our society has led us to completely conflate self-esteem and body esteem.

Self-esteem refers to how you think and feel about yourself

as a total package—your personality, your role in relationships, your accomplishments, your morals, your values—everything that contributes to who you are as a person in the world. Body esteem refers to how you think and feel about your body—your size, your shape, your hair, your features—all of those attributes that contribute to your physical appearance. If you are fortunate enough to have wrapped your head around this distinction and have managed miraculously to remain sheltered from modern society for your entire life, then you can successfully separate your self-esteem from your body esteem. But most of us have not been so fortunate. Whereas body esteem is supposed to be a minor component of self-esteem, in our society, body esteem often eclipses self-esteem and becomes the primary and sometimes only dimension on which women evaluate their self-worth. Even if they are successful businesswomen, wonderful mothers, Olympic athletes, scientists, or models, a bad hair day can bulldoze any positive thoughts about who they are, giving all the deciding power to how they look.

We're going to explore why and we're going to learn how to disentangle self-esteem from body esteem.

On the most fundamental level, body esteem is easier to deal with than self-esteem. Self-esteem includes so many intangible, abstract, and nonvisible factors. It is precisely because appearance is concrete, changeable, and visible that it's easier for us to focus on body esteem. It's easier to lose five pounds than to address a fundamental worry that you are not good enough. It's easier to pay fifty dollars for a fancy antiwrinkle cream than to have a long hard thought about aging. But these quick fixes are just Band-Aids. They might give you a brief boost: "I feel good in these shoes," or "I feel more assertive with my new breasts." But they don't address the core self-esteem issues that plague you.

Although the landscape for women has changed considerably since I was a young girl, women are still too often silenced by society. And even though society has changed, many of the warnings that were uttered when we were girls have not eroded with time. "Don't be too smart; don't be too loud; don't be too opinion-ated; don't eat too much in public; let the boys win." In fact, many of those internalized messages contribute to the continuous nega-tive self-talk that women and girls tell me is going on in their heads all the time. I hear this in my practice, in the workplace, and even in my daughters' schools. Look around you. Every time we see a picture of the Senate, the House, the Supreme Court, the astronauts, a meeting of world leaders, the Nobel Prize–win-ners, and even top chefs, they are overwhelmingly male. On some level, we are getting the implicit message that this is not our world. When we see our male colleagues making more money than we do for the same work, on some level we know that this is not our world. Since this is not our world, rather than acknowledging our ire and fighting for justice, instead we blame ourselves. "I'm not good enough." "I took time off to have children, so it's my fault." "I'm a bad negotiator." Rather than staying in the ring and putting up a good fight, women retreat and self-blame.

Psychologists call this behavior learned helplessness. If you expose a dog to electric shocks and teach her that there's nothing she can do to escape them, eventually she'll just give up trying to escape and sit down and endure the pain. It's an animal model of depression; the dogs look sad, dejected, and hopeless. So, un-able to escape being shocked, women retreat to the weight and appearance battlefield where we can at least have a sense of con-trol and experience some minor victories. Although that allows us to be seen, our voices are still not heard. Women don't spend so much time on weight and appearance because we are vain. We do it because it is the only venue in which we can fully express ourselves. The more we hide who we are, run from our opinions, and remain silent, the more we become weight ob-sessed, ping-ponging between starvation and overeating as we strive for the elusive thin ideal. Will we ever find the healthy and stable middle ground that allows us to eat well, be active, treat our bodies and minds with the respect they deserve, and allow our voices to be heard? How do we get out of this tortured cycle?

How do we finally allow self-esteem to become uncoupled from body esteem so that we and others can value us for who we are rather than how we look?

Part of the answer lies in recognizing and taking charge of the insidious negative self-talk that invades our thinking in childhood and persists into late adulthood. We get hints of this internal chatter when little girls say they should go on a diet or that they're not pretty enough. We hear it when our daughters doubt their ability to get into the college they dream of. We endlessly compare ourselves with other girls and women—whether real or Photoshopped. We rarely give ourselves compliments; we just constantly point out our flaws, our failures, and our shortcomings. We apologize for everything. "Sorry" seems to be women's favorite word, as if we don't have a right to be here. This constant negative chatter in our heads mirrors what is being said or implied about us in the outside world. We always fall short of the ideal woman who is portrayed as smart, thin, rich, a mother of four, the perfect partner, never tired, and able to bake cookies from scratch while preparing a briefing for tomorrow's court appearance.

These unwinnable comparisons feed into this uniquely female brain chatter that is akin to personalized torture. We insult ourselves with phrases we would never think of uttering to other people. Mean girls aren't just on the playground—they're inside our own heads. Negative self-talk about appearance generalizes to negative self-talk about other areas—competence, lovability, personality, and intelligence. What effect does this negative self-talk have on our outlook toward life, our self-esteem, our accomplishments, our relationships, and ultimately our children? How does the negative self-talk get there? Why are we so down on ourselves? How has self-denigration become such a defining feature of the modern woman?

In Part One, we cover the female life cycle—from birth to death—and explore how we feel about ourselves and our bodies at each age. We'll explore how society conflates body esteem and self-esteem and—with every available psychological, economic, and interpersonal tactic it can muster—ensures that we will never be at peace with our bodies, believing that there is always something we could and should strive to make better. Since body esteem and self-esteem are so often intertwined, no wonder our self-esteem suffers too.

We will learn how to separate body esteem from self-esteem. But it is not an easy task in our world. Recognizing and understanding all of the factors that contribute to women feeling badly about ourselves is a necessary first step in making this separation and taking control of all of the negative commentary that goes on in your head and chips away at both types of esteem. Revisiting the way these internal and external forces affect us across the lifespan will set the stage for you to identify and take control of your own internal self-talk, and it will help you mentor your daughters, nieces, granddaughters, and the women and men around you. In Part Two, I will give you the tools and exercises you need to do just this. After completing the second half of this book, you should be well on your way to separating your self-esteem from your body esteem and to treating yourself with the respect and admiration you deserve.

This book is for all women, regardless of income, size, shape, race, ethnicity, and age. Negative self-talk does not discriminate, and we all need help to ensure that we can experience positive, uplifting, and respectful internal dialogue so that our voice can be heard and we can make this our world too.

PART ONE

How We See Ourselves from Kindergarten to the Nursing Home

CHAPTER 1

From Elementary to Middle School: Loss of Identity

"What's a daughter? Just a reminder of the pain . . . a
younger version of oneself . . . who will do all the same
things, cry the same tears. I try to forget I have a daughter."
—Fiona "Fee" Cleary, *The Thorn Birds*

My first child was a boy. I love him with all my heart, but he is different than I am—starting with the anatomy! When I got pregnant with my second child, I knew she was going to be a girl. I dreamt that she was a girl; I felt in my bones that she was a girl. When the amnio results came back, it was just confirmation of what I knew—that she indeed had two X chromosomes and anatomical features that were familiar to mine. Even though I had known it instinctively, I was thrilled by the official news. As a woman, something about having a girl is truly magical. That single phrase—"It's a girl"—conjures up a kaleidoscope of images of what it means to be a girl and to be a woman raising a girl. Whether girls follow the path of pink bows, patent leathers, and Barbie dolls or scraped knees, tree houses, frogs, and lizards, at first they're invincible. They can be a princess, they can be Dora the Explorer, or they can be both. You marvel at their intense friendships, their creativity and imagination, their compassion, and their boundless energy. But then, far too early, the world starts chipping away at them in very subtle ways. As the late congressional representative Shirley Chisholm said, "The emotional, sexual, and psychological stereotyping of females begins when the doctor says, 'It's a girl.'"[1]

You notice that she stops raising her hand in class even when she knows the answer. You comfort her after she has been teased about her weight and you have to hold yourself back from going after the teasers. You hear the dreaded *"Mommy, does this make me look fat?"* and she refuses to take her towel off at the swimming pool. The transformation has begun. Your benevolent princess or fearless explorer has been broadsided by reality. All of those wonderful and magical images you had of raising a daughter shatter when reality slaps her in the little face.

Freud said "the first ego is a body ego." What he meant was that the first things we are aware of and respond to are basic biological bodily signals such as hunger, fullness, pooping, and pain. But these are hardwired signals related to survival in the world. As little children, we are granted a brief grace period when we blissfully enjoy the complete separation of body esteem and self-esteem. Maybe as toddlers, before we become aware of the fact that people make judgments based on appearance and weight, we can play, explore, fantasize, and revel in the experience of being human without reference to or awareness of others' evaluations of our physical appearance.

But something starts to happen—slowly and insidiously. Our mothers put bows in our hair and dress us in pretty dresses. Dad says, "You look pretty today." Grandparents take us clothes shopping and see outfits that have our favorite princesses on them and we want one too. Our peers start to talk about who is pretty and who is popular. Ever so gradually, we start to become aware of the external eye. The external eye is the lens that belongs to others and makes judgments about us based on our appearance—our skin color, our hair, our weight, our eyes, our size, our shape. That once-carefree nature becomes buried in self-consciousness. Awareness of the external eye and the development of self-consciousness mark the first step toward the inexorable intertwining of body esteem and self-esteem.

The Early Years: Princesses and Tomboys
Girls have rich fantasy lives and try on many identities in their formative years. In the safety of their own bedrooms, with their dress-up-clothes boxes and dolls, in the books they read and the

shows they watch, they are experimenting with the question "Who am I?" Whereas boys are often encouraged to "be all that you can be," girls still live in a world that focuses more on "be what you should be." Maybe you're old enough to remember the book *Nurse Nancy* from your childhood. If you are too young, this was a book about a very helpful girl who dressed up as a nurse and helped patch up the neighborhood boys when they scraped their knees playing ball or other manly games. But when things got tough, it was Dr. Dan who came to the rescue.

I loved that book when I was a little girl. My mother read it to me over and over again. It even came with colored Band-Aids! Thirty years later when I read my old tattered copy to my kids before they could read, I confess to having changed the words. I always read it as "Doctor Nancy" and "Nurse Dan." No disrespect at all to nurses, but I wanted my kids to know that girls could be doctors and boys could be nurses! My little secret got outed years later when we were packing boxes for a move and triaging my kids' old children's books. My daughter came across an old book she recognized vaguely, but it was called *Nurse Nancy*. She was puzzled. The pictures were just as she remembered, but she asked, "Mom, is there another book? This one is *Nurse Nancy*, but I remember you reading *Doctor Nancy* to us." She caught me, and got a good laugh out of my editorializing.

In these early years, no one has yet challenged little girls' notions about what they want to be when they grow up. At first when they are reading books and learning about life, they don't "see gender." Both boys and girls can be astronauts and both can be ballerinas. People let them have their little fantasies because they're still too young to "understand." I remember attending a preschool event with one of my daughters. She came home with a declaration that "she had found the boy with whom she wanted to have babies." Intrigued, I asked what it was about him that made him such a good prospect, and her choice had something to do with sharing, being nice, and having a very cool lunch box. I marveled at her definitiveness. She clearly believed she had the right to choose her man. She evaluated the important parameters and she made her choice. Two days later, she came home and just as definitively said this chap was no longer under consideration because he had knocked her tower of blocks down. She retaliated by knocking his down too. Just like that— you're a good guy, I like you; then you're off the list for behaving badly. If only it could stay that simple!

Soon the societal message about what is valued about girls and women starts to worm its way into their vulnerable minds. If you avoid television, the movies, magazines, the checkout counter at the grocery store, lunch boxes, peers, and if you make your own clothes and breakfast cereal, you might escape being brainwashed, but if you are exposed to any of those things, your chances of being inoculated against the appearance culture are low.

If you consider the stereotypes that engross our daughters, two of the common ones are the princess and the tomboy. Of course it is not just princesses and tomboys and no gray area in between, but for the purposes of illustration, focus on those two extremes. The princess is clear. She's pretty, special, thin, has a tiny waist, is in need of rescuing, and girls long for her life. There's always a guy in the picture, there's something desirable about him, and her life revolves around catching him. The princess is an interpersonal beauty. Girls live out their fantasies and desires by identifying with these princesses. They can go through their princess phase with full regalia and their own little kingdom. They imagine a life of luxury and opulence—not like their mom, who is washing clothes and doing dishes like the scullery maid.

The tomboy provides a desirable alternative for girls who just aren't into the princess scene, as well as for girls who may try on several different identities. The tomboy might be strong, adventurous, scientific, and typically androgynous. Tomboys are generally not the pretty ones because, of course, the myth prevails that you can't be smart and pretty at the same time. The tomboy is a complicated character. She is a little awkward, not the most popular, sometimes a bit of a pain because she is thinking and asking questions all the time. She is often valued for her skills but seldom loved by the prince type, although her parents may love her.

It is so uplifting to watch little girls get completely immersed in fantasy play. They are Jasmine or they are Velma on *Scooby-Doo*; just like you were Ginger or Mary Ann from *Gilligan's Island*. But this too is time limited. The problem emerges when the fantasy world and reality clash. Little girls can remain safe and carefree in their worlds of play only until the outside world starts infringing on them. Once they realize the tooth fairy was Mom or Dad, the fantasy bubble starts to burst. It is with that bursting bubble that we begin to hear the first utterances of negative self-talk. That slap of reality increases the gulf between who the little girls want to be and who they are beginning to think they are.

The Story of a Princess

Maya was a six-year-old girl living with her family in Wisconsin. She loved anything that had to do with princesses. Her favorite game was Pretty Pretty Princess. She most loved playing with her dad because she could make him wear bracelets and necklaces, and that made her laugh. She practically memorized every movie with a princess theme that came out. Her mom would often find her deep in her princess fantasy play in her bedroom. She had princess costumes of every color, tiaras, jewelry, and glittery slippers. There was never any question what Maya was going to be for Halloween! One day Maya was watching a princess movie all dressed up in her own pretty princess costume. She was dancing and singing in her room, completely lost in her own fairy princess world. With the DVD still on, she caught a glimpse of herself in the mirror. She looked at herself, then back at Princess Jasmine, then back at herself in the mirror again. She placed her hands on her stomach, then on her hips, and tried to suck in and stand on her tippy toes. When she could suck no further, she said to herself, "Princess Jasmine's tummy doesn't stick out like mine! She's skinny and pretty." Zing. That brief moment of comparison, and her fantasy bubble burst. She turned off the DVD and took off her princess costume and buried it deep in the recesses of her closet. Then she went downstairs to find comfort in cookies and chocolate milk. That was the end of her princess phase. Her mom never did understand why Maya stopped being interested in princesses almost overnight.

Maya made it to age six before that defining moment when she realized that she looked different from Princess Jasmine. That's as long as the grace period lasts and about all the time we have to truly be ourselves free from the external eye. Once elementary school begins, that precious protected time, the time we were so thrilled to experience with our daughter, starts to be challenged by the outside world—and it all starts with appearances. By age six, children are already aware of the societal bias against fat.[2] Children who are overweight internalize this message early, and they can see the difference between themselves and their toys. A full 90 percent of girls in the United States between the ages of three and eleven own a Barbie doll.[3] Although other doll trends have come and gone, none has the staying power of Barbie. It is not just overweight children who can perceive the difference between themselves and Barbie—it is every girl who isn't the kid equivalent of five foot seven, blonde, with 32.4-16-28.6 measurements. (Yes, those are Barbie's actual measurements, which correspond to one in 100,000 women in the real world.)

BIG-SCREEN PRINCESS VERSUS
A REAL PRINCESS'S TALE

Millions of girls around the world have been captivated by the princess theme that appears in many children's movies and merchandise. These animated, flawless beauties are unrealistic role models for young girls to emulate. Their lives are filled with turmoil and distress, and the only way out is through the aid of a knight in shining armor. They fit the same mold—unrealistically thin, effortlessly gorgeous, and they always attract the most handsome men (love based on appearance). Since they are animated, they *can* be perfect! Adults realize this, but children are less able to distinguish between reality and unobtainable fantasy. This may set some girls up to try and attain this perfectionism and beauty to achieve the "happily ever after" they so badly desire.

What about a real princess's life? Victoria, the Crown Princess of Sweden, was born in 1977. In many ways, Victoria has fundamentally changed royal traditions. She was designated Crown Princess in 1979, stepping ahead of her younger brother, which was sealed with a parliamentary change to the Act of Succession that introduced equal primogeniture (royal succession that does not give preference to boys over girls or vice versa). Victoria is currently the only female heir apparent in the world.

In 1997, the Royal Court conceded that all was not well with Victoria. Pictures confirmed that her weight had dipped dangerously low, and she was indeed suffering from anorexia nervosa. She went to the United States for treatment while studying at Yale University, away from the watchful eye of the Swedish public. Speaking about her period of suffering, the Crown Princess explained, "I felt like an accelerating train, going right down . . . during the whole period I had eating disorders and was aware of it, my anguish was enormous. I really hated how I looked like, how I was . . . I, Victoria, didn't exist. It felt like everything in my life and around me was controlled by others. The one thing I could control was the food I put in me.'[4] Giving hope to millions who suffer from this disorder, Victoria recovered. On June 19, 2010, she was married to her personal trainer, Daniel Westling. Once again, Victoria bucked royal tradition by marrying a commoner. Although the wedding was of fairy-tale proportions, Victoria's story reveals clearly that even the lives of real princesses are not perfect.

Elementary School

Elementary school marks considerable developmental change for girls both in how they feel about their bodies and how they feel about themselves. Surveys of elementary schools reveal that 40 percent of elementary school girls and 25 percent of elementary school boys want to be thinner.[2] By late elementary school around half of girls are dissatisfied with their weight and shape and have already developed the adult female pattern of pervasive negative body esteem. Interestingly, at this age, a difference emerges between white and African-American girls. The African-American girls show a glimmer of resilience. Many of them want to be bigger at this age and continue to have higher body esteem throughout life.[5]

What about self-esteem? Elementary school is where body esteem for girls and boys starts to diverge and then remain different across the life span. Before elementary school, girls and boys feel equally positively about themselves. By late elementary school, on average, girls have already become dissatisfied with themselves. This graph illustrates perhaps one of the most upsetting findings in child-development literature. This study by Baldwin and Hoffman analyzed several years of data from the Family Health Study.[6] They studied 762 children ages eleven to sixteen. As you can see, around age eleven and twelve, girls and boys score similarly on tests of self-esteem. Then, after the age of twelve, girls' self-esteem takes a nosedive. As boys maintain a positive self-perspective throughout this observation period, with a brief exception during the transition from middle to high school, girls start out feeling just as positively about themselves as boys, then go to the absolute basement. This graph, adapted from Baldwin and Hoffman, depicts the diverging curves between the sexes from ages eleven to twenty-one.

There are several take-home messages from this study. First, self-esteem is not stable: It changes over time. Second, self-esteem fluctuates more in girls than in boys. Baldwin and Hoffman hypothesize that how one feels about the changes that are going on in one's body may lie at the root of these different patterns. Whereas the changes in girls' bodies during puberty move them further away from the societal ideal (from thin and androgynous to curvaceous and sexual), the changes that occur in boys' bodies move them closer to the societal ideal (from scrawny and lanky to muscular and strong). So the fact that bodily changes in puberty bring boys closer to their ideal and take girls further away from theirs might contribute to this depressing divergence in adolescence.

Just as their bodies are changing and moving away from the thin ideal, girls are also starting to be confronted with limitations and prejudices. I was fortunate that my parents never dissuaded me from any of my fantasy jobs—"garbage man," firefighter, archaeologist, president. Never once did they say that I could not do what I wanted because I was a woman. Well, maybe with the exception of garbage man—that career path didn't thrill my mother. But what they said diverged completely from my actual experience. All around me, I knew no women in anything but support jobs and very few mothers who worked outside of the home. My mom helped out in my grandfather's store, my paternal grandmother was a seamstress, and my maternal grandmother never worked a day in her life. I knew a grand total of one female physician—my ophthalmologist. I thought she was totally cool and she had very cool office equipment. I remember her very French accent: "Do you see better vis zis one, or zat one?" But,

SELF-ESTEEM RATINGS OF GIRLS AND BOYS FROM AGES ELEVEN TO TWENTY-ONE

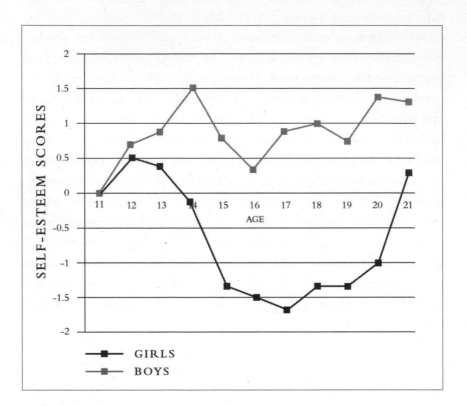

even though she was highly respected as a physician, women in the community would often comment on her appearance and "excuse" her for not being fashionable or having the right hairdo. Although she was absolved, the fact that her appearance wasn't up to par was duly noted. For heaven's sake, the woman was probably operating on twenty eyes a day and they still gave her a hard time for not having her nails done! So although I was supported in my fantasies, the *reality* of what I experienced in the world around me was different.

When does this subtle socialization begin? I was in the fourth grade, probably around ten years old. I was in science class and we were studying astronomy. I loved astronomy. I had books on astronomy. I joined a science-by-mail class about as- tronomy where I got great books and awesome stickers of the planets and stars. My teacher, we'll call her Miss Riley, asked the class a question about the planets. I, obviously still suffering from the delusion that girls and boys got called on with equal fre- quency, nearly jumped out of my chair, dying to answer. I an- swered the question correctly, completely, and enthusiastically, and Miss Riley responded, "Um, hmm, anyone else want to add to that?" Then Donald raised his hand. Donald's dad was a pilot, and from Miss Riley's perspective probably a pretty good-looking guy. Donald basically said the exact same thing I said. At which point Miss Riley went weak at the knees, gushing over his an- swer. "Exactly! Well done, Donald. You and your dad must talk about the stars all the time since he flies up in the sky every day." Well, *Pfft*, I thought. I was still young and brash enough to raise my hand again and say, "But Miss Riley, that's exactly what I just said!" Clearly, that didn't get me any points with Miss Riley ei- ther.

Decades later, when I visited my youngest daughter's ele- mentary school classroom, I was appalled to see that some things still hadn't changed. Boys were still getting called on when girls had raised their hands first. Boys were getting more positive comments and strokes from the teachers. And boys' work was more prominently displayed and showcased around the class- room. On parents' night, I watched as teachers were more likely to engage boys' parents in conversations than girls'! I was right back in Miss Riley's classroom—forty years later!

This gender bias is borne out in research. The results of a 1992 American Association of University Women Report called "How Schools Shortchange Girls"[7] were illuminating and dis- turbing. Girls receive significantly less attention from teachers in the classroom than boys do, and teachers give more esteem- building encouragement to boys than to girls. If a boy calls out without raising his hand, teachers are more likely to listen com- pared to when a girl calls out, when teachers cut them off and remind them to raise their hand first if they have something to contribute. Even when boys do not volunteer or raise their hands, teachers are still more likely to encourage them to give an answer or opinion. A Scandinavian study concurs. Even in egalitarian Scandinavia, boys are given more attention than girls.[8] Male teachers start to pay girls more attention when students get older, but female teachers always give more attention to boys regardless of the students' age.

Whether this is overt discrimination remains debatable. But focus on the powerful message that being ignored sends. The enthusiasm we initially have to participate actively in the world is gradually extinguished as we accumulate more and more experiences of being ignored or undervalued. It can make us feel unnoticed, invisible, and irrelevant. Some girls may shrink into silence, others may persevere and continue to bang their heads against the recognition wall, and others may find other ways to get themselves recognized, even if it means acting out or dressing provocatively. Negative attention is, after all, better than no attention at all. Our institutionalized failure to recognize the valuable contribution of little girls may be an important contributing factor to many of the challenging behaviors that we see in girl circles, including bullying, oversexualized behavior, and oppositionality. Beneath the surface, these subtle and insidious messages whittle away at girls' self-esteem day by day, year by year. Astonishingly, teachers are often not aware that they give differential attention to boys. The pervasive ignoring and the constant undervaluing all convey the message, *"This is not your world, this is his world."*

Even so, girls are doing well in school. In fact, they are outperforming boys in a number of subjects across the age span. According to Drs. Dan Kindlon and Michael Thompson, authors of *Raising Cain*, a book about the academic problems facing boys, girls outperform boys in elementary school, middle school, high school, college, and graduate school. Girls are doing better despite being ignored.[9] This elementary school scenario prepares them well for later life. It's the childhood equivalent of less pay for equal work.

Sticking with the situation of elementary school girls, what is the impact of this on their immediate world? This is precisely the juncture at which all of the appearance focus begins. Children long for a world that is theirs. If girls are systematically excluded and undervalued in the school setting—even if they are outperforming boys—then they need to create a separate micro-environment in which they can get kudos, succeed, be noticed, and belong.

Again, I learn from observing my children. In one of my daughters' schools, they alternate health class and PE across semesters. So there is one semester in the year when they don't benefit from the daily physical activity you could and should get as a child (and as an adult) via PE class. During her health semester, I noticed that she was absolutely climbing the walls when she came home from school. She reported that she was going stir-crazy sitting down all day. I knew she still had a recess period and naïvely asked why she wasn't getting any physical activity then. The picture she painted of the playground was demoralizing. While the boys were running around shooting baskets, playing four square, and engaging in other physical activities, the girls were sitting at picnic tables painting their nails and reading teen magazines! The girls who weren't into nail polish or *Teen Cosmo* had no place to go. The boys didn't want them, and if they did play with the boys, they got teased by the girls. If the girls started up a game on their own, the boys rapidly conquered their space, reclaiming their playground territory.

It struck me that this was the first evidence I saw of girls using physical appearance to create a world that is all their own. The boys were not welcome in that fingernail-painting world, and the girls could carve out their private space to talk, interact, and belong. They hear the messages, they see their mothers and aunts and grandmothers occupying this world, and, at least on the outside, they get more praise for participating in that world than they do for answering questions correctly in class. It becomes their retreat.

There is a big trade-off for this sense of belonging. The appearance world, although inviting, is rife with traps of its own.

Building Our Identity, or How Other People's Labels Shape Our Self-Perception

"She's so pretty." "She's really slimming down." "What a young lady she's become." There are a litany of stock comments that relatives and friends heap on girls that they would never heap on boys. Or the male equivalent has very different connotations. A highly accomplished colleague of mine has two children. Her daughter is about two years older than her son. She recounts an experience she has every time she goes to visit her in-laws. At first sight, within earshot of the kids, her father-in-law makes an opening comment about his grandson—like how strapping he is, how much energy he has, or how funny he is. His remarks invariably emphasize her son's power, wit, growth, and personality. He then launches into his opening dialogue about his granddaughter, which has a completely different look and feel and invariably focuses on physical appearance. The latest comment was how pretty she has become and that she is "slimming down nicely." My colleague has had to develop a debriefing for her daughter, explaining why Grandpa says such things, but even with careful debriefing, these comments stick and send a message. First, they convey that your brother is valued for his strength, his humor, and his intelligence and you, little girl, are valued for your looks and the size of your body. And, in case you missed the subtle subtext, it also conveys the message that you didn't used to be quite as pretty as you are now and thank heavens you are finally getting out of your chubby phase! If you hear these comments often enough as a child, no matter how resilient you are, no matter how much buffering your mother provides, and no matter how many other things you have going for you and you value about yourself, the comments get under your skin and stick with you.

Here are some examples of appearance-based comments that were uttered during childhood but have stuck with women throughout their lives.

Patrice, now thirty, has a vivid memory of her fifth-grade teacher making sure she was in the back row during the annual class picture. Her teacher simply said, "Patrice, you're bigger than the other girls so you should be back here," and ushered her to the back row of the bleachers so only her face would show in the picture. Now, Patrice was indeed taller than the other kids, but she was also heavier. She never knew which attribute her teacher was talking about when she positioned her in back, but for the rest of her life, that statement—"Patrice, you're bigger than the other girls"—haunted her regularly. Not surprisingly, in just about every group and family picture for the rest of her life, you could only see Patrice's head from the back row.

On a personal note, I had one large grandma and one thin grandma. My large grandma was a seamstress and she made lots of clothes for me, which meant frequent measuring and fittings. I was probably about eleven, and as she was measuring me, she said, "You have a figure just like mine." I remember looking at her and taking in what was nearing 200 pounds, then looking down at myself, panicking a little, and wondering what similarities she was seeing that I was somehow missing. When I asked what she meant, she said that just like her, I had a "little waist and that fills out again at the hips." For years that phrase went through my head every time I tried on a pair of pants that looked great on the hanger but were clearly cut for people who have a different body type from mine. On the one hand, she was absolutely right, I was not a rectangular person, but, in my child brain, I thought, "If I weren't built like Grandma, I could wear those cool pants!"

What makes these comments particularly sticky is that you hear them with a child brain. Your brain isn't developed enough to evaluate them critically. Plus, they most likely came from someone older whom you were expected to love or respect. Patrice could not say to her teacher, "Wait a minute, I want to be up front with my best friend Suzy." I could not say to my grand-mother, "Grandma, we have very different body types."

The reason phrases like that stick with us when we are young is that we look to others' perceptions of us and comments about ourselves to help us build our own identity. In childhood and adolescence, we are beginning to weave the story of who we are and what makes us unique in the world. We compile libraries of phrases uttered by others like "She's pretty," "She's fat," "She's built like me," "She's slimming down." Those phrases become incorporated into our self-perception and build our inner narrative of who we are. Precisely because we hear them with a child brain and incorporate them into our self-definition, they often remain unexamined for the rest of our life. These seeds get planted early, grow wild, and never get pruned.

In defense of well-meaning people, most of the time friends and relatives are not intentionally setting out to plant mind bombs in our little girls' heads. In fact, it is more likely that they simply have no other blueprints for behavior. They live in the same world we do and have probably faced the same discrimination. So, if anything, their intentions might be good and they could be welcoming the girls into the world of appearances that they too have made their own. It's okay to tell your daughter that she looks pretty; just make sure to praise her for all of the other wonderful features you value about her as well, and more often than complimenting her appearance.

By the end of elementary school, many girls are well on their way to having an internal library of negative self-comments. You may actually remember the first time you experienced negative self-talk or the first time that a self-critical comment hijacked your self-esteem. For some, this can be quite a defining event and can mark the first step toward developing enduring problems with self-esteem, social anxiety, eating disorders, or depression. We're talking about the process of external comments permeating our defensive shields and becoming part of our own internal dialogue about ourselves. To illustrate this, let's take two ends of the continuum. There is an adorable Internet video—"Jessica's 'Daily Affirmation'"—of a positively exuberant little girl in her pajamas who climbs up to her bathroom mirror to deliver what can best be described as an "I love my life, I love myself" diatribe. "I can do anything good . . . I like my mom . . . I like my hair . . . I like my haircuts . . . I like my stomach . . . I like my house . . . My whole house is great . . . I can do anything good . . . better than any-one."[10] She declares this with enthusiasm and launches her little day with a complete self-esteem boost. Contrast this with another YouTube video in which an older girl has a completely different experience looking into the mirror. In this clip, rather than having the world at her feet, this young woman has been beaten down by the world. The image she sees in the mirror reflects her fears about who she is and distorts her self-perception—in this case blinding her to life-threatening anorexia nervosa.[11]

The core difference between these two videos is the emergence of self-consciousness, or becoming aware of the external eye. These negative self-comments are a by-product of self-consciousness. They are cued from the outside—perhaps an innocuous comment or maybe a truly malicious one. But they worm their way into your head and begin eating away at your self-esteem. They emerge from and exacerbate self-consciousness. If you go to the pool in the summer, boys run around with abandon, swim trunks falling down, bottoms exposed, tummies sticking out, running when they should be walking, barely paying attention to the people around them. They're not even aware that other people might be looking at them until the lifeguard blares a whistle and tells them to walk, not run—then their response is "Huh, what, who me?" Then turn your gaze to the girls. Some of them have towels wrapped around their waists, some have shorts on over their bathing suits, and some wear T-shirts. They are hiding their maturing bodies. They are aware of being watched by the external eye—maybe hyperaware. Girls are considerably more likely than boys to be self-conscious once they reach adolescence. Between the ages of eight and eleven, girls and boys differ in self-consciousness by only 2 percent, but by age fifteen the difference increases to 24 percent! This self-consciousness is most likely related to girls' heightened concern about others' attitudes toward them and their tendency to see themselves through the eyes of others.[12] No single institution does more to increase self-consciousness than middle school. Middle school marks the decline.

Middle School Sucks

Alicia, age twelve, decided to go to her first middle school dance. She wore her usual jeans and a T-shirt. When she arrived, all the other girls had on miniskirts, camis, makeup, and high-heeled shoes. One of the girls said to her, "It's a dance, not a camping trip, stupid!" Alicia went into the bathroom, looked at herself in the mirror, and thought, "You are so dumb. You'll always be a tomboy. Well . . . whatever . . . you'd look fat dressed in their kind of clothes anyhow." She pulled out her cell phone, called her mom to pick her up, and never went to another school dance.

Middle school is a sociological disaster. Whoever decided it was wise to put prepubertal sixth graders together with hormonally ridden eighth graders knew nothing about child development. It's tough for boys, too, as the vertically challenged and hairless roam the halls with next year's smelly, hirsute high school JV football team. When you walk through middle school halls, the main thing you notice is bodies. There are bodies sprouting everywhere. You are surrounded by puberty. Puberty marks the landslide for self-esteem in girls. Early in elementary school, girls and boys are equally likely to raise their hands in class, hang upside down on the monkey bars, and play dodgeball—then the bodily changes that inevitably occur during puberty are accompanied by new internal dialogue and new observable behavior. Our society no longer bestows any glory, pride, or ceremony on someone who is becoming a woman. In stark contrast, late bloomers are envied and even worshipped as having lean and curveless bodies to die for. What girls say to themselves becomes even more undermining: "Don't show them how smart you are! Don't eat that much in public! Guys don't like girls with appetites. No more playing, no more climbing trees, no more dodgeball . . . paint your nails during recess. Where's your makeup, you look pale! You could never fit into that . . . hm . . . but maybe you should try. STOP! Don't put that in your mouth."

In middle school, girls start actively trying to manage their appearance. Of course it starts in elementary school, but by middle school, the train is out of the station. Clothing, shaving, makeup, and heels become part of the morning ritual. The daily "I can do anything" affirmation transforms into a daily inspection.

The sobering fact is that around 30 percent of ten-to-fourteen-year-olds are actively dieting.[13] Over 80 percent of ten-year-olds are afraid of being fat.[14] As early as the preteen years, girls will withdraw from life-engaging activities like giving an opinion, going to school, and going to the pool because they feel badly about their looks. Girls' self-esteem and self-confidence plummet as they transition from elementary to middle school. Depression, anxiety, self-harm, and disordered eating all start to enter the picture. Middle school is especially tough for girls because everything happens at once. Boys mature slightly later, so they are spared the simultaneous onslaught of so many social and biological changes. For girls, in middle school they experience the puberty-related weight gain and fat redistribution, dating, fast realization of limited options in career and sports, sexual harassment, teasing about bodily changes, and exposure to over-sexualized dressing and behavior in their older schoolmates. Middle school makes them grow up too fast. By middle school, 40 to 70 percent of girls are dissatisfied with two or more parts of their body, and it is usually the areas that are associated with the changes in fat distribution that occur during puberty (stomach, thighs, hips, breasts, buttocks). Body satisfaction hits rock bottom between the ages of twelve and fifteen.[15] According to Levine and Smolak, in industrialized countries, body image (including appearance satisfaction) is probably the most important component of an adolescent's self-esteem—especially in girls.

Girls are not alone in their struggle with negative body image; increasingly men and boys are also suffering from body-image concerns and have unhealthy desires to be thin and more muscular. Instead of the "thin body ideal," men see media messages that support a larger, muscular, lean ideal body. This is often recognized at young ages, around six or seven years old, when boys begin to play with action figures that undoubtedly have unrealistic bodies.[16] However, what perpetuates this image and what might lead to body dissatisfaction in adolescents and men is the increased viewing of these images in popular male magazines, television shows, and movies.[17] Boys with low self-esteem are at greater risk for body dissatisfaction, and this is especially true if they feel that there is a perceived pressure from media both to lose weight and gain muscle.[18] Similarly, weight-loss behaviors are more common in boys who feel pressured by the media to look a certain way.[19] Lacking confidence and self-esteem may be preventing some men and boys from buffering the impact of unhealthy, unrealistic societal messages.

In an intriguing twist, some boys and men look at themselves in the mirror and constantly see a body that is too small and weak. They may develop what is known as muscle dysmorphic disorder, in which they develop an unhealthy obsession with gaining muscle and maintaining leanness.[20] Like those suffering from eating disorders, males suffering from muscle dysmorphic disorder often have a highly distorted view of their body and what it actually looks like. Unfortunately, this can lead to health risks in the forms of excessive exercise, strict dieting, and anabolic steroid use. It is also the case that some men will withdraw from social situations because they are embarrassed about how "small" their body looks, when in reality they are muscular and toned. Muscle dysmorphia is sometimes referred to as "reverse anorexia nervosa" or "bigorexia" in the world of competitive bodybuilding and weightlifting.[21]

The roots of preoccupation with body size and muscularity in boys are noteworthy. Much as with women, body esteem and self-esteem are linked in males who succumb to appearance pressures. A study of one hundred male bodybuilders revealed that 21 percent reported having been bullied as children, which was also associated with lower self-esteem.[22] When we are examining what is happening with young boys, it is clear that the media-portrayed muscular thin ideal is being internalized by young boys at increasingly younger ages. A study of 248 middle school boys found that those boys who acknowledged a muscular ideal were more likely to endorse weight control and muscle-building techniques.[23]

Especially in this era of heightened awareness of childhood obesity, a healthy focus on weight and fitness is to be commended. What becomes concerning is when it crosses the line into an unhealthy obsession that negatively affects both body esteem and self-esteem of not only our girls but our boys as well.

Peers, Family, and You Matter
This section is not about blame. The world has erred for far too long blaming parents, blaming peers, and blaming the individual for struggles with problems like depression, anxiety, and eating disorders. Rather, this section highlights who matters when it comes to building your self-esteem and body esteem. The opinions of people who are closest to us matter the most, but how we interpret those opinions is also important—and our interpretations don't always match their intentions.

One of the most important factors that influences body dissatisfaction and appearance focus in adolescent girls is how caught up in appearances their peers are. If your peers are all about appearance, if they judge and tease others about appearance-related issues, your satisfaction with your own body is likely to be lower. This makes perfect sense. If you hear your friends commenting and teasing others about their weight, you know that you could be next on the chopping block. So you become more focused and more dissatisfied with your own looks. Girls as young as nine who watch TV and movies that have appearance themes and then talk about the shows amongst themselves also experience greater body dissatisfaction.[24] Girls who perceive their friends as having strong opinions about appearance and who value those opinions are more likely to develop problematic eating habits and have lower body satisfaction.[25] A girl's group of friends or clique that she spends time with significantly influences her degree of concern with her body image and her dieting behavior.[26] If you look at members of a specific clique, girls share similar levels of body-image concerns, dietary restraint, and use of weight-loss behaviors. Not only are their levels of body esteem similar, but so are their levels of self-esteem.[27] Girls' friendship circles converge on both self-esteem and body-esteem dimensions, and, no surprise, they are related. As body esteem goes down, it drags self-esteem with it. What we don't yet know is which way the relationship goes. Do girls who are appearance-focused seek each other out to form groups, or does being around appearance-focused girls make you more focused on appearance? Experience (and the movies) would suggest that it's not an either-or situation. Recall the Pink Ladies and Sandy Olsson (played by Olivia Newton-John) in the movie *Grease*. The Pink Ladies sought each other out to form a tight group, and Sandy transformed herself to fit in. It goes both ways!

The extent to which parents and other family members are invested in appearance also influences girls' focus on appearance. This effect can be both direct and indirect. Often it can be completely inadvertent. Direct comments about weight and shape, comments about developing bodies, actively putting children on diets to lose weight, and teasing can all have a negative impact on a girl's body esteem. Indirect effects refer to modeling behaviors. As a parent or relative, you can talk up a great game in terms of body shape and weight acceptance, but your actions speak louder than your words: if you display your own body dissatisfaction by saying things like "This makes me look fat" or "I can't eat that or I'll blow up," or if you see a large woman on the street and are the first to comment, "Oh, who let her out of the house today?" or "Does she really want to be seen on the beach looking like that?" children are absorbing and interpreting all of your comments, and they fear that regardless of what you *say* to them, this is what you are really thinking on the inside. They'll wonder if when you say, "I love you just the way you are," you really mean, "I love you even though you're a little chunky."

But to cut parents a break, we have no training in this area. Especially now with our culture challenged by rapidly escalating rates of childhood obesity, we have no script for how to talk about weight and shape with our children. In fact, we are terrible when it comes to a basic skill such as judging whether our children are in a healthy weight range. Pediatrician Eliana Perrin, M.D., M.P.H., and colleagues equipped practicing pediatricians with a tool kit that included an easy-to-use chart to map body mass index (BMI, a measure that accounts for both weight and height and, in children, sex and age as well), and a series of questions and suggestions to help parents start the conversation. "Parents don't recognize weight problems or don't know how to make things better, and even if they do, there are often barriers to healthier eating or more activity for these families," she said. Her tool kit helped parents become more accurate judges of their children's weight, led to improved dietary behaviors in children, and reduced time spent in front of various types of screens—known as "screen time." "We found something we can do to help stem the obesity epidemic," Perrin said.[28] Clearly, parents can learn if someone takes the time to teach them.

The fact that the first father stepped inadvertently into a weight and appearance minefield shows that even the most educated and powerful men in the world need guidance when it comes to talking about their daughters' weight. Interviewed by *Parents* magazine in November 2008, President Obama said, "A couple of years ago—you'd never know it by looking at her now—Malia was getting a little chubby," ABC News reported.[29] What a firestorm that comment started. The blogosphere was rife with speculation that President Obama and the first lady's campaign against obesity were going to cause a backlash of eating disorders. But what it really showed is that dads (even the first dad) need help when it comes to understanding how to talk to their daughters (and wives) about weight. Does a comment like the president's cause eating disorders? Of course not. But it could sting. Our weight and appearance are tied deeply with our emotions and self-concept. Talking about our children's weight is not like talking about some other index—the pollution index is up today, Dow Jones is down. Comments on weight and shape are emotionally loaded precisely because they cut to the core of self-worth and identity. Parents are our greatest allies in building self-esteem and body esteem; they just need the tools to do so effectively.

In addition to peers and family members, your own personality traits may render you more or less vulnerable to comments made by those around you. It's not just whether teasing or insulting happens, but a combination of it occurring and your response to it. People exist who get teased about their weight and shape or other aspects of their appearance or behavior and it simply doesn't get to them. Their internal psychological Kevlar allows insult bullets to bounce right off them. If you are impervious to your environment, you are protected. If, however, you are sensitive to your environment and if you are keyed into other people's motivations and feelings, then you are more likely to be wounded by teasing or insulting comments.

Ironically, we value and foster girls' ability to be empathic. Our capacity to empathize with others is probably a combination of hard wiring and learning. This is a gross overgeneraliza-tion, but I have observed that in many instances women tend to be more empathic than men. Or perhaps a better way to phrase it is that their thresholds for concern or even awareness are set differently. For most guys to be concerned, someone has to be bleeding out, whereas women rush to help at the first sign of a scratch. This enhanced sensitivity to others can also make girls more sensitive to criticism, which can influence how vulnerable they are to teasing.

If you are highly sensitive to criticism, you are more likely to perceive criticism in situations that are open to interpreta-tion. So let's say you are growing breasts and feeling somewhat self-conscious about it. Aunt June says, "My, you're filling out nicely." Perhaps not the most sensitive comment, but definitely an ambiguous one. If you are impervious, you think June is just one of those aunts who feels compelled to comment on your changing body. You give her a goofy look, run away, and erase the comment from memory. If you are more sensitive to criti-cism, you might wonder what Aunt June was really trying to say. Was she saying that you're too fat? Did you need a different bra? Was your shirt too tight? You would be more likely to interpret her comment as a criticism, have a negative emotional reaction, and store the comment in your personal archive. So it is not just the event of teasing, or the event of something being said about your body; it is the combination of the event and your reaction to it. We can only do so much about controlling the events around us, but in Part Two of this book, we can arm you well for chang-ing your reactions to them!

A primary task of adolescence is identity formation, and we do that in part by looking to others to reflect back to us who we are. It is an unfortunate truth that for many of us during that process, the negative comments are more likely to stick than positive ones. Sometimes innocuous comments cut deeply and stick forever, echoing in our minds for decades afterward. You may never be completely able to erase the tape that plays those comments back in your mind; however, you can change your response to them and how they affect you.

Go back in time to examine some of the comments that you recall from your youth. Start by dusting off some of the cobwebs in your self-commentary library and listing some of those comments that were made about you or to you when you were younger. Ultimately, the goal is to provide you with tools to change your internal response to those comments, but for now, just start by cataloging those comments.

One of the best ways to change your response to insults is to externalize them. These comments often feel so insulting that we don't share them with anyone. We carry them around in the shadows, sometimes for decades, incorporated into our identity. Sharing them can be amazingly liberating. It shines light on them and allows others to help you put them in their rightful place. Ask a fundamental question, namely, Was the speaker a complete jerk who doesn't deserve to take up any of your brain real estate, or was the person well-meaning but clueless and deserving of your forgiveness?

Sunny Sea Gold, health articles editor at *Glamour* magazine and the founder of HealthyGirl.org, was inspired by a reader to make a list of all of the hurtful things people had said to her about her body over the years. Sunny posted her own story about when she was fourteen, right at the pubertal transition, and at a family reunion an older male relative patted her roughly on the area right around the love handles and said, "Boy, kid, you'd better start layin' off of the potatoes." As a fourteen-year-old, she was mortified and spent the rest of the reunion wrapped in a blanket and isolated from her family. When she revisited that comment years later with her adult brain, she decided the relative, although clueless and insensitive, meant no harm, and she was able to forgive him. But please! she exclaimed. It is hard enough going through puberty with your body popping out all over the place for everyone to see, let alone having an older male relative

NEGATIVE COMMENTS INVENTORY

Age	Comment	Who said it	Situation	How it affected you then	How it affects you now
12	She's really developed quite the pear shape, hasn't she?	Skinny, cigarette-smoking aunt	Family holiday dinner. Said it to my mother within earshot.	Confused, upset, became obsessed with reducing my hips.	Still obsessed with reducing my hips, still always look at myself and see a pear.

Print your own table online at www.womaninthemirrorbook.com.

comment about it. People chimed in from around the globe with memories of mean things that had been said to them about their bodies when they were young that stayed etched in their minds—"sausage fingers, tree-trunk legs, thunder thighs."

Exercises: Starting Your Negative Comments Inventory
Take an inventory now of all of the negative things that you can remember people have said about your body or appearance when you were young. If there's nothing on your list, congratulations, you dodged that bullet! For now just fill in these columns. We'll

come back to this inventory in the second half of the book and apply your grown-up brain to evaluating them in order to reposition them in (or maybe even evict them from) your brain forever. Once you complete your inventory, read through it carefully and hold on to it, because you will expand it in the next chapter when we move on to high school.

CHAPTER 2

The Ins and Outs of High School

"You got your freshmen, ROTC guys, preps, JV jocks, Asian nerds, cool Asians, varsity jocks, unfriendly black hotties, girls who eat their feelings, girls who don't eat anything, desperate wannabes, burnouts, sexually active band geeks . . ."

—Janis, *Mean Girls*

Peyton was a junior in high school in Virginia. She was in the top 2 percent of her class, the assistant editor of the school newspaper, on the varsity field hockey team, taking four AP classes, and she was getting ready to start the college search. She wasn't popular in the cheerleader kind of way, but she had lots of friends and people liked being around her. Even though it looked to the casual eye as though she was enjoying her days at school, hanging with other girls, eating lunch and talking together, even doing some dating, no one knew the private torture she endured 24-7. Inside, she was panicked that she wasn't going to get into a good college and that her parents and teachers would be disappointed in her. Even though her classmates were her "friends," they were also all competitors. She always sat with the same group of girls at lunch. Peyton made sure she was last through the line—on purpose. She had to inspect what everyone else got first, because in her mind she heard the command "You *have* to eat less than they do!" Outwardly, she was engaged in conversation with her friends, but on the inside, she was doing calorie math. Her thoughts were, "Count their calories. Do *not* eat more calories than they do!" She would check out all of the girls at the table and compare who was skinniest today—was it Emily, was it Sydney, was it Jenna? If the answer wasn't Peyton, she would go into panic mode, her thoughts becoming, "Don't touch that roll, it will put me over. I don't care if I'm hungry. I have to stop eating!" To the observer, Peyton was just having lunch with her friends, but in her head she was engaged in a cutthroat competition to be the one at the table who ate the least. But she was the only one competing. Eventually, this internal struggle got her in trouble. Her coach noticed that she had no energy on the field, and Peyton noticed that she would be reading the same page over and over again in her AP history book, but nothing was sticking. The cutthroat competition that she was engaged in had led Peyton down a dangerous path toward an eating disorder.

Our educational system is broken, and it feeds into girls' self-esteem crisis. With few viable vocational options that don't require a college education, every student is competing for college entry. Kids are doing four, five, six, seven hours of homework every night, sacrificing sleep, nutrition, physical activity, family, and friends just to make themselves attractive to college-admissions committees. High school is no longer experiential; it is not about growing and developing in the here and now; it has become entirely preparatory for the future. Teachers can no longer foster creativity, growth, and exploration but rather are forced to teach to the test. Students are forced to be oriented toward tomorrow and to fret over whether they will get into their dream college—even if they don't really want to go to college. The end result is extreme pressure including the pressure to be someone you might not really want to be.

Teachers are forced to shove content down our children's throats in a desperate race to cover the prescribed curriculum rather than support their development as citizens of the world. Learning has become superficial. At the end of high school, our children look back and realize they have spent the past four years in front of a computer screen wondering if more of the same lies ahead.

This pressure is resulting in increases in depression, anxiety, self-harm, eating disorders, and suicide in high school children. Depression in children is serious—it is estimated to affect about 5 percent of adolescents.[1] Estimates of the prevalence of deliberate self-harm, such as cutting, scratching, and burning, vary widely by region, but there is evidence that it is becoming more common. Factors commonly associated with self-harm are thoughts of suicide, low self-esteem, depression, impulsivity, family dysfunction and conflict, bullying and intimidation in school, and poverty.[2] Suicide is a major cause of death among adolescents and rates are more quickly rising in teens than in other age groups. Out of the four million suicide attempts in the world, 90,000 adolescents successfully commit suicide.[3] Finally, reports from the Centers for Disease Control indicate that the percentage of youth between four and seventeen who were given the parent-reported diagnosis of attention deficit hyperactivity disorder (ADHD) increased from 7.8 percent to 9.5 percent, and there has been a 21.8 percent increase in ADHD diagnoses between 2003 and 2007.[4] In part, we may be getting better at detecting and taking symptoms seriously in youth. On the other hand, we have to seriously explore whether aspects of our children's lives are fostering this rise in worrying symptoms and behaviors.

A documentary, *Race to Nowhere*,[5] offers a poignant glimpse into the inner struggles of high school students around the country. The internal and external pressures to succeed weigh enormously on the shoulders of youth, leading to exhaustion and occasionally tragic outcomes.

Our children's lives are scheduled down to the minute with classes, clubs, sports, lessons, and community service—not stemming from a passion for volunteering, but, again, to impress the admissions committees. What if your child isn't really college material? What if your child is intelligent in a way that is not captured by the SAT or the ACT? What if your child would do better with an apprenticeship or would benefit from taking a few years off between high school and college? We are funneling all of our children down the same cattle chute to college, even if they don't belong there. And when they don't measure up on the metrics that are ultimately not appropriate for them, their self-esteem takes another hit.

Do you really care whether your mechanic read Kierkegaard or if your favorite artist took calculus? What's wrong with letting them spend more time in shop or the studio to nurture their talents and passions? Don't send them to Princeton if they would be happier under a car or covered with paint. We preach tolerance of diversity of racial and ethnic backgrounds, but we are losing our rich tolerance of diversity of intelligence.

Peyton, in the beginning of the chapter, was under enormous pressure. Granted, some of that pressure came from who she was by nature, but her school mirrored and exacerbated the pressure she put on herself. She wanted to foster close friendships with her friends, but she knew that many of them would be applying to the same colleges as she and that they would not all get in. They didn't talk openly about the fact that they were in direct competition with each other, but it seemed to be an unwritten subtext. Whose CV was stronger? Who had more community-service hours? Who had the highest GPA? Who was going to be valedictorian?

With girls, in addition to the academic realm, much of this interpersonal competition gets hijacked into the realm of physical appearance and weight. Just as Crown Princess Victoria of Sweden intimated about her eating disorder, girls can feel as if everything in their lives is controlled by others and the only thing they can control is the food they put into their mouths. According to Project EAT, in a survey of 1,396 high school girls, 19 percent reported chronic dieting and 57 percent engaged in unhealthy weight-control behavior.[6]

High school girls know on one level that there is something inherently wrong about the focus on weight and appearance, yet this knowledge is not sufficient to change their behavior and thoughts about themselves. The Girl Scouts of America conducted an online survey in 2010.[7] They contacted one thousand girls aged thirteen to seventeen. These were not just Girl Scouts, but represented American girls overall. The sample was balanced by age, race, and ethnicity—13 percent were African-American and 13 percent were Hispanic, and the online invitations were nationally dispersed so that the United States population was fairly well represented. The most striking results of the survey, which was called Beauty Redefined, were some puzzling contradictions that emerged. Nine out of ten American teenage girls feel pressured by fashion and media industries to be skinny. Although 75 percent of girls stated that they would be more likely to buy clothes that they saw on "a real size model" than on a superskinny model, over 40 percent said they preferred to see the latest fashions on skinny models rather than full-sized women! Although 65 percent of girls thought the body image represented by the fashion industry was too skinny, 63 percent said it was unrealistic, 47 percent said it was unhealthy, and 28 percent said it looked sick, over 60 percent of the respondents compared their bodies to fashion models and 47 percent said that fashion magazines give them a body image to strive for! Finally, 31 percent of respondents claimed that they starved or refuse to eat in order to lose weight. So on the one hand, girls seem to be aware that the standards set by the fashion and beauty industries are unrealistic and even sick, but that knowledge is not sufficient to protect them from engaging in behaviors to try to achieve that unrealistic ideal.

Where Do I Fit In?

So much of high school is about fitting in somewhere, or becoming at peace with not fitting in. One look at a yearbook and it is clear that high school is a time when your identity becomes defined by what you do—what clubs you belong to, whether you were an editor, a captain, a homecoming queen, a cheerleader, a volunteer, a National Merit finalist, a member of the Asian club, the Hispanic club, or the Model United Nations. High school is also the time when your identity gets reduced to a one-liner: She was most likely to . . . succeed, go to jail, become a millionaire. As you join different clubs and try out different social groups, you are testing out new sides of your identity. There are many facets to these decisions. "Is this something that I want to make part of my personal history, or is this something that doesn't fit with who I am or who I want to be? Is the topic of personal interest or relevance to me? Do I like the other people who are in the group? Are they like me or different from me? Are there things about them that I would like to be more like? Do I agree with the values of the people in the group? Do I feel like an outsider in the group, or do I feel like I do or could belong?" These questions resonate not only with your interests and values but also with your religious, ethnic, and racial identities.

All of these questions are further embedded in our racial and ethnic identities. To what extent can your ethnicity protect you from insults to your self-esteem and body esteem? In a study we conducted in 2008 with over four thousand women across the United States, it seems clear that no one is immune. The negative dialogue seems to have no hesitation crossing racial and ethnic borders. White, African-American, Asian, Latina, and Native American women all suffer with some sort of dissatisfaction about their bodies and appearance. There are some subtle differences. African-American girls and women seem to be more tolerant of larger body sizes, and Asian girls and women tend to diet less. But weight isn't the only dimension of discontent. No sooner do they catch a break in the weight realm than new discontents emerge. "I have to straighten my hair. I have to lighten my skin. I have to use more makeup to make my eyes look more Western. I have to get a breast reduction to get rid of my curves. I have to get breast implants to get more curves." All of these commands give the same message—it's not okay to look like you; you have to look like the mythical idealized "her." Although minor movements ripple through the fashion and advertising world to increase diversity of color and size, the vast majority of appearance role models continue to be tall, thin, white young women. The message is that you need to go to any measures—from makeup to surgery—to make yourself look more like "her."

This intense desire to achieve body ideals takes on different forms across cultures. In Asia, for example, dieting can take on extreme forms, possibly due to cultural perceptions of beauty. According to sociologist Mary Gee from the University of California at San Francisco, the stereotypical Asian-American woman is petite and thin. In addition to striving for that petite ideal, some resort to plastic surgery and other forms of body modification to emulate American ideals of beauty and success, whether it's double-eyelid surgery, skin whitening, or disordered eating behaviors.

Behaviors can get even more extreme, as reported by the *New York Times*. According to Philippa Yu from the Hong Kong Eating Disorders Association, the magic number that Asian girls and women are striving for is one hundred pounds, no matter what their height. Sing Lee, director of the Hong Kong Eating Disorders Center at Chinese University, adds that excessive exercise is typically not an approach taken by Asian women, as muscles are not considered to be feminine. For that reason, Asian girls turn to more extreme methods such as pills, herbs, and even swallowing parasites for weight loss. The Hong Kong Health Department went so far as to issue a warning that these parasites can cause abdominal pain, vomiting, diarrhea, and even death.[8]

According to a Puerto Rican researcher who studies eating disorders and body image in Latina girls and women, the biggest struggle she hears from Latina girls is disliking their more curvaceous figures. They most commonly express the desire to reduce their breasts and hips and to become more rectangular and less overtly sexual.[9] In *Hijas Americanas*, Rosie Molinary conducted a survey and interviewed over eighty women who self-identified as Latina and were living in the United States. These rich interviews revealed complicated effects—both positive and negative—that straddling two cultures can have on your self-esteem and body esteem. She notes that many Latinas reported feeling caught between two standards of beauty, leaving them either not feeling beautiful in either culture or feeling beautiful in one but not the other. She described them feeling as if on the precipice of judgment, caught between American pop culture and the values and cultural traditions of their families.[10]

Beyond body image, we face other challenges to our core identity in high school and beyond. One look at the cafeteria provides all the data needed to confirm that true integration eludes us. In addition to the clear racial and ethnic clusters, high school fosters clustering based on socioeconomic status (preps and poor kids), psychopathology (cutters and stoners), antisocial behavior (hoods), and brains (nerds or geeks). Belonging or being perceived to belong to any of these groups can lead to instant stereotyping and stigmatization. Often these identities are hard to shake, even if you do undergo radical change over the summer. Labels are sticky and can follow you from class to class, from year to year.

Most mothers can share the challenges that their daughters have faced with stereotypes and stigmatization, but Lisa Rubenstein, correspondent for the Raleigh *News & Observer*, has had the unique opportunity of rearing three girls of different racial, ethnic, and religious backgrounds.[11] Lisa is a self-described Caucasian-American Spanish-speaking Jew married to a Hindu Indian raised in Ghana who sports Canadian and U.S. passports. As Lisa reports,

> My youngest daughter, with her black eyes, brown skin, and curly hair, helps white people diversify the guests at their children's birthday parties. My middle daughter's Swahili name makes her a target for school clubs and teams that are seeking to add cultural breadth to their populations. My eldest daughter's brown skin and straight hair identify her as the Latina who will bring closure to the yawning achievement

gap every time she takes a seat in a high school honors class. The problem is that my kids are neither black, nor African, nor Latina. My youngest doesn't get credit for being Indian, even though she has spent time visiting her relatives in Delhi and the Punjab, eats chapattis with her dinner, and has grandparents who tell her Hindu folk tales. Instead, it is her skin color, identifying her as born of a black and a white parent before we adopted and raised her, that helps observers to classify her as African-American. No one understands how she can be Indian, and no one remembers that she is half Caucasian. My middle daughter, whose skin is as white as mine, doesn't get any credit for being African-American even though she was born in Mozambique and lived in southern and eastern Africa for four years. My eldest daughter, of Jewish and Indian heritage, doesn't get credit for working hard on projects and staying awake late to prepare for tests; it is assumed she does well because it's in her genes.

Although few of us have experience with as much diversity as Lisa, we all see the impact of stereotyping and stigmatization on our children in high school. These various groups and cliques are like magnetic forces that draw you in while you constantly evaluate whether it is safe to be labeled part of any group. Will you be seen as too alternative, radically green, too ethnic, too nerdy, too girly? The safest option seems to be remaining flavorless, or, as many girls who try to diet into oblivion seem to do . . . just to disappear.

CYBERBULLYING: THE NEW LOCKER ROOM

Bullying is aggressive. It is intentional and harmful and its hallmark is an imbalance in physical or psychological power. Although the school bully has been around forever, with increased awareness of the long-term detrimental effects of bullying, educators have renewed their efforts to reduce bullying in schools.

In the past, bullying was a face-to-face enterprise. Whether it happened in the classroom, at recess, in the locker room, or on the playing field, typically the bully was there to push around his or her victim—either physically or verbally. Children could go home and have temporary respite from the torture—at least until the next school day.

Now children's lives are drastically different, thanks to the Internet. Over forty-five million children between the ages of ten and seventeen in the United States use the Internet every day. Homework is often assigned that requires Internet use, and children and teens often have multiple chat windows going when they are supposed to be doing their homework. Most social interactions among children online are not monitored by adults.

This is a perfect setup for cyberbullying. In many ways, it is easier to bully online because a certain degree of anonymity is guaranteed. You no longer have to have the guts to bully someone face-to-face: All you have to do is hit Enter.

Studies have documented intimidation, humiliation, gossip, slander, and taunting through e-mail, instant messaging, chat rooms, social networking sites, cell phones, and blogs. Suicides secondary to cyberbullying have received national attention. We have no idea how many other problems such as depression, alcohol and drug use, anxiety disorders, eating disorders, and self-harm may have cyberbullying at their roots.

What we know is that Internet bullying peaks in eighth grade and declines in eleventh grade. Girls and boys are equally likely to bully via the Internet. The same sorts of situations that are associated with verbal bullying seem to be associated with Internet bullying. Bullying is often about establishing and maintaining a social hierarchy. The more connected that kids feel with their school and the more positive the school climate, the less Internet bullying occurs.[12]

One of the scary features of Internet bullying is how fast and far information can travel. A devastating rumor can be sent to hundreds of recipients with one keystroke. Unlike in the locker room, your friends can't rush to your defense as effectively. What is said about our children on the Internet is now another source of their emergent identity. Cybercommentary gets incorporated into their negative self-talk even more indelibly than verbal commentary because there is a digital trail. What they say and what is said about them online now contributes to who they see themselves as in the world.

There is no perfect solution to cyberbullying, but there are safeguards. Given that Internet is required by so many schools and given that the Internet is a vast and wonderful resource that we want our children to have access to, all we can do is apply intelligent parenting to the Web as well. Talk to your children about what they do online. Have access to their accounts and let them know they can and should talk to you about unpleasant things that happen either to them or to their friends or classmates. Read up on effective Internet parenting. For excellent tips for parents, kids, and schools, start at www.wiredkids.org. Most important, get to know your children's friends. Before the Internet, we would either have met our children's friends and their parents face-to-face or at least talked with them on the phone. We could use our parental antennae to gauge how comfortable we were with these new friends. Remember the phrase, "I don't approve of [insert name here]" which meant you were most definitely *not* going to their house on Friday night. Now our children have many "friends" whom we have never met or talked to, whose parents we don't know, and, quite frankly, who might not even be kids. Give your parental antennae a chance and try to meet the children with whom your child has a virtual relationship.

When we write guidelines for Internet monitoring, we are typically thinking about protecting the victims of cyberbullying, but they are equally important for parents whose children might be the cyberbullies. In several suicide cases, cyberbullies have been charged with crimes ranging from "unrelenting bullying" to statutory rape. Monitoring your child's Internet use can prevent her or him from being a victim or an aggressor.

Being Overweight in High School

What happens to the overweight or obese teen in high school? Size is yet another critical dimension on which our children are teased, judged, and excluded. Major differences exist across racial and ethnic lines in terms of obesity. The numbers from the National Health and Nutrition Examination Survey (NHANES) study are striking. When you define obesity in children as greater than or equal to the sex- and age-specific ninety-fifth percentile from the 2000 CDC Growth Charts, nearly 20 percent of boys ages twelve to nineteen and 17 percent of girls are obese. Within these categories, Mexican-American boys and black girls are at greatest risk.[13]

Although the basic equation is well-known—not enough physical activity and too much food—it is critical to go back a step and explore the factors that lead to that increased energy intake and decreased energy expenditure. As mentioned at the start of the chapter, children are stressed. They get too little sleep, have no time to care for themselves, have been robbed of physical-activity time by increasing pressures to cram ever more content into their tired brains, and they are overscheduled to the point of missing regular and family meal times. Especially when we are growing, our bodies crave sleep and regularity—our high school–aged children are deprived of both. Non-nutritious, calorie-dense school lunches, unsafe neighborhoods, increased screen time, sugar-sweetened beverages, and the lack of physical activity during school hours all contribute to the problem. Add the stress of success into the equation, and you have the perfect storm for the development of obesity and stress eating.

Obesity strongly influences how adolescents feel about

PREVALENCE (PERCENT) OF OBESITY AMONG U.S. ADOLESCENTS AGED 12–19, FOR SELECTED YEARS
1988–1994 THROUGH 2007–2008 FROM THE NHANES STUDY

	1988–1994	1999–2000	2001–2002	2003–2004	2005–2006	2007–2008
Boys, All	11.3	14.8	17.6	18.2	18.2	19.3
Boys, Non-Hispanic white	11.6	11.8	16.6	19.1	15.5	16.7
Boys, Non-Hispanic black	10.7	21.1	16.7	18.4	18.4	19.8
Boys, Mexican-American	14.1	27.2	21.8	18.3	25.6	26.8
Girls, All	9.7	14.8	15.7	16.4	17.3	16.8
Girls, Non-Hispanic white	8.9	11.0	13.7	15.4	13.5	14.5
Girls, Non-Hispanic black	16.3	25.2	22.0	25.4	29.8	29.2
Girls, Mexican-American	13.4	19.3	20.3	14.1	25.4	17.4

Excludes pregnant females.

NOTE: Obesity defined as body mass index (BMI) greater than or equal to sex- and age-specific 95th percentile from the 2000 CDC Growth Charts.

themselves and how they are perceived by their peers. Overweight adolescent females who correctly perceive their weight report lower self-esteem.[14] The negative self-perceptions seem to get worse with increasing weight. Obese youth report higher body dissatisfaction than overweight youth, who report more body dissatisfaction than normal-weight youth. Obese youth have higher depression scores and evidence greater depressive symptoms and negative self-esteem.[15] Obese children are also less likely to be named as a friend by other peers, are thought of as more aggressive and disruptive, and are more likely to engage in socially withdrawn behaviors. Their peers also rate them as less athletic and less attractive than others.[16]

In addition to overweight and obesity, we have seen a rise in binge eating in the past decade, which is often referred to as loss-of-control eating in children and adolescents. Binge eating is defined as eating an unusually large amount of food in a short period of time and feeling out of control. With loss-of-control eating, you sense that you just can't stop once you have started. About a quarter of adolescents who seek treatment for obesity report binge eating.[17,18] Unsurprisingly, youth who report binge eating also experience more depression, anxiety, low self-esteem, body dissatisfaction, and weight concerns.[19] Adolescents who are overweight and also experience binge eating are at particular risk for other mental health problems.

Addressing overweight in high school children is challenging. First, programs for this age group need to be effective and nonstigmatizing. Second, many of the approaches that have been developed to increase diversity tolerance of race, ethnicity, and religious background in high schools need to be applied to size-diversity tolerance. Size-diversity programs appear to have beneficial effects on how high school students think about and act toward each other when it comes to weight and shape acceptance. Of concern, this acceptance and tolerance does not seem to translate into how they feel about themselves. It is hard to blame them, as their feelings and behaviors reflect the world around them. The powerful messages that bombard them from society are more pervasive and penetrating than our diversity interventions are.

Chevese Turner, CEO of the Binge Eating Disorder Association, underscores that size acceptance must be internalized by the individual before it can permeate the larger society. She notes that we can teach anyone the proper way to treat another person, but the juxtaposition of the messages we get daily about body size is in direct contradiction with size-diversity tolerance programs. Explains Chevese, "On any given day, we hear over and over what we are doing wrong with our bodies and how to change them. We see spokesperson after spokesperson touting diets and toned bodies, telling us how much better their lives are now that they've lost thirty pounds. Now we're being told that our lack of concern for our bodies is costing the hardworking tax-payers more and more money, and individual freedoms are being infringed upon by those who take up more than their fair share of space." How can these messages not lead to further stigmatization and self-hatred? The fear of being teased, bullied, and treated as an outsider is real. According to Chevese, fat is the last bastion of socially accepted bullying because of the pervasive belief that fat is a result of lack of will and laziness.

These negative self-thoughts affect life and accomplishments. Adolescents who are overweight complete less education than their non-overweight peers.[20] Since the 1960s, we have known that obese students have lower college-acceptance rates than their non-obese peers despite equivalent academic records.[21] Obese girls are only half as likely to attend college.[22] And it's not just education: In a national study of men and women ages eighteen to twenty-five, obese women earned 12 percent less than non-obese women.[23]

The take-home message is that education and direct experience may help youth develop greater diversity tolerance in others, but additional means are necessary to ensure greater self-acceptance. As in the Girl Scouts' survey, the girls seemed to know intellectually that the fashion-industry ideals were unrealistic and even sick, but that knowledge was not enough to stop them from engaging in unhealthy weight-loss behaviors themselves. Dealing with the rise in childhood and adolescent obesity is not a simple public-health intervention: Michelle Obama's "Let's Move!" campaign illustrates the breadth that any public-health intervention needs to have in order to tackle this problem. But we must tread carefully. Our interventions can't be so focused on numbers on the scale that we further foster failure. Nor can we be so focused on weight-loss outcomes that we inadvertently encourage unhealthy weight-loss behaviors that would propel yet more students down the path of eating disorders. The enormity of the task can be daunting, especially in light of the massively powerful interest groups (e.g., Big Food and Big Beverage companies) whose products and marketing need to be turned around in order to do their part. You can avoid these pitfalls by focusing on one child at a time and empowering families and schools to foster healthy, self-esteem-preserving change.

Graffiti

If you really want to know what is going on in high school, go to the bathroom. Bathroom-stall graffiti is a rich chronicle of high school subculture and a glimpse into the minds of both the tortured and the torturers. Graffiti is no longer just who loves whom inside a heart with a date, which used to provide juicy soap-opera gossip; graffiti today borders on libel and reveals the depths of despair and hatred that many high school students experience. The occasionally artful scratchings reveal a broad array of "anti-" feelings—anti-gay, anti-smart, anti-liberal, anti-conservative, anti-fat. Here's a snapshot from one stall: I ♥ Justin Bieber, Justin Bieber is gay, You're gay, John is gay, Ron is a faggot, I hate school, I hate my life, I'm fat, There must be two people inside Jenna's body, I want to die, I have a gun, I sit in this bathroom every day during lunch and I'm miserable, Chenelle is a slut . . . and explicit sexual drawing after drawing notating which students engage in which explicit behaviors. Interwoven with explicit personal messages are bold and threatening gang tags and monikers. And this is high school! Fourteen-year-old freshmen are bombarded with this kaleidoscope of hate and despair, fearing what would or could be written about them. Although cleaning staff are charged with wiping or painting over the offending dialogue, the history remains like an archaeological dig.

The bottom line is graffiti is vandalism that tends to be committed by juveniles. Like cyberbullying, graffiti is a way to vent anger, frustration, or abuse indirectly without confronting the source face-to-face. Like cyberbullying, with graffiti, word travels fast and sticks. For gang members, tagging is a rite of passage—the more daring and challenging the tag, the higher up you can ascend in the graffiti subculture. It achieves rebellion and status in one act. Assaultive graffiti empowers the writer—at least in the short term. Self-loathing graffiti allows the writer to express his or her despair publicly, but rarely leads to detection or intervention.

The domain of graffiti is relevant insofar as it is yet another stage on which our self-esteem and body esteem can take a battering. Building proper defenses, discussing graffiti openly, and helping our children develop more Teflon than Velcro responses to these illegal assaults is another important step in empowering them against stigmatization and abuse.

High School Athletics

Athletic pursuits can also deeply influence both body esteem and self-esteem in girls. Title IX did women an enormous favor by guaranteeing them equal access to education and activities (which has come to include sports). More girls today participate in team and individual sports than ever before. Sports have enormous health benefits and can positively boost self- and body esteem. However, there is a darker side. Many sports, especially those with emphasis on weight and appearance for success—such as figure skating, gymnastics, ski jumping, cycling, and wrestling—can also take a serious toll on athletes' self- and body esteem and can serve as triggers for eating disorders. But these are not the only sports associated with increased risk. In fact, it is not so much the sports that place athletes at risk but the people involved in the sports. A soccer coach who thinks winning is related to his or her team being at "fighting weight" can be as detrimental as a skating coach who weighs you in public. It's not the sport, it's the people in the sport.

High school athletes are often not just focused on winning in the here and now, but also on the impact that their current performance will have on their success in obtaining college athletic scholarships. Pressure from coaches, family members, and even the media can prompt an unhealthy obsession with training and lead to overexercising, unhealthy dieting, and unhealthy weight-loss practices to achieve goals set by coaches. The team weigh-in is perhaps the most humiliating of all sports practices, with its public shaming and implication that if you are over your fighting weight, you'll take down the team. Gymnastics and skating coaches who send home BMI report cards to the family from summer training camps—not focusing on their children's accomplishments or, for that matter, whether they are having fun but whether they are losing weight—completely obscure the point of participating in high school athletics.

The fact that it is the people not the sport per se that contribute to eating disorders was illustrated vividly in a frank *Huffington Post* interview with Jenny Kirk, the highest-ranked former singles figure skater to discuss her personal struggles with an eating disorder.[24] Before her eating disorder prompted her to leave the sport, Kirk won the World Junior Championship, medaled five times at the U.S. national championships, and qualified for the world team three times. Her exit robbed her of the opportunity to be selected for the 2006 Olympic team.

Kirk explained:

> For me personally, I started to control the types of food I was eating—think labeling foods "good" and "bad"—after a disappointing finish at the 2003 National Championships. At the time I believed that if I became very aware of the types of food that were going into my body, how hard I was working out off the ice, and how much I weighed, then I would be able to control my results on the ice. There are so many things in skating that a competitor can't control, particularly the

judging, and I felt that if I were a certain weight, I would feel more in control of all those external variables. What really happened, though, is that the disorder started to control me, and it took over my life.

She went on to explain that at the higher levels of competition, everything about a skater is scrutinized—by coaches, by judges, by commentators. It is not just about athletic achievement but about performance, about body type, hair color and style, and even about costuming. Discussing her diminishing energy as her eating disorder progressed, Kirk recalled, "I remember as I fell deeper into the disorder, it became increasingly difficult for me to find the energy needed to complete my run-throughs. Although I probably should have understood that this meant I had to eat more, I punished myself, thinking that my stamina was lacking because I was out of shape and eating too much. For me, it didn't matter that I was losing muscle strength, because every time I looked in the mirror I felt that my muscles were too big."

Kirk estimated personally that 85 percent of female skaters struggle with eating disorders or disordered eating. Earlier studies of college athletes suggest the numbers are somewhat lower, but higher than in the general population. In a study of Division I NCAA athletes, 9.2 percent of the females were identified as having clinically significant problems with bulimia, and 2.85 percent as having a clinically significant problem with anorexia nervosa; 10.85 percent of the females reported binge eating on a weekly or greater basis, and 5.52 percent of the females reported purging behavior (vomiting, laxatives, diuretics) on a weekly or greater basis.[25] More recent studies indicate that sports anxiety, or worries about performance and competition, is a particular risk factor for the development of eating disorders in female athletes.[26]

Focusing specifically on the health of female athletes, the female-athlete triad is a syndrome consisting of three conditions: disordered eating, amenorrhea, and osteoporosis. It can affect any active female, not just competitive "athletes," and it is a major problem in high school and beyond.

The troubles begin when more calories are burned than are consumed. This can occur simply because of a high level of activity, but often it stems from an intentional restriction of food intake. Body-image problems or pressure to be thin for a sport (particularly sports like gymnastics and figure skating that emphasize leanness) can cause females to develop disordered eating behaviors and deprive themselves of the calories they need. Poor nutrition and reduced energy availability (in the form of calories) cause the body to reduce or cease its production of important hormones like estrogen. This can lead to irregular periods or even amenorrhea, a condition in which a woman goes three or more months without having a period.

The lack of necessary nutrition and hormones leads to bone loss and eventually osteoporosis. Bones need calcium and vitamin D as well as reproductive hormones like estrogen to maintain their strength. Without these substances, bone loss will occur, putting the female at risk for fractures. Active young females with amenorrhea can have bones similar to those of fifty- to seventy-year-old women.

It is not known exactly how prevalent this serious syndrome is. Disordered eating behavior has been reported in between 15 to 62 percent of female college athletes and amenorrhea in between 3.4 to 66 percent of female athletes, compared with 2 to 5 percent in the general population.[27] Coaches may falsely believe that amenorrhea is a normal consequence of training. Keep in mind that disordered eating, amenorrhea, and osteoporosis exist on a continuum: A person does not need to have a severe eating disorder or have missed three periods in a row for her health to be affected.

Roberta Sherman and Ron Thompson, two of the gurus of eating disorders in sport, emphasize that sport participation per se is not the problem, but rather the risks that are sometimes found in the sports environment. They call upon coaches, sport governing bodies, and parents to move beyond the continued emphasis on the purported relationship between weight and leanness and sport performance. They urge replacement of the "thinner is the winner" belief with a balanced approach that performance is enhanced through health and nutrition.[28]

One truth about high school is that it is a complex time. Teens can experience enormous growth and development, but they can also be stressed and abused. Regardless, high school represents a defining time. During high school many features of your personality and interpersonal style get defined. People continue to change and evolve, but many of the core traits are becoming defined during this age.

A danger in the high school years is when youth go underground with their thoughts and feelings. The pinball-machine atmosphere of social, academic, and athletic demands can be bewildering to the rapidly developing adolescent brain. Keeping the dialogue alive during the teen years is not always easy, but it's a worthwhile goal in order to protect teens from being overwhelmed or finding outlets for their confused thoughts and feelings that do more harm than good.

Exercises: Revisiting Your High School Labels
Take yourself back to high school in order to continue building your internal self-portrait and to help you further understand how your own self-esteem and body-esteem library was built. Where and with whom did you sit in the cafeteria? Or did you avoid the cafeteria altogether? What labels did you get in high school? Or did you stay under the radar screen to remain label-less? What critical comments or epitaphs defined who you were becoming, and what groups did you belong or not belong to? What physical or personality characteristics did your peers judge you on or define you by? (Print this series of questions at www.womaninthemirrorbook.com.)

A sample of someone's high school labels assessment: I was fat. I avoided the cafeteria entirely because I didn't want to be seen

eating. I brought my lunch and would find a room to sit somewhere alone and eat. I was quiet and never said anything in class
because I didn't want any attention to be drawn to me. My grades
were average. I got teased walking down the hall. Boys would
plaster themselves up against the wall to make room for me and
then imitate me waddling. High school for me was all about getting out of there. My identity when I left was the fat loner.

CHAPTER 3

Transition to Independence

The period of time after high school is usually a time of increased independence, a time when you may continue your education away from home or work full-time for the first time. Whatever the transition, it often involves moving out of the family home and learning how to navigate the adult world on your own.

Not everyone goes to college, but lots of people do. Or they have similar experiences that mark a new degree of independence from their families. Some of the factors covered in this chapter are specific to college life (exams, living in a dorm, cafeteria food), but others are shared by everyone in the transition to the independent phase of life (increased autonomy, future planning, eating on your own, increasing financial independence).

It seems the minute you graduate from high school, everyone's focus is on "what's next." Even if every bone in your body is begging for a summer off to recover from senior year, the pressure starts immediately. Whether it is starting the new job or preparing for college, the clock starts ticking feverishly. When you were in high school, all you wanted was to get out. Now, being cut loose puts you face-to-face with some daunting freedoms.

The Transition Years: When Self-Esteem and Body
Esteem Collide

As we transition to independence, we are faced with even more profound external evaluations of who we are, how we perform, how we compare to others, and how we look. Whether it is performance on a job interview, an audition, or a college-entrance interview, the level of scrutiny by the outside world—and, as a natural extension, the degree of self-scrutiny—increases astronomically. As we are no longer living at home, after these experiences we can't retreat to a trusted safe place in our home—our bedroom, a favorite tree in the backyard, an old stuffed animal. Rather, we return from these evaluation events, filled with emotion and even self-doubt, to a messy roommate, a dripping faucet, an empty refrigerator, bills to pay, or any number of situations that require our adult attention.

It comes as no surprise that the transition years are prime time for the development of eating disorders: The environmental and social conditions are ripe for a collision of self-esteem and body esteem in vulnerable individuals. To understand why this is such a high-risk time, it helps to understand the actual landscape of eating disorders. We talk about three or four basic presentations.

Anorexia nervosa is probably the most widely publicized eating disorder, and it is also one of the most deadly. Anorexia is marked by emaciation, weight loss, or low weight, a relentless pursuit of thinness, an intense fear of gaining weight, unwillingness (and often inability) to maintain a normal or healthy weight, and disrupted eating behavior. Other features include distorted body image (seeing oneself as fat even though underweight) and an intense fear of gaining weight. As a side effect of starvation, menstruation can stop, increasing the risk of later osteoporosis. Eating, food, and weight control become obsessions. Some who have anorexia recover with treatment after only one episode. Others get well but have relapses. Still others have a more chronic form of anorexia, in which their health deteriorates over many years as they battle the illness.

People with anorexia are up to ten times more likely to die as a result of their illness than peers without the disorder. The most common complications that lead to death are cardiac arrest and electrolyte and fluid imbalances. People with anorexia nervosa are also fifty-seven times more likely to commit suicide than their healthy peers.[1]

Many people with anorexia have coexisting psychiatric and physical illnesses, including depression, anxiety, obsessive behavior, substance abuse, cardiovascular and neurological complications, and impaired physical development.[2] Other symptoms may develop over time, including:

* thinning of the bones (osteopenia or osteoporosis)
* brittle hair and nails
* dry and yellowish skin
* growth of fine hair over body (i.e., lanugo)
* mild anemia, muscle weakness and loss
* severe constipation
* low blood pressure, slowed breathing and pulse
* drop in internal body temperature, causing a person to feel cold all the time
* lethargy

In terms of psychology, people with anorexia are often perfectionistic and anxious; they have a strong need for control, plus feelings of guilt and self-hatred, social withdrawal, depressed moods, and sometimes other self-harming behaviors.

Bulimia nervosa is characterized by recurrent and frequent episodes of eating unusually large amounts of food and feeling a lack of control over the eating (i.e., binge eating). This binge eating is typically paired with a type of behavior that compensates for the binge, such as purging (e.g., vomiting, excessive use of laxatives or diuretics, fasting, and/or exercising excessively). Unlike people with anorexia, people with bulimia can fall within the normal weight range for their age and height. But like people with anorexia, they often fear gaining weight, want desperately to lose weight, and are intensely unhappy with their body size and shape. Usually, bulimic behavior is done secretly, because it is often accompanied by feelings of disgust or shame. The bingeing-and-purging cycle usually repeats several times a week and often several times a day. As with anorexia, people with bulimia often have coexisting psychological problems such as depression, anxiety, and/or substance abuse. Many physical complications result from bulimia, including electrolyte imbalances (which can lead to heart failure), gastrointestinal problems, cardiovascular problems, and oral and tooth-related problems.[3] Other symptoms include:

* chronically inflamed and sore throat
* swollen glands in the neck and below the jaw
* worn tooth enamel and increasingly sensitive and decaying teeth as a result of exposure to stomach acids
* gastroesophageal reflux disorder (acid reflux, gastric reflux, GERD)
* intestinal distress and irritation from laxative abuse
* kidney problems from diuretic abuse
* severe dehydration from purging of fluids

Other psychological features include perfectionism, self-hatred, depression, feelings of shame, and a tendency to isolate oneself. Often dependencies on alcohol, drugs, medicines, compulsive shopping, or other self-harming behaviors can occur.

A more recently described presentation also seen on college campuses is unofficially called *purging disorder*. In this variant, people engage in compensatory behaviors such as vomiting or laxative abuse in the absence of binge eating. So they may purge after small amounts of food or after no food at all.

Finally, the most common eating disorder is *binge eating disorder*, or BED. People with BED eat an unusually large amount of food within a distinct period of time and feel a loss of control over their eating. Unlike people with bulimia, they do not regularly use inappropriate compensatory weight-control behaviors such as vomiting or using laxatives. Thus, BED is often, but not always, associated with overweight and obesity. BED is not yet recognized as an official eating disorder, but it will be in the next version of the Diagnostic and Statistical Manual of Mental Disorders.[4] Previously used terms to describe these problems included compulsive overeating, emotional eating, or food addiction. BED is often marked by several of the following:

* rapid consumption of food
* uncomfortable fullness after eating
* eating large amounts of food when not physically hungry
* feelings of guilt, shame, disgust, or depression after overeating
* eating alone to avoid embarrassment
* coexisting psychological problems including anxiety and depression
* more health problems, stress, trouble sleeping, and suicidal thoughts than people without an eating disorder

People with BED often feel badly about themselves and may miss work, school, or social activities to binge eat. They also experience guilt, shame and/or distress about the binge eating, which can sadly lead to more binge eating. It is estimated that approximately one fifth of the people who seek professional treatment for obesity meet the criteria for binge eating disorder.

Even though eating disorders clearly occur across the lifespan, the transition years are a particularly high-risk time. The average age of onset for anorexia nervosa is 18.9, for bulimia nervosa 19.7, for purging disorder 20, and for binge eating disorder 25.4.[5,6] Overall, eating problems appear rampant in college, and studies at American universities have found between 11 and 20 percent of women have full-blown eating disorders, with up to half reporting at least one eating-disorder symptom, and up to two thirds reporting dieting behavior.[7,8,9]

Causes of Eating Disorders: Nature and Nurture

Eating disorders have been misunderstood for decades. People often falsely believe that eating disorders are choices and that they are caused by people trying to diet down to reach some thin ideal. Eating disorders are disorders, not choices. From a scientific perspective, we still don't completely understand what causes eating disorders. We do know that they are caused by a complex interplay of both genetic and social factors.[10] People are often surprised to hear that genes play a role in eating disorders precisely because there is so much misinformation about eating disorders in the popular press. Eating disorders existed for hundreds of years in both Western and non-Western regions of the world. Eating disorders also run in families. The disorders are more common in relatives of people with eating disorders than in relatives of people without eating disorders. Because of shame and stigmatization, you may not be aware of people in your family who have suffered. Of, if they are older, they might never have actually received a diagnosis or proper treatment—but, for example, everyone might know that "Aunt Louise ate like a bird" or "Joan always goes to the bathroom after meals."

From decades of family studies, twin and adoption studies, and now studies that are actually designed to identify genes that influence risk for eating disorders, we can say with confidence that over half of the liability to all eating disorders is due to genetic factors, and environment is to blame for the rest.[11] In fact, eating disorders are classic examples of where genes and culture collide. The environment might be the trigger that releases the underlying genetic predisposition. That is, even if you have some genes that place you at risk, if you never go on your first diet, you may never develop an eating disorder. Ultimately, genes load the gun, but environment pulls the trigger. Here are some examples of the role the environment or social factors can play:

* In modern Western societies, there is intense pressure on women (and men) to be thin and fit. In recent decades the

role models for beauty have become increasingly thin. These role models have become so thin that very few healthy women in the population are actually that size! The same is true for male models and athletes.

* As the thin ideal has become tinier, there is more pressure to diet and exercise excessively, and a corresponding increase in eating disorders. The current "ideal" body shape for women as advertised by the fashion industry is closest to that of the prepubescent, immature girl's body. All of the digital editing and Photoshopping also makes people think perfection actually exists and is attainable. For most mature women, achieving this body shape would require losing so much body fat that it would become impossible to maintain normal menstrual functioning, normal interest in sexual activity, and normal levels of reproductive hormones.

* Advertising is putting the same pressures on men but is focusing more on leanness and low body fat. Dieting or exercising down to these extremely low weights can have similarly problematic sexual and hormonal consequences for men.

* Everyone living within modern Western society experiences some of these societal pressures towards thinness. We encounter them every day on the TV, in magazines, and even standing in the checkout line in grocery stores. These media images can attract us like a nasty magnet, even though they can make us feel worse about ourselves and even more inadequate than before.

College: The Pressure Cooker

Going away to college is a huge transition and can be one of those environmental triggers for individuals who are genetically predisposed to eating disorders, as well as for individuals who have lower genetic risk. College entry is both exciting and horizon broadening but also a source of new stresses and pressures. Before you even get there, you torment yourself: "I've got to lose weight before I go; I need new clothes; I have to get a tan." Fearful of first impressions, or wanting a fresh start from high school, you go for a complete physical and personality makeover before you even leave home. When you get there, the social comparisons start immediately; it can be like middle school all over again. "She's thinner than I am; she's prettier than I am; she's more popular than I am; I have to lose weight to fit in!" Balancing this, the first months of college are filled with discovery and experimentation as you meet new people, explore new topics, join new clubs or sports—but as

That was then . . . high school	This is now . . . college
Parents and teachers played a role in reminding you about your responsibilities and schedules.	You are in charge of your schedule. No one tells you when to sleep, eat, or do your homework.
You may have had your own room or lived only with family members.	You share a room with someone and a building with lots of strangers.
You likely went to school with people in your neighborhood or city.	You go to big classes with people from all over the country and the world.
Your curriculum was largely determined for you.	You declare a major and make choices about classes.
Tuition and books were probably free. Parents paid the bills and took care of most financial worries.	College is expensive! You may have a tight budget, school loans, and financial stressors.
You had established friendships and family support.	You form new relationships while still working on old ones that are important.
You made some decisions and choices, but priorities and goals were often reinforced by parents.	You face moral and ethical challenges that require you to examine your values.
You had opportunities for some meaningful extracurricular activities.	You have opportunities for more extracurricular activities than you can imagine.

the year progresses, freshmen women describe feeling less competent, becoming more uncomfortable with their weight, making lower grades than expected, and encountering increased stressors in their living environments. Over the course of the first year of college, women's self-esteem actually decreases!

Fundamental changes occur between high school and college. (See table on opposite page.)

This is really an enormous shift in responsibility, and there is very little burn-in time. The stress and excitement can be exhilarating but also exhausting. For many, college is hardly a reprieve from struggles with body esteem and self-esteem; in fact, for many they get worse during that time.

Monique's Story

Monique was transferring to a new, more prestigious college after being very successful at a smaller college. She had been voted vice president of her class, made all A's, was a member of the tennis team, and had a fairly active social life. Toward the end of her freshman year, she felt some of her friends pulling away from her. She decided it was probably because they were envious she was transferring. Although being left out hurt her feelings, she just continued to focus on her own goals and looked forward to moving to a new town and a new school.

Monique had always tried to eat relatively healthfully; however, due to all of her athletic activity she basically ate whatever she wanted, thinking nothing of eating fast food a few times a week or drinking a lot of soda every day. Before transferring, she thought it might be a good idea to learn more about healthy eating. She wasn't going to be able to play tennis at her new school, and she was worried about gaining weight. Monique's dad was a runner, but he blew out his knee and started dieting to watch his weight. Monique read some of the nutrition books, low-fat cookbooks, and "calorie comparison charts" that her dad had bought. She was mortified that she had eaten almost all of the foods in the "Ten Foods You Should Never Eat" chart. The more she learned about the health benefits of each and every fruit, vege-table, and whole grain, and all the harmful ingredients in pro-cessed foods, the more she couldn't believe what she had been putting into her body! She decided to make it a priority to avoid all "bad foods," fearful of what harm she may have been wreak-ing upon her physical health. No longer ignorant of the nutri-tional value of each and every food (including caloric value), she felt very responsible and disciplined now that she planned and controlled exactly what she put into her body.

As the weeks of summer wore on, she became more obsessed with reading her cookbooks and nutrition manuals so that she could plan out perfectly healthy, calorically conscious meals for the next day. As a side effect of eliminating soda, fried food, and the majority of processed foods from her diet, Monique began to lose weight. Although it wasn't her intention to lose weight, it was certainly a nice side effect. People commented on her extratrim figure and she felt a strange sense of pride when she started fitting into smaller clothing styles. She even got a boyfriend that she felt "lucky to be with," but her "superhealthy" diet made it hard for them to go out to eat or have much fun together. When he broke up with her, she was devastated and vowed to lose more weight so she would never have to feel rejected again. Monique missed a period, but she didn't worry because she knew her body was ex-tremely healthy as a result of ridding her diet of all harmful foods. She also began to weigh herself daily just to make sure she wasn't eating the wrong foods or eating too much, as she saw her weight as a direct consequence of every morsel she put into her body. The daily weighing ritual—which at first was a time of amazement and elation filled with thoughts such as "My body is so healthy I'm fi-nally getting to my natural size!"—began to be a time filled with intense anxiety with thoughts that she might have put on weight and thus must not be eating a perfectly nutritious diet.

When Monique got to her new college, people never com-mented on her weight. They all only knew her as a slim person.

She feared she wasn't special, pretty, or smart enough to fit in. Whenever she ate something she saw as bad, she berated herself for not having more willpower and would try to make up for it by exercising an extra hour or two the next day. Every now and then she induced vomiting because she felt the need to get all of the bad food out of her system. This didn't happen very often, but when it did she would be exhausted and unable to get her work done.

No one seemed worried about Monique. While thin, she was not less than 85 percent of her normal weight and had only missed one period—she surely wasn't anorexic. Simultaneously, even though she was purging some, it wasn't more than once a week and she wasn't bingeing, so she surely wasn't bulimic. However, she clearly had some serious disordered eating patterns and problems. She was beginning to experience intense anxiety surrounding the thought of regaining lost weight, and the majority of her time and energy was devoted to maintaining this extreme health regimen. Her resident advisor (RA) began to notice that Monique rarely came to hall parties to celebrate birthdays, and when she did she brought her own snacks, organic carrots and water. When her grades dropped, her RA talked with her about how unhappy she seemed and suggested that she go to the counseling center. Monique was annoyed, thought her RA was envious of her weight, and didn't really think she had a problem. To get the RA off her back, she agreed to schedule an appointment with a nutritionist at campus health services. She was sure the dietician would be impressed with her knowledge and diet and would tell her she was on her way to optimum health. Just the opposite happened! The dietician expressed her concern about Monique possibly having an eating disorder and explained that it was a serious threat to her physical health and was probably interfering with her quality of life and her studies. As a result, Monique agreed to continue seeing the nutritionist and a counselor to explore the thoughts and feelings about her eating and weight. She began to realize she was losing what was most important to her—time with family, building friendships, being an athlete, and doing well in school.

This scenario is played out at countless colleges and universities across the country every year. Girls underperform, skip semesters, drop out, or are asked to take leave secondary to the development of eating disorders on campus. Dormitory janitors tell horror stories about clogged toilets due to frequent purging. Tuition money is lost and girls get out of sync with their class when eating disorders interfere with their college experience.

Some myths about college play right into college girls adopting unhealthy eating disorders, and perhaps the biggest culprit is the myth that all girls gain fifteen pounds during their freshman year of college. The fear of "the freshman fifteen" can propel desperate measures to inhibit weight gain to ensure that "it doesn't happen to me." But how real is the freshman fifteen? In a study of 149 students tested first in September of their freshman year and again in April, 63 percent gained weight, 13 percent stayed the same, and 24 percent lost weight. Overall, the increase in weight was 3.36 pounds (hardly fifteen). Even if you just looked at the students who gained weight, their average increase was 7.3 pounds.[12]

Another study tested both women and men on college campuses to see if the myth held for both sexes and also tried to see what factors were associated with weight gain. They studied 265 men and 341 women and found that on average, men gained 3.5 pounds and women 4.0 pounds. Weight gain tended to happen early in the year (i.e., before November) and weight stabilized as the year progressed.[13] Factors that were associated with weight gain differed between the sexes. For the guys, weight gain was associated with intense workouts and high levels of sports participation. So it looks like their weight gain might be more related to muscle mass than increases in fat (although this was not measured directly). For girls, however, the only factor associated with weight gain was having a good relationship with their parents. These were parents who were described as uncritical and who allowed their daughters to be independent. Now just how that translates into weight gain was never quite explained, and indeed it might not be explicable. Some other factors that the researchers did not measure might be stronger predictors. But the important point is, in both of these studies, the freshman fifteen was shown to be a complete myth. Not only doesn't everyone gain weight, but even those who do gain much less than fifteen pounds. To put it into even better perspective, people of the same age who aren't in college are gaining weight too, on average 1.72 pounds. So it's definitely worth watching your habits when you get to college, but obsessing about a myth can only cause you harm and could launch an eating disorder.

Clearly, college is a time that can exacerbate both eating disorders and problems with weight control. What is it about the college situation that makes it such a high-risk time? Before leaving for college, we are typically still eating the food that is in the home, typically bought by the parents—probably supplemented by some of our own social eating. Access is somewhat restricted by virtue of the fact that parents are the primary shoppers. Eating is somewhat monitored—hopefully some meals are still eaten together as a family, and the primary shopper usually keeps tabs on what is being eaten and whether the amounts seem reasonable. I do know my mother didn't prepare a cafeteria buffet every night and we definitely didn't have ice cream available for sundaes after every evening meal. We had one shared meal. Everyone ate the same thing, and dessert wasn't always included.

When we go away to college, the food landscape changes dramatically. Depending on living arrangements and meal plan, some changes can include:

* twenty-four-hour access to calorie-dense foods
* tight budget for meals
* late-night pizza

* skipping meals because of oversleeping or class schedule
* limited kitchen and cooking resources
* limited storage space for food
* buffet-style cafeteria food
* caffeine
* availability of alcohol
* additional eating episodes after drinking alcohol
* availability of marijuana
* additional eating episodes after smoking marijuana

All of these factors require considerable self-regulation in order to maintain a balance of caloric intake and output. What college students report is that evening dorm-room eating ends up almost constituting a fourth meal. There are no weight consequences to these additional calories if they are offset by increased physical activity. So if your college schedule means lots of long walks across campus from class to class, and playing team or intramural sports, you might end up being one of those students who does not gain any weight. But if all of your classes are in one building and you don't exercise, then you might gain weight in college.

There are also additional factors that aren't directly related to food that can affect eating, such as:

* lack of sleep
* lack of regular exercise and sports participation
* different peer-group norms
* increased sexual activity

These changes both are influenced by stress and can cause additional stress. Sleep deprivation is linked to poor eating habits and weight gain. A lack of sleep is caused by extra stress (like cramming for an exam), but it also creates additional stress (being too exhausted to study). Then, even worse, students will start to have difficulty distinguishing between tired and hungry, and they might develop the habit of eating to stay awake, when what their body really needs is sleep. Or they might opt for a large designer coffee that gives them the caffeine burst but adds lots of high caloric hitchhikers such as cream, flavoring, and added sugar.

Research has begun to shed light on the association between sleep and weight. An extensive study of over nine thousand people who participated in the National Health and Nutrition Examination Survey I (NHANES I) first weighed participants in 1982–1984.[14] They were followed up in 1987 and gave a self-reported weight. At that first measurement, people who reported averaging fewer than seven hours of sleep per night were more likely to be obese. What was interesting is those people who reported less sleep were also more likely to become obese during the follow-up interval. There are several hypotheses as to what is going on with this relationship, including a hibernation hypothesis (that less sleep could be interpreted by the body as a sign of short summer nights, which is a signal to start storing fat because winter is coming) as well as a hormonal hypothesis: Levels of appetite hormones such as leptin and ghrelin as well as insulin sensitivity are affected by sleep deprivation and could influence weight gain over the long haul. A study published in 2005 in the journal *Sleep*[15] found that sleep-deprived teens consumed 2.2 percent more calories from fat and ate more snacks than those who slept eight hours or more a night. They also ate more total calories. The recommended number of hours of sleep for teens is nine, but that rarely happens. In short, sleep patterns that are established in college, especially if they are maintained afterward, could very much influence your weight trajectory throughout your life.

Gaining a few pounds is not that big a deal, but what becomes worrisome in college is when those few pounds are met with drastic measures to lose them. Word travels fast on college campuses, and there are certain technologies and fads associated with extreme weight control. Girls will often try things in pods (the same way they go to the restroom), and for many, experiments with diets, supplements, and herbal extracts will remain just that—experiments. But in every pod there are one or two girls who succumb to the extremes and the experiment morphs into a frank eating disorder. Without the day-to-day oversight of parents and siblings in the house, days, weeks, and months can go by without major changes in weight and behavior being detected. Or, more commonly, roommates or teammates suspect that something is wrong but they don't know what to do and are afraid to say anything.

This can all happen quite fast. Female students report increased eating-disorder symptoms from September to April of their freshman year. This also means an enormous amount of change within the first semester of college.

Another major change that occurs during the transition years is the availability of alcohol. It's hardly news that drinking occurs on college campuses, but one of the biggest myths is that most students are drinking heavily in college. A research project by the Higher Education Center for Alcohol and Other Drug Prevention called the *Survey of College Alcohol Norms and Behavior* was administered to three hundred randomly selected students at each of eighteen participating colleges.[16] Seven out of ten students (69.2 percent) overestimated the number of drinks their peers consume per week. Students actually drank on average about 4.7 drinks per week, but their fellow students perceived their peers to be drinking on average 9.01 drinks per week. Apparently it is easier to remember the few students who were trashed and acting ridiculously and to estimate drinking rates based on them than to pay attention to all of the people who remain sober and sane. These sorts of misperceptions alter our sense of what "normal" or "typical" behavior is and can contribute to students drinking more than they normally would just to be like everyone else.

Binge drinking in college has been on the rise, particularly in women, and it is associated with binge eating. Drinking leads to disinhibition of all types, making people more likely to act impulsively and put their health at risk. Alcohol consumption has been linked to an increase in having unplanned and unprotected sex and to an increased risk for obesity. People who binge drink also tend to have poor diets, greater body dissatisfaction, and unhealthy weight-control behaviors. Aside from binge drinking, simply having a few drinks at a party can trigger tendencies to overeat for some people.

The *New York Times* described a phenomenon of college women skipping meals in order to expend most of their daily caloric intake on alcohol.[17] The horrible term *drunkorexia* was coined. Because food restriction is a risk factor for overeating or a binge, this strategy not only backfires but is a recipe for disaster. Not only that, but starving in order to drink can drastically affect your academic performance.

FACTS AND TIPS FOR COLLEGE EATING

* Get your head out of bed, and eat! People who skip breakfast sabotage themselves. They set themselves up both physiologically and psychologically to overeat the rest of the day. Plus, if you want to get up in the world, you've got to get up in the morning.
* Get a good night's sleep. A number of studies have found that sleep-deprived adults and children are at greater risk of being overweight. Creativity and problem solving require a rested brain.
* Keep alcoholic beverages to a minimum. Beer, wine, and liquor don't provide nutritional value and can cause blood-sugar spikes and dips. They may make you more likely to eat when you are not hungry.

* Try to eat food items high in calcium. Your late teens and early twenties are important years in osteoporosis prevention.
* Pay attention (okay, this goes for class, too). Try to eat mindfully, not mindlessly. When we are eating and multi-tasking, we don't enjoy what we are eating and can quickly lose track of how much we are eating.
* Pay attention to serving sizes. You may be eating more or less than you think.
* Be sure to eat enough. Prepacking healthy snacks for busy days can help you eat healthfully and have plenty of energy to get through your day.
* Make your plate colorful—not monochromatic. Different fruits and vegetables offer different health benefits.
* Plan regular opportunities to exercise a few times a week. Studies have shown that exercise can decrease anxiety and depression. Exercising with friends or in a recreational group can help prevent overexercising and adds a social benefit.
* Listen to your body. Pay attention to its hunger signals and learn to eat when you are hungry rather than when you are stressed, anxious, angry, tired, or even joyful.

Source: Pathway to Awareness in College Eating (PACE): http://www.pace.unc.edu/team.[18]

Sexual Orientation

College is also a time when many people consolidate their sexual preferences. Especially if your high school was very traditional or intolerant, college might be the first time when you can seek out and discuss your preferences with peers. Research consistently shows that gay men have worse body satisfaction than straight men, and gay male college students report higher overall body dissatisfaction than straight students. Gay students also admit to feeling "terrified of being fat" as well as "feeling fat despite others' perceptions" at higher rates than their straight classmates. They have high body dissatisfaction even when at their ideal body weight. Also, gay men who are more invested in the gay community report the highest levels of body dissatisfaction, and their desired appearance focuses more on leanness than thinness.

The reasons for heightened body dissatisfaction in this population are not clearly understood, but some theories suggest a variety of influences. First, gay men believe that men are more likely to judge partners (male or female) based on physical appearance. They also know that the relatively low numbers of gay men in the community can make finding a partner even more difficult. Thus, the dissatisfaction is related to a desire to attract a suitable partner. Simultaneously, being gay in a world that can be hostile and discriminatory can cause significant distress, and disordered eating can manifest in an attempt to cope with personal and sexual concerns.

In a raw and revealing memoir, Frank Bruni, former *New York Times* restaurant critic and author of *Born Round*, recalls his college days at the University of North Carolina as a prestigious Morehead Scholar.[19] Having kept his weight under control in high school as a competitive swimmer, the transition to a more sedentary college lifestyle gave his waistline the opportunity to catch back up with his appetite. At the same time, he entered the gay dating scene completely self-conscious about his body and weight. Bruni recalls, "It was Haagen-Dazs or love. I couldn't have both." Frank descriptions of his nighttime binges in the newsroom, developing a purge map of the university where he could vomit undetected, and episodes of overwhelming weakness from laxative abuse underscore the private pain and self-consciousness of a college-aged gay man suffering from an eating disorder during the difficult transition years. Despite vows to himself to be candid about who he was and what he felt in college, the inner torture he experienced unfolded on the appetite and body-esteem playing field.

In addition to body dissatisfaction, gay men report almost all eating-disorder behaviors at higher rates than straight men. One study reported that the proportion of gay and bisexual men with disordered eating symptoms was ten times higher than among heterosexual men (10 and 1 percent, respectively).[20] A sociocultural explanation for these differences holds that values and norms in the gay male community place greater focus on physical appearance, and gay men feel pressured to confirm to these ideals.[21,22]

Applying the same sociocultural perspective to women, one proposal holds that lesbian and bisexual women adhere less to the standards of feminine beauty espoused by Western culture than heterosexual women and thus may be protected from eating disorders. There is mixed support for this in the literature, with some studies revealing that lesbian and bisexual women have lower levels of body dissatisfaction and eating disorders than heterosexual women.[23,24] Other studies find no differences.[25,26]

A comprehensive study of white, black, and Latino heterosexual, gay, and bisexual women and men revealed that gay and bisexual men had a significantly higher prevalence of bulimia and other eating disorders, but there were no differences between heterosexual women and lesbians and bisexual women. Eating disorders also did not cluster in one race or ethnicity, although Latino and black gay or bisexual men had particularly high rates of eating disorders.[27] This is consistent with reports from university campuses in Puerto Rico, which identified high rates of binge eating, vomiting, and laxative use among male students regardless of sexual orientation.[28]

College as the Solution

Colleges can also be part of the solution to the body-esteem and self-esteem whirlpool. What better time to set the stage for a lifetime of healthy behaviors and attitudes? Although we have seen vividly how body esteem and self-esteem can collide during the college years to result in eating disorders or weight gain, college campuses have become increasingly aware of their responsibilities to foster healthy lifestyles in students, because the years kids spend in college often establish patterns for the rest of their lives.

Many colleges have taken advantage of widespread Internet on campus to develop screening and detection programs for a number of health problems like depression and alcohol abuse. At UNC Chapel Hill, a program is being piloted called Pathway to Awareness in College Eating (PACE).[29] In this program, freshmen are invited to complete an online survey to screen for disordered eating. Depending on their results, they are offered a menu of options for intervention. Those with few or no symptoms are provided complete access to an extensive library of online information about eating disorders, nutrition, and college health. They also participate in ongoing monitoring so that any new symptoms that emerge can be detected as they go through their college years. Individuals who are showing some symptoms are invited to participate in online therapist-led chats. They too participate in ongoing monitoring. Individuals who are clearly symptomatic are immediately referred for face-to-face care. By establishing a baseline at the beginning of freshman year and following students throughout their four-year stay, programs like PACE can detect individuals who are starting to show symptoms, or who are showing worsening symptoms, and ensure that they get referred to the proper level of care promptly. The goal of such programs is to reduce the number of new cases and to improve detection before the eating disorder becomes so severe that their lives and their education become compromised.

A second powerful movement has transformed the way weight and shape are discussed and experienced on college campuses, and it's coming from an unlikely source—sororities! Previously vilified as the sources of body competition and disordered eating, sororities—at both the local and national level—have teamed up with eating-disorders-prevention researcher Carolyn Becker, Ph.D., of Trinity University in San Antonio, Texas, to develop a program that is spreading around campuses to empower women to not have to fall into the eating-disorder and appearance trap while in college.

Reflections: Body Image Program was started by the local sororities at Trinity University and then made available throughout North America for any sorority (and even some non-sorority groups) by the Delta Delta Delta sorority (also known as Tri Delta). As the first peer-led, evidence-based eating-disorders prevention program shown to truly work, Reflections purposefully does not focus on eating disorders, but rather emphasizes creating and reaffirming positive and healthy personal body image through a variety of structured small-group discussions, activities, and exercises.

Reflections has a proven track record—not only for improving body-image issues, but for encouraging healthy confrontation and communication skills as well. [30] The results are impressive:

* Eight months after the program, 53 percent of women who have participated at one school no longer felt strongly that their weight influenced how they felt about themselves as a person.
* 48 percent of women at one college who said they "felt fat almost every day" before the program felt that way never or less than half the time up to eight months after the program.
* Over half of participants who felt their shape often interfered with their ability to concentrate before the program experienced a dramatic decrease well after the program.

The Reflections program helps college women take control of their own destinies, their own bodies, and their own inner dialogues. Its goal is to change the conversation to create a more positive body image for women everywhere. Tri Delta has broadened the impact of this program by launching Fat Talk Free Week. During this week, women and girls throughout the world (not just college women) are encouraged to ban "fat talk" from their vocabulary. This is such a fundamental component of taking charge of your inner dialogue and separating your body esteem from your self-esteem that an entire chapter is devoted to eliminating fat talk in Part Two of this book.

Fat talk describes all of the statements made in everyday conversation that reinforce the thin ideal and contribute to women's dissatisfaction with their bodies. Examples of fat talk include "I'm so fat," "Do I look fat in this?" "I need to lose ten pounds," and "She's too fat to be wearing that swimsuit." Statements that are considered fat talk don't necessarily have to be negative; they can seem positive yet also reinforce the need to be thin: "You look great! Have you lost weight?"

Fat Talk Free Week is a five-day public-awareness effort sponsored by Tri Delta, The Center for Living, Learning and Leading, and many other invested partners. The campaign was intended to draw attention to the damaging impact of fat talk and the thin ideal on today's women. Dr. Becker explains, "Reflections and Fat Talk Free Week exist thanks to a realization that organized groups of women [i. e., in this case sororities] have enormous power to create change when given the right tools. These programs were born out of a respectful partnership between the best prevention science available and true respect for community power, along with a healthy dose of serendipity. The take-home message of Reflections is that scientists need community partners and communities need science if we really seek to create change." Dr. Becker and the countless women who have put time, energy, and creativity into this program illustrate just how strong women can be when they join together with the goal of reducing or eliminating talk that is damaging to the self and to other women.

Diploma in Hand

Somewhere around junior year, it strikes students that the end is nearing. Even if you are working your way through college, there is still succor in being part of a university community. You belong and you have at least short-term direction. Crossing the hump of sophomore year makes you realize that you will soon be on your own. The free-floating anxiety about your future that permeated the end of high school returns with a vengeance in college when you begin to think about next steps—job market, graduate school, time off. Plus, with the pressure to pair up, if you have not found what looks like a permanent partnership, you start worrying that the pickings are going to get slim once you leave school.

If job and partner are not in place, graduation can be a bittersweet event. On the one hand, you have completed a praiseworthy accomplishment—you have your degree. On the other, especially in difficult economic times, uncertainty makes it hard to celebrate without overtones of anxiety and worry.

Exercises: Transition-Year Challenges

Returning to your ongoing inventory, chronicle any negative comments that you might have accumulated and archived during your transition to independence years—whether that was college, your first job, or the first time you moved out of the house. Comments made during this phase of life can be particularly sticky because they often have an evaluative component about your general competence. In college or at your first job, you're being evaluated by peers, colleagues, supervisors, teaching assistants, and professors. In college, every day seems to bring some sort of evaluation. We're judged socially, emotionally, and academically, and we have many public experiences of either making the cut for something or being cut. From rushing sororities to test grades to academic honor societies to promotions on the job—there is constant judgment of whether you are good enough. If you make the cut, those organizations or groups become part of your world. If not, again you face the chant of "that's not my world." Looking back, include both comments and experiences from that period of life that worked their way under your skin and challenged your self-esteem. If you don't have any examples, then you have gotten out of jail free and you can head right to the next chapter. But if you did experience some negative comments, take a moment and catalog them now before moving on to the next chapter. Here's a sample of an event to get you started:

TRANSITION-YEAR COMMENTS

Age	Comment or event	Who said it, did it?	Situation	How it affected you then	How it affects you now
18	Rushed a sorority with my best, friend Beth. She got in, but I did not!	Cathy L., sorority sister, broke the news with a sweet smile.	In the sorority commons room with 25 other girls.	Devastated, envious, felt rejected. Wished my friend would back out but she didn't. Would never be my world!	Still *hate* driving past the sorority house because they rejected me!

Print your own table online at www.womaninthemirrorbook.com.

CHAPTER 4

Marriage and Family . . . or Not!

After you have finished your education and established yourself professionally, you embark upon a stage of life when difficult choices need to be made. Decisions about whether to enter into a permanent relationship, get married, and have children are central organizing principles of your life. If you do have children, you must wrestle with balancing the demands of work and family. Whichever path you are on, you feel scrutinized by others—by mothers and grandmothers, by other women, by the men in your life, and especially by yourself.

Women's bodies undergo enormous change during this phase of life. You starve to fit into your wedding dress, you gain weight after you get married, you expand to have babies and breast-feed, and by your mid- or late thirties the aging process is quietly marching along. If you have chosen the partner and family route, you look across the fence at friends and colleagues who have opted out of this lifestyle and occasionally envy them for how much time and money they must have to work with and pursue their own interests. If you've opted out of the partner and family script, sometimes your biological clock starts ticking in a panic or you worry about being destined to a lonely and disconnected future. Regardless of which path you choose, you fret.

To Partner or Not to Partner?
When you hear someone say, "I'm glad I'm married—it seems so much harder to find someone these days," you probably remember

your mother saying the same thing about her generation. If it keeps getting so much harder, we're going to be extinct. But with Germany at zero population growth and Italy actually experiencing negative population growth, maybe it really *is* getting harder.

Somewhat ironically, we're going through puberty earlier and reproducing later. Although this pattern is good for the tampon industry, it has complicated women's lives. Women are capable or reproducing long before society is ready for us to reproduce. We *look* ready to reproduce before we are mentally prepared to deal with being sexual.

The pressures to "partner up" may have started as early as elementary or middle school, but when all of your friends start sporting engagement rings and you still haven't found Mr. Right, panicked negative self-talk sets in. If you are searching for Ms. Right, your negative self-talk will be somewhat different.

Regardless of your sexual preference, the attributions can be the same. After a series of failed relationships, the internal chatter turns to asking yourself what is wrong with you. "I'm too bossy, I'm too demanding, I'm too old-fashioned, I'm too liberal," and of course women commonly settle on "I'm too fat," since that is easier to do something about. So you sweat and starve and go to extremes to get your weight down to the point where no one wants to be around you because you are miserable and no fun! That strategy backfired!

Lily was incredibly desperate to get married because of the pressure she felt from her family, friends, and most of all from herself. Her negative self-talk focused on her inadequacies in selecting men and keeping them around. She worried that she was too demanding, bossy, smart, and successful—all of the qualities her mother told her would scare men off.

Out of desperation, she convinced herself that she loved a man with whom she had very little in common. He was less educated than she, not social, boring, did not like her friends, and didn't even like Lily all that much, but she nevertheless managed to get him to the point of proposing. It was apparent to everyone around her that this situation was forced and wrong, but all she cared about was the ring. Once she had the ring, she could appease the external eye. But everyone around her knew this relationship was doomed. The relationship ended up being a financial disaster for her because she went in half with him on everything, determined that this was going to be a till-death-do-us-part scenario. But they didn't even make it to the altar. After they dissolved the engagement, her negative self-talk became even more self-blaming and nihilistic and she believed she would never find a man because she was somehow fatally flawed.

Jessie spent five thousand dollars on a wedding dress that she purposely bought too small so she would be forced to lose weight in order to walk down the aisle. She was determined to be the bride she always imagined she would be. She wanted everyone to look at her and say what a great figure she had. Two months before her wedding, she was exercising every day, cutting down on carbs, and staying away from sugar completely. With a week to go before the big day, she had her final fitting and she was *still* having trouble with the zipper. As she was standing in the dressing room, the thoughts going through her head were painful: "I blew it—I'm a loser. I look like a sausage in this dress!" But, still determined, she decided that rather than having the dress let out, she was going to give it one more push. She figured that if she started taking some of those water pills, she'd get less puffy and there would be a chance she could fit into her dress. So for the last week, while she was running around finalizing flowers, guest seating, menus, and orchestrating out-of-town guests, she skipped meals and popped handfuls of over-the-counter water pills. No surprise, the numbers went down on the scale. On the morning of the wedding, she was exhausted and haggard, but all she cared about was that she got that dress zipped up! But what a price she paid. As she walked down the aisle, she barely registered seeing her husband-to-be waiting for her at the altar; all she could think about was what the people watching her were thinking. She made it through the ceremony even though she was a little light-headed and worked her way to the reception. She was completely dehydrated. While working the receiving line, she had a glass of champagne on an empty stomach. She started to feel dizzy, excused herself, and went to the ladies' room. When she didn't return several minutes later, one of her bridesmaids went in after her and found her passed out on the bathroom floor. The pressures to be the "perfect bride" turned what should have been the best day of her life into a trip to the emergency room.

You find someone whom you love and with whom you want to spend the rest of your life. You exchange rings; you glow with promise, excitement, and love. You decide to formalize your commitment with a wedding and you buy your first bridal magazine. Unless you have been a bridesmaid before, you have no idea what's awaiting you. A whole industry designed to transform what should be the most wonderful day of your life into the most stressful! Why do they do it? Why are wedding-dress sizes different from regular sizes? Why, if you wear an 8 in the real world, is your wedding dress a 10, or even a 12? This is a conspiracy! You look at a bridal magazine, see a dress you like, go to a store, try it on, and you're two or three sizes bigger than you thought you were. Your reaction: *"I HAVE to lose twenty pounds before the wedding . . . ALL eyes will be on me!"* So you embark on the search for invitations, cakes, flowers, and bridesmaids, not in a nourished and healthy state but completely food deprived and irritable. The glow from your engagement fades to a hungry pallor as you test your self-worth every morning on the scale.

Weddings are a lightning rod for negative inner dialogue that robs us of a pivotal life experience. Prichard and Tiggemann unveiled the intentions of 879 Australian brides-to-be recruited from five bridal Web sites.[1] Before the wedding, close to 75 percent of the sample planned to exercise more and follow a "healthy eating plan," over 35 percent planned to cut fat or carbohydrates from their diets, and on average they were hoping to lose over eight kilograms (eighteen pounds) by their wedding day! These authors cried out for a healthier bridal body ideal. Special events like weddings become not about the love you share with someone else but about how you look, what people are saying about your body, and the number on the scale. It pulls you out of the here and now and traps you in your distorted self-perceptions—a supremely lonely place—isolated from those you love and the life around you.

Wherever a wedding is taking place, the inner thoughts of brides and grooms are strikingly different. Let's start with the guys. "The penguin suit is irritating, the collar is cutting into my neck, I can't wait till this ceremony is over, I need a drink, I'm gonna score tonight!" Okay, I'm sorry, gentlemen, I don't really mean that (well, maybe I do). Let's just say that part of their brain is looking forward to the after-party. The rest of their attention is, of course, focused on their lovely bride, and they are probably just a little worried about what they are committing to!

As the bride walks down the aisle, she sees the groom waiting for her, she has her dad on her arm, but all she can think of is how fat she looks. "Is my stomach sticking out? Is this dress flattering? Should I suck in more?" Granted, everyone actually *is* staring at her. If you have even a smidgen of shyness or social phobia, walking down the aisle is a nightmare, but if you're worried about your weight, you don't even focus on your groom, this life-changing experience, or the joy that you could be feeling because you have been removed from the here and now by your negative self-talk.

Marriage, Self-Esteem, and Body Esteem

You survive the wedding and the knot is tied. What's next? What happens to body esteem and self-esteem as you cross the threshold from single to married life? Decades ago when marriage meant giving up your life for your man by just about every metric except the economic one, marriage was not to women's advantage.

With the evolution of the nature of marriage, things are not quite so bleak—although they're not entirely rosy either. Never-married women (whether cohabitating or living alone) tend to have higher body mass indices than married or divorced women,[2] but married women do not report higher self-esteem than single women.[3] One large study with adult women in the community also found that married women were less likely to report intense dieting, suggesting that marriage may offer some protection against this potentially harmful eating behavior; but there were no differences between married or cohabitating and single women in terms of binge eating or weight concerns.[4] Marriage and becoming a mother were both associated with significant decreases in scores on scales that rate bulimia and the drive for thinness.[5]

Although marriage might offer some protective effects against disordered eating attitudes and behaviors, it does not make women's lives any easier. In fact, marriage means busywork for women—but not for men! According to a University of Michigan study, having a husband creates an extra seven hours a week of housework for women.[6] In contrast, having a wife saves men from about an hour of housework a week. The good news is that the amount of housework done by U.S. women dropped from twenty-six hours a week in 1976 to seventeen hours in 2005—but that's on top of their day jobs! For men, it has climbed a little—from six hours 1976 to about thirteen hours in 2005. Children add a whole new dimension. Married women with more than three kids did an average of about twenty-eight hours of housework a week, whereas their married male counterparts chipped in only about ten hours every week.

It has been argued (by many comedians especially) that this housework differential is an artifact of women having unrealistic standards of cleanliness and tidiness, but in reality it is because maintaining standards of sanitation and livability still fall on our shoulders. If women were content with their families wearing dirty clothes, having dirty dishes stacked up in the sink, and eating take-out pizza every night, then their hours of household chores might decrease and be on par with those of men. But women continue to retain disproportionate responsibility for sanitation, decorum, and nutrition that drive those hours up.

Even so, women still get married. Even if they get divorced, they get married again. The institution has changed but it is here to stay. Women seek out marriage for several well-documented reasons, one of which is reproduction.

Pregnancy and Your Body
Samantha was pregnant for the first time and she had no idea what to expect. She had suffered from bulimia when she was younger and had struggled with her body image as far back as she could remember. Her friends told her she would just love being pregnant because she could eat whatever she wanted without feeling guilty. She started out like gangbusters and gained twenty pounds in her first trimester. She was actually okay with the weight gain until her first prenatal visit. The nurse was merciless in admonishing her about the weight gain and told her in no uncertain terms to put the brakes on the eating for two. Needless to say, the nurse didn't ask about any history of eating problems and didn't provide any guidance (aside from a pamphlet on nutrition during pregnancy) about how to get her eating under control. Samantha was mortified. She started fasting before every prenatal visit to avoid the embarrassment of being humiliated by her nurse again. For two days before every visit, she restricted herself to two hundred calories per day, determined to "make weight." Then after the appointment, she just felt like her bones were hungry, for days she felt like she could eat everything in sight—and she did. Even though she fretted about what the extremes of fasting and binge eating were doing to her baby, the fear of humiliation was just too much to bear.

Pregnancy is the ultimate out-of-control body experience. This is a time of life when many women claim to hear multiple competing scripts in their heads. The old script doesn't stop. You see your pregnant silhouette in the mirror and you say to yourself, "You're fat!" But for many women, a healthier set of challenging scripts emerges at this point to counter that old dialogue that say, "Wait a minute, I'm not fat, I'm pregnant." The reproductive years are complicated for both body esteem and self-esteem. Not only is your body undergoing real changes, your hormones are rising and falling with abandon sometimes from one minute to the next.

From your first prenatal visit (and every one thereafter), the first thing your obstetrician's nurse does is plop you on the scale. Just like at a fish market, she'll call out and record your weight. Especially if it's your first pregnancy, you have no idea what's normal. Instead of asking how you feel about your weight, she writes it in your chart and rotely moves on to blood pressure. You listen to other women, read magazines, scour the Internet and the mommy blogs, and talk with your female family members— all to get an idea of what's normal—but everyone seems to tell a different story. So ultimately you're not sure which of your own scripts to listen to, and you might wonder, *Hey, maybe I am fat after all!*

Pregnancy gets you coming or it gets you going. Some women have easy pregnancies and then their labors and deliveries are horrible. Some women have wretched pregnancies, then the babies slip out like Jell-O. You can't compare and you can't compete. Most of all, you can't predict!

We tend not to respect the realities of pregnancy enough. We set up a series of expectations for pregnant moms both during pregnancy and afterward that are tailor-made to further erode self-esteem and body esteem. The biggest culprit is the culture of "should" that surrounds pregnancy and the postpartum—you "should" work up to the day you are due, you "should" be able to lose your baby weight within six weeks, you "should" be able to breast-feed without any guidance, you "should" be able to go back to work after six weeks as if nothing ever happened. The second-biggest culprit is the culture of fear that we have created around pregnancy—don't eat this, don't go there, don't get exposed to that—or your child will come out a three-headed hermaphrodite with attention deficit hyperactivity disorder! All of this can make a mother so anxious and obsessed that her levels of cortisol (the primary stress hormone) alone can affect her unborn child.

It is no surprise that you are supposed to gain weight during pregnancy. Astonishingly, the guidelines about how much weight you should gain during pregnancy have varied considerably across the decades. Currently, the recommendations differ depending on your body mass index (BMI) before pregnancy. Body mass index is a measure of weight that also accounts for height. It is measured in kg/m^2. The easiest way to calculate your BMI is to go to a reliable BMI calculator such as that provided by the National Institutes of Health (www.nhlbisupport. com/bmi).[7] If you want to do the math, take your weight in pounds and multiply it by 703, then divide that quantity by your height in inches squared. (BMI = weight (lbs) × 703/ height (in)^2.) If your pre-pregnancy BMI is less than $18.5 \, kg/m^2$, your recommended weight gain range is twenty-eight to forty pounds; if you are $18.5–24.9 \, kg/m^2$, then twenty-five to thirty-five pounds; if you are in the overweight category (BMI 25.0–29.9), then it is recommended that you gain between fifteen and twenty-five pounds; and if you are in the obese range (BMI greater than 30), then eleven to twenty pounds.[8] But the worst thing to do is to become obsessed by these numbers. They are guidelines, not rules, and focusing on numbers rather than healthful nutrition can do more harm than good to both mother and baby.

The best advice is to avoid extremes. Don't go hog wild and eat like crazy, thinking that eating for two means a ticket to the all-you-can-eat buffet for nine months. And don't restrict. Don't let that script that keeps telling you you're fat deny you and your baby the nourishment that you both require. Now, this is advice for women who have never had problems with eating disorders. Advice for those who have is more complicated. The first piece of advice is to find an obstetrician with whom you can talk about your eating disorder even if it was something in the past. We have done a fairly good job bringing depression out of the shadows and getting obstetricians and midwives to talk about histories of depression and what that means for risk of postpartum mood disorders. But we still don't have them talking openly about eating disorders. The reason for that is so many physicians still think that eating disorders are just choices—eat a little more or eat a little less. Well, we all know it isn't that simple.

In fact, in a large study we conducted in Norway with over forty thousand pregnant women, we tracked the course of eating disorders during and after pregnancy. What we found was striking. There was a subset of women for whom pregnancy offered a reprieve from their eating disorder. These women seemed to be able to adopt healthy eating behaviors while the baby was on the inside. Another group of women did not experience this grace period and continued to suffer from eating disorders throughout the pregnancy. Finally, what we didn't expect was that a substantial number of women actually developed eating disorders for the first time during pregnancy. The most common eating disorder to develop during pregnancy was binge eating disorder.[9] Mothers with eating disorders also had different nutritional profiles than moms with no eating disorders during pregnancy, and they tended to breast-feed for shorter periods of time. What you eat during pregnancy matters—both biologically and psychologically. Find a doctor with whom you can discuss this frankly so that you can get nutritional counseling and psychological support as needed both during and after pregnancy.

We completed another study at a psychiatry clinic that specializes in treating women who have mood disorders associated with pregnancy. Of all the women presenting for postpartum depression, a whopping 30 percent reported histories of eating disorders. Had we not asked, they would not have revealed their histories, as these women were only presenting for the treatment of depression, not eating disorders.[10] Women typically try to hide their eating disorders from their providers for fear of being criticized or poorly understood.

Your body is basically taken over by your baby when you are pregnant. Many women find that self-consciousness can rear its head again during pregnancy. In the early months before you have told anyone you're pregnant, as you start to challenge the zippers and buttons of your clothes, you wonder if people are thinking that you are getting fat. You're being wise and cautious by not telling people that you're pregnant until twelve weeks, but you want to just yell out, "I'm gaining weight because I'm pregnant!!" You feel like you need to justify yourself and apologize for weight gain that you can see and feel but that others most likely can't perceive at all. With the exception of highly body-competitive women, people notice much less about each other's appearance than we think. For precisely this reason we need to develop an app to give our partners a heads-up when we get a haircut so their phone can remind them to say, "Nice haircut!" Otherwise, chances are they won't even notice such a major change let alone a subtle increase of a few pounds.

But then once you do announce your pregnancy and once you do start to show, your body is no longer your own. A junior colleague who was about six months pregnant flopped down in a chair in my office, exasperated. "If one more person comments on the size of my belly, I am going to scream," she exclaimed. In the course of a free afternoon that she spent at the pool with her son, people commented, "You're big for six months," "You're small for six months," "You're carrying high, it must be a boy," "Are you gaining more weight than last time?" and her favorite, "*Qué grande!*" She then complained that everyone seemed to think that because she was pregnant, her belly became public property and they all had the right to touch her expanding abdomen. She just wanted to scream, "Get your paws off my body!"

This is one of the mysteries of pregnancy—why interpersonal boundaries completely change and people think they have the right to touch you in ways they never would if you were not pregnant. There is absolutely no "should" about being required to let other people touch your belly when you are pregnant. Touching your belly is a privilege that you invite others to do—an experience over which you have the last say. It's okay to build a fence around your belly. You wouldn't let a stranger just come up and touch your baby after she or he was born, and you sure wouldn't let a stranger come up and touch your belly when there was no baby in there. So hands off unless you have an invitation!

But these are not easy waters to navigate—especially with well-meaning relatives and especially if your culture of origin condones or even encourages such practices. For example, Wendy was finally at the point of agreeing that it was okay to protect her belly from random hands reaching out to touch her. When she finally got up the courage to restrict someone's touch, she found that she felt enormously guilty. The thoughts in her head were, "Maybe the woman was just trying to bond with me; maybe this is the way women show community in this day and age; maybe there is something evolutionarily significant about women getting overinvolved with each other's pregnancies; maybe I hurt her feelings by telling her it made me uncomfortable when she touched me." This is a continuation of the tortured inner female dialogue that continues throughout the reproductive years. Although Wendy believed intellectually that she had a right to tell people, "Hands off," when push came to shove, she felt completely guilty for setting a limit—to the point where she wondered whether being assertive was worth it. It was almost easier for her to endure the misery of being inappropriately touched than to make her preferences known. This is a fundamental challenge. You have the right to negotiate, the right to be assertive, even the responsibility to your daughters to be strong role models—but you can't always do it because the internal doubt dialogue gets in the way. The only way to get past that hurdle once and for all is to deal with the internal dialogue directly.

In the United States, in many jobs, you are expected to be

back to work six weeks after giving birth. This is patently ridiculous. Nowhere are the policies as mother-unfriendly as in the United States. Other places, such as Germany and the Scandinavian countries, have protected "mother time" in which your job has to be kept for you for up to a certain period. Denmark even mandates paternal leave by granting fifty-two weeks total of parental leave, eighteen of which must be taken by the mother, two of which *must* be taken by the father, and the rest of which can be divided as the parents see fit![11,12] Remarkably, their companies carry on, their departments thrive, and the mothers (and fathers) seem much happier!

Our six-weeks-if-you're-lucky system is structured so that you should be completely prepared to come back to work and there should be no visible traces that anything happened. Basically the expectation is to have the baby, pull yourself together, fit back into your work clothes, find a placement for the child, and get yourself back to work. No fatigue, no decrement in performance, and no distractions from that pesky little limpet. Leave no trails. If you're lucky, they'll set aside a stall in the bathroom or some dingy little room where you can pump, but don't take more than fifteen minutes, and let's not have this breast-feeding whim go on for too long, please. You get questions like, "Are you *still* breast-feeding?" suggesting subtly that it's time to move on.

But the whole pregnancy experience is surrounded by additional "shoulds." The tabloid baby watch is replete with miracle stories about celebs giving birth and getting right back to work without batting an eye. Heidi Klum walks the Victoria's Secret show six weeks after giving birth. Natalia Vodianova on the runway just two weeks after delivery. (Don't forget that Ms. Vodianova suffered from an eating disorder and represented the Council of Fashion Designers of America on a panel defending the fashion industry's stance on eating disorders.) When you read these miracle stories, the thoughts that go through your head are, "If they can get back to work that fast, then I should be able to too." But there are serious differences between their lives and yours. These women have twenty-four hour personal trainers, chefs, nannies, and personal assistants, and they are so popular and rich that people work around their schedules—they don't clock in according to their boss's schedule!

Here is how absurd it is to think that you can get back to work full throttle after six weeks (and this isn't even considering whether you had a C-section or vaginal delivery). Six weeks after giving birth, your hormones are still all over the map. Regardless of whether you are breast-feeding, you're probably still not menstruating, so that is one concrete indicator that those pregnancy-related hormones have not yet stabilized. You're not sleeping. Before pregnancy, women sleep on average 412 minutes per night and report a sleep efficiency (ratio of the time spent asleep to the time actually in bed) of 93 percent. At three to four weeks postpartum, you are down to 379 minutes with a sleep efficiency of 81 percent.[13] You're also not thinking clearly. Women talk about "pregnancy brain" and memory problems. Well, they're real, especially if you're not sleeping.[14] Yet we expect you to be back operating heavy machinery, flying airplanes, performing surgery, cleaning teeth, teaching school, whatever your job might be in this somnambulistic state. You can probably pull yourself together and do it, but definitely not at top efficiency. Chances are the pressure to be back at top form so soon takes a toll on not only your health but also your self-esteem and your body esteem.

When you are torn between having to go back to work or losing your job because you want to be with your child; when you go back to work but you still feel puffy, as if nothing fits, and your breasts hurt because you can't get away to pump, it is only natural that you ask yourself, "Am I doing the right thing?" You look around and see someone else who seems to be doing it with more ease, and you feel inadequate as a mother and inadequate in your job. Your self-esteem and your body esteem can take a hard knock at a time when you deserve to be fully experiencing the marvels of having a new child.

In an entertaining and enlightening book called *Does This Pregnancy Make Me Look Fat?*, activist Claire Mysko and model Magali Amadei developed a "Healthy Beauty Pledge" for mothers and mothers-to-be to help them reclaim their bodies and their minds and to cleanse them of the "shoulds" and myths that drive new mothers to extremes.[15] Some of their pledges:

* Acknowledge that there is no such thing as the perfect body or the perfect mommy.
* Take care of myself and take time for myself even if some days I can only manage one-minute increments.
* Give up the mission to get my "prebaby body" back and start focusing my energy on moving *forward* in my new life.

Claire and Magali advocate for less emphasis on losing the baby weight right after pregnancy and more emphasis on dealing with eating and weight issues in mothers-to-be. Acknowledging the percentage of women in the country who struggle with eating and weight, they emphasize that we should help them to establish healthy eating patterns *before* even getting pregnant. Those healthy patterns would then be able to continue during and after pregnancy and replace the desperate dash to drop the pounds after giving birth.

Claire and Magali are alluding to a common script that women share after giving birth: As soon as the baby is out, they no longer have an excuse to be above their pre-pregnancy weight. They were given a brief reprieve while carrying the baby, but as soon as they are home from the hospital, their get-out-of-jail-free card expired. Weight loss becomes a motivating factor in several parenting issues—such as finding child care so you can exercise, and even whether or not to breast-feed.

Breast-feeding definitely has advantages, but it is a personal choice. The United States doesn't make it easy to breast-feed for long. On average, around 71.4 percent of U.S. children receive some breast milk, but by three months only 51.5 percent of infants were receiving it; at six months, these rates drop to 35.5 percent.[16] In contrast, in Norway 99 percent of women initiate breast-feeding, and the proportion of breast-fed infants is 96 percent at one month, 85 percent at four months, and 80 percent at six months.[17] Obviously, their working-mother policies facilitate breast-feeding and make it easier for mothers to choose this option. In the United States, the choice can be agonizing and inappropriately influenced by other people's perceptions and judgments. Remember, it is much harder to be resilient to judgments from others when you are a hormonal roller coaster. The United States has sacrificed breast-feeding for productivity. In fact, we historically farmed our breast-feeding duties out to wet nurses so that we could get on with our lives. Now we farm them out to multinational corporations who don't have a hope in the world of ever creating formulae that come close to the biological complexity of breast milk.

I have a personal story that helped me understand the challenges American women face when it comes time to making the decision to breast-feed. It never crossed my mind not to breast-feed. As a scientist, I did the research and understood the immunologic benefits to the baby, and as a psychologist I valued the bonding time with my babies. I didn't discuss it with anyone and I didn't make my decision public in any way. I just did it. My first child was born in the United States, and women who had been mothers in the sixties, which was the heyday of baby formula, often made comments like, "Oh, dear, breast-feeding, that's so old-fashioned. We never did that. How are you going to go back to work?" Just the subtle innuendo that they had evolved beyond breast-feeding and somehow I was reversing evolution with my decision could really have gotten under my skin had I been more sensitive and less clear in my decision.

Then I had the remarkable fortune of having two babies in

New Zealand, where the support for breast-feeding mothers is universal. Not only did I receive wonderful preparation in the hospital, but breast-feeding was condoned everywhere and anywhere, and a nurse came to my house every week as a matter of routine care, checking in on the health and development of my babies. She also checked in on how breast-feeding was going. I was even excused from jury duty secondary to breast-feeding obligations! After I went back to work, no matter what I was doing, our nanny would show up, knock on the door, announce that it was lunchtime, and I would just carry on with whatever I was doing—whether it was a meeting with a student, a staff meeting, or a teleconference, and my babies would be fed. We simply made it happen, and no one batted an eye. I took this arrangement for granted and assumed that breast-feeding in public was just as natural as seeing someone sitting on a park bench reading a book.

Then, on a trip back to the States with three children in tow, one still breast-feeding, I was in the Honolulu airport waiting for a flight and it was my daughter's "lunchtime." On cue I started feeding her, and all of a sudden I felt this unfamiliar wave of self-consciousness. I turned bright red when I realized everyone was looking at me because I was brazen enough just to be breast-feeding right there in public at the gate. One flight across the Pacific, and suddenly feeding my child was something to be ashamed about. It's not like I was being immodest in any way—I had a blanket over me—but I had not made the effort to find some slimy little bathroom stall or "family bathroom" to go breast-feed out of the sight of onlookers who might be offended. I was ready to get right back on the plane and return to New Zealand, but I soldiered on, modifying my behavior so as not to offend the delicate sensibilities of an American public who seemed to have forgotten the biological purpose of mammary glands. I marvel at the newly engineered breast-feeding slings and harnesses that look more like belaying equipment. Perhaps they do make it easier for Mom to breast-feed, but they have the obvious desired side effect of hiding the whole process from the outside world. A simple choice becomes complex if your inner dialogue takes you to complicated places when it comes to the decision to breast-feed. Much of the decision ends up having more to do with feelings about yourself and your body (and other people's feelings about your body) than the health and well-being of your children.

One hotly debated topic is whether breast-feeding helps with postpartum weight loss. A large Danish study suggests that women who breast-feed do return to their pre-pregnancy weight faster than women who do not.[18] But this reflects breast-feeding at Danish rates and for Danish duration, not the short periods that many American women breast-feed. Many women are simply not prepared to eat the additional three hundred to five hundred calories per day that are required to sustain breast-feeding and would rather switch to a bottle so that they can get right back to their rigorous exercise routines without having to worry about sustaining their milk supply.

One very concerning new development is women using pumping as a means of expending calories. Pump purging, for lack of a better term, refers to women who continue to pump long after their babies have weaned in order to shed the additional six hundred–ish calories a day that breast-feeding entails. These women continue to pump solely for purpose of weight loss. The pump-and-dump mentality to shed pounds definitely qualifies as an extreme weight-loss behavior. There are better ways to achieve your healthy weight goals, and if you are thinking about this approach, reach out for help, because this is a mind trap that you need help to climb out of immediately.

MOMMY MAKEOVER SURGERY

In our haste to return to our prebaby shape and weight, plastic surgeons have yet another suite of options for you—Mommy Makeover Surgery. Life starts to imitate Photoshop as women opt to undergo postbaby "reconstruction." A quick trip to www .yourplasticsurgeryguide.com will pummel your body esteem. This site expertly gets you to focus on all of the postbaby gravity effects that a little surgery can fix! The message is that you can work and have a family too, but just don't let anyone see it. There's no room for bodies that have visible traces of having had children. You need to look corporate and contained in order to maintain your place in the world. If you don't, it's your fault for not taking advantage of the tools that are out there!

Here's an excerpt from the advertisement, with my commentary inserted:

Pregnancy takes its toll on your body, especially your breasts and abdominal areas. (*These guys are geniuses to recognize that your abdomen and breasts change during pregnancy!*) **"Mommy Makeovers Counter the Physical Effects of Pregnancy"** On average, most women gain 25 to 35 pounds during pregnancy. This weight is stored as fatty tissue in the breasts, abdomen, flanks (love-handles), hips, lower back, buttocks and thighs. The breasts also grow due to weight gain and to prepare for nursing. But don't despair, a mommy makeover can help you look your best again. (*So, they state clearly that "your best" doesn't mean how you looked during pregnancy—that was clearly "your worst." "Look your best" to them means looking like you never had a baby.*)

Once a woman finishes breast-feeding, the breasts deflate further and begin to sag. For example, some women need (*need?*) breast augmentation to correct severely deflated "pancake" breasts, while others may need (*need?*) breast implants in combination with a breast lift. Still, some women may actually desire a breast reduction with a lift. In the abdominal area, many women need (*need?*) a full abdominoplasty with tightening of the muscle layer as well as removal of the excess skin and fat, while some may need (*need?*) a mini-abdominoplasty. Some women may also benefit (*benefit?*) from liposuction to sculpt the back, hips and thighs; and smooth out their contours. Finally, an increasing number of women (*increasing?*) have also been requesting a buttock lift as part of their mommy makeover. (*Once they "take care of" all those unsightly baby-related problem areas. Then they'll invite you back for their antiaging package!*)

www.yourplasticsurgeryguide.com/trends/mommy-make over.htm

Motherhood

You survive pregnancy and the postpartum period, buy the socially expected high-tech stroller and the mommy van, get your child into the right preschool, when you start to realize that someone forgot to tell the moms in your neighborhood that they left middle school over a decade ago. The self- and body-esteem gauntlet continues. At your neighborhood pool, the PTA meeting, or even in church, the external eye still seems focused on you. The torture and judgment continue. We torture ourselves, and frankly, we torture each other.

From your children's preschool to senior year in high school, there is always one mom who is the class supermom. At one level, more power to her: Every teacher deserves a supermom in her classroom. This mom organizes events, handles the e-mail list, gets people to bring things in for celebrations, reads to the kids, and sometimes even substitute teaches. She is the cheerleading captain for the parents' team. Often she doesn't work, or if she does, she is an insane multitasker who has mastered the art of being in two places at once (or she has an identical twin).

In the best of all possible worlds, you could just be thankful that she has the energy to do all of this so the rest of the mothers don't have to. But instead your inner dialogue makes you feel guilty for not doing as much as she does. "If Lucinda can do it, I should be able to do it." "She brought in homemade truffles for the class and all I could muster up was paper plates." "What is wrong with me—I'm a *bad mother*."

Nowhere is this more evident than planning the birthday party. A friend was working on deadline for a major presentation at work as her daughter's four-year birthday approached. She lived in a typical suburban neighborhood where she was one of the few working moms. She had inadvertently gotten sucked into the one-upmomship associated with children's birthday parties: She was spending more time obsessing about the theme of the party than her upcoming presentation. In the neighborhood that year, things had started rather lowbrow with a Chuck E. Cheese extravaganza (only one kid vomited), then there was the inflatable moonwalk in the front yard (one kid broke her ankle), then there was the rent-the-whole-skating-rink party of thirty kids (no reportable injuries), the professional clown (made two kids cry), the rent-a-pony (front yard clean up was ugly).

Even though rationally my friend knew that this whole birthday-party-competition scene was completely over the top, she was paralyzed by the decision. The worst insult she could imagine would be some kid saying, "That was a boring party." She was even more paralyzed about what the moms might say: "Ah, that Amy, you know she works, bless her heart, I guess she just didn't have time to organize a fun party, or maybe they're hurting financially. What does her husband do for a living again?" Spear through her heart. She became completely paralyzed by the decision and could not focus on work. After several conversations, I managed to shake some sense into her and remind her that some of the most memorable birthday parties that we attended as kids involved nothing more elaborate than pin the tail on the donkey or running through a sprinkler! It's not about the mom and her social status in the neighborhood, it's about the kid's birthday.

With some trepidation, she went with a retro "design your own pizza" birthday-party theme. The kids had a blast making everything from traditional cheese pizza to peanut butter and Nutella pizza. The kitchen was a mess, but the kids were happy and talked about their crazy designer pizzas for years to come. Plus she didn't have to spend four hundred dollars on a pony or a clown or a skating rink. And no one got hurt.

The comparisons and competition and one-upmomship don't stop after preschool. "How many AP classes is *your* daughter taking?" "What college did *your* son get into?" But the goal is to rise above the petty competition and learn how to keep the innuendo from permeating your inner dialogue and your inner evaluation of your worth as a parent. Your self-evaluation has to remain independent of the critical and competitive judgment of others. This is accomplished by seeking out those people who love hearing about your children and their accomplishments and love talking about theirs, but don't compare or compete. It's not easy in the suburbs and it's not easy if you have an opinionated family, but liberating your inner self-evaluation from the critical evaluations of others is an important step in conquering negative self-talk. Remember to only respect the opinions of people you respect. The rest don't deserve any real estate under your skin.

Opting Out

We have been hearing more about women who choose not to deal with the dual stress of working and raising children. Of course we *can* juggle work and family, but what if we don't *want* to and we have the means to opt out? Obviously, everyone does not have the choice to be a stay-at-home mom, but the stories are borne out in the data. In a 2005 *New York Times* piece, Louise Story reported on e-mail surveys with Ivy League students, including 138 freshman and senior females at Yale.[19] Around 60 percent of the young women reported that they planned to cut back or stop working entirely when they had children. About half of those women said they planned to work part-time, and about half wanted to stop work for at least a few years. Now, of course what young women predict about their behavior and what they actually will do when the time comes may not be the same, but another report about women who actively withdrew from the workforce sheds additional light on the topic. Again from the *New York Times*, Lisa Belkin reported that the U.S. census showed that the number of children being cared for by stay-at-home moms increased nearly 13 percent in less than a decade, while the percentage of new mothers who went back to work fell from 59 percent in 1998 to 55 percent in 2000.[20]

One piece of the puzzle is women opting not to work. A second piece reveals that women are also putting the brakes on how high they climb in their jobs. Ms. Belkin reported that 26 percent of women who were poised to break through to senior levels of management did not want to be promoted. Likewise, of the 108 women who had appeared on the *Fortune* magazine list of the fifty most powerful women over the years, at least twenty had chosen to leave their high-powered jobs, most voluntarily, for lives that were less intense and more fulfilling. Maybe for some women, having or doing it all is simply too much and not worth the hassle.

This is wholly understandable. On a panel of "successful academic women" I attended, three of four confessed to having stay-at-home husbands who cooked, drove the children around, and took care of other household chores. It's easier to be successful when you have a wife or a husband who takes care of all of those time-consuming tasks. I interviewed a man for a senior position and he praised his wife for her support. He complained about the price he had paid for success, stating, "Well, sometimes it means I'm sitting at the kitchen table with my computer checking e-mail while my wife is cooking, but she understands." I confess to having felt little empathy at that moment. What I said out loud was definitely different from what was going on in my head. Luckily my editor was on the job that day. I said, "Well, it's wonderful that you have enjoyed that kind of support." In contrast, I thought, "Do you seriously think I am going to sympathize with you because you were sitting at the table with your computer while your wife was cooking dinner for you? I want a wife like that too! Let's see you try cooking dinner, helping your kid with homework, and chairing a teleconference at the same time!" I didn't recommend him for the position.

Regardless of your path—wife, partner, single, mother, career woman, or some combination of these, there is always someone out there poised to judge. One thing women all seem to have in common is that we are permeable. We vary individually by degrees, and our permeability can also vary over time, but we notice when the external eye is focused on us and that self-consciousness transforms to negative inner dialogue.

Exercises

Returning to our ongoing exercise, continue by documenting how the external world has passed judgment on how you have traversed (or are traversing) this stage of life. Only include experiences that you have actually had. If you have never been pregnant or never worked outside of the home, then focus on other important aspects of your twenties and thirties that have contributed to your self-esteem and body esteem. For many, the child-rearing period extends well into your forties and fifties and sometimes even beyond. Make this exercise your own and tailor it to the specific circumstances of your life.

After you have filled out this table, take a look back at the previous tables you completed. You are well on your way to excavating many of the negative comments that have come from the outside that form the foundation for your own personal negative internal dialogue. Hold on to those tables, as there are a couple more decades to cover. Some of you might have already

CHALLENGING COMMENTS IN ADULTHOOD

Comment	Situation	Effect it had on you
"Qué grande!"	A woman talking about my pregnant belly when I was at the pool with my son.	I tried to be understanding, but it made me feel like a whale. I just wanted to cover up.

Print your own table online at www.womaninthemirrorbook.com.

experienced these later decades; for the rest of you, what's coming might just be preparing you for the future or may help you understand your mothers and grandmothers more. These collected comments provide the grist for the mill in Part Two, when you will learn how to transform negative internal dialogue into respectful self-commentary.

CHAPTER 5

The Sandwich Generation

When you are in your forties and fifties and both your children and parents are dependent on you, your own needs are heavily punctuated by the needs of the generations behind you and ahead of you. You finally sit down to do something, carve out a few hours for yourself, and someone needs you. A call from your parents about a computer glitch, a call from your son in college, a medical form that needs signing for sports, questions about college applications, or the omnipresent "Honey, did you see my [insert misplaced husband object here]?" Your thoughts are, "Why can't I ever sit down for a few minutes without someone needing something from me?" It's true: As a sandwich-generation woman you are a resource, a facilitator, and the glue that holds the generations together. You are a pediatrician and a geriatrician—equally competent in splinters and prostates. But as rich as these years are, they just happen to correspond with some rather precipitous aging. Some people say the stress of being in the sandwich generation makes you age, but more likely than not that aging process would be going on anyhow—these two processes are simply correlated in time.

The forties and fifties are a complicated stage of life for both body esteem and self-esteem. You aren't a spring chicken anymore. Depending on where you live (compare L.A. or Miami with Fargo or Berkeley), women your age might be going to extensive lengths to re-create their youthful bodies and faces. It's Saturday morning, you're un-made-up, uncoiffed, wearing sweatpants and a T-shirt, dropping your kid off at soccer, on the phone with your mother discussing a medical issue, checking e-mail on your Black-Berry, and trying to decide what to make for dinner. Joining you on the sidelines is an artificially tanned, preternaturally pert, Botox-paralyzed soccer mom who clearly has her personal trainer on speed dial. What goes through your head? Suddenly you are reduced to Maya comparing herself with Princess Jasmine, or Alicia at that middle school dance, or Peyton counting her calo-ries in the high school cafeteria. You freeze-frame your hectic morning and say to yourself, "God, I look frumpy." All that you are, all that you do, all the help that you give other people, and one middle-aged princess in your peripheral vision can bring you down. Even at this stage of life, your body esteem and self-esteem remain deeply intertwined. Until the moment that she arrived on the scene, you had actually been juggling all of those balls pretty well. You and your daughter had found a song on the radio that you were both singing along with (a rare moment) and you weren't even thinking about how you looked. It was Saturday soccer, not a night at the theater. Your self-esteem and body esteem were bliss-fully separate and neither was occupying your conscious thoughts. Then you let the princess burst your bubble and they collided again.

Body Esteem in Your Forties and Fifties

The changes to your body are so gradual and you have been so busy that you might not really have noticed. Or you might have wondered whether gravity was pulling some of your bodily fea-tures toward the ground, but you weren't quite ready to admit the extent of it. Sometimes there is a defining moment when it hits you that you aren't young anymore.

Sara, forty-five, was looking for a dress to wear to a friend's wedding. She found a beautiful silk halter dress. She loved the colors, she loved the texture; she thought it was perfect for the wedding. She put it on and even twirled around in the dressing room like a little girl. She felt pretty. Oh, so pretty: She heard

Natalie Wood's voice singing in her head as she danced around in front of the mirrors. She then asked the opinion of the sales associate who suggested they call the "undergarment consultant" to help her figure out what kind of a bra to use with the dress. The consultant was a tiny woman about fifteen years Sara's senior. She had half glasses on, a tape measure around her neck, a dark blue dress, and clunky black shoes. She looked like a third-grade teacher from the 1950s. But the woman didn't mince words. She took one look at Sara, one look at the dress, and she said, "No, that dress is not for you. Your boobs already dropped. No bra can fix that. Find another dress." And she walked out of the dressing room! Sara was dumbstruck. The I-feel-pretty soundtrack screeched to a halt and suddenly she wasn't pretty at all. Her boobs had dropped. What did that even mean? She tried tying the halter a little tighter and examined herself from the front, the side, the back. Oh my God, she thought, my boobs *have* dropped! When the hell did that happen? She left the store, went home, locked herself in the bathroom, took off her clothes and bra, and, as if for the first time, realized that her breasts were indeed no longer as pert as they had been before! After that day, every time she stepped out of the shower and found herself square with the mirror, she heard that underwear consultant's voice in her head saying, "Your boobs already dropped."

Normative Discontent

In 1985, Rodin, Silberstein, and Striegel-Moore[1] coined the phrase "normative discontent" to describe the nearly universal unhappiness that women feel about their bodies. On some level, we all hope that we'll age out of this normative discontent. As we mature, have more concrete roles in life, become more sensible and grounded, perhaps we won't dislike our bodies as much. Unfortunately, the research does not support this theory.

The evaluation of our appearance is related to our self-esteem no matter what our age. In fact, body dissatisfaction in women is remarkably stable across the lifespan. Some of the best work in this area comes from an Australian research group led by Marika Tiggemann. They have shed clear light on how women's perceptions of their bodies and their self-esteem evolve over time.

One of the techniques used to measure body satisfaction is the silhouette technique. You show women an array of silhouettes ranging from thin to overweight and ask them to choose the silhouette that best captures what they look like now and the silhouette that best captures how they would most like to look. The discrepancy between the two measures is a measure of body dissatisfaction. As women age, they gain weight. U.S. statistics indicate that women in their thirties weigh about 8.8 pounds more than those in their twenties, women in their forties weigh about 6.6 pounds more than women in their thirties, and women in their fifties weigh about 1.2 pounds more than women in their forties. Weight starts going down again in their sixties and seventies when health problems increase.[2] Women's silhouette selection for how they look now increases across the decades, indicating that they realize this increasing trend. In parallel, their ideal silhouette choice also increases with age, suggesting that they lighten up a little in terms of their desired shape and weight. *But* the discrepancy stays the same. So the net effect is that body dissatisfaction stays the same across the lifespan. No matter how old women are, they're never happy with themselves.

Despite this stable body dissatisfaction, women actually experience an increase in self-esteem as they approach their forties and fifties. So self-esteem and body esteem experience somewhat of an uncoupling in middle age. Tiggemann believes that as women age, even though their bodies deviate more from the youthful thin ideal, they develop cognitive strategies that allow them to be more accepting of their aging bodies. This allows them to preserve their self-concept and their self-esteem even as their body dissatisfaction persists. Moreover, just how much your body esteem and self-esteem separate from each other depends on how important appearance has always been to you. If your identity is very much dependent on your physical appearance, body dissatisfaction will continue to heavily influence your self-esteem throughout life.

The nature of the strategies that women use differs. Every woman has to hone her own path to self-esteem in this age band. When asked, women talk freely about their experience of aging. Jeanine Cogan, coach and policy director of the Eating Disorders Coalition, frames the problem, "As a forty-five-year-old woman who has watched my hair gray, my running legs turn to cottage cheese, my butt loosen, my arms sag, my face soften and little lines creep in around the eyes and mouth, the aches and pains in my back and elsewhere settle in—my slightly righteous 'Love your body no matter what' mantra has weakened. When I fit the beauty ideal, I rejected it. Now that I no longer do, there is a sense of loss that hits me at times."

Some women adopt a strategy that allows them to view their changing body as a chronicle of their life. Amy Pershing, a forty-four-year-old social worker, says, "I feel my body is the one pure truth teller; all my wrinkles, bumps, cellulite, scars, aches and pains are my body bearing witness to my journey. It looks and feels the way it does because I have *earned* it. I am proud she has survived; I have not always made her journey easy." It is not as if these strategies make you look into the mirror and always love your wrinkles, but they can help you come to terms with them. The wisest of women admit to still having occasional battles with intertwined self-esteem and body esteem and still needing to actively combat negative self-talk, but they work hard to maintain peace with their aging bodies. If all of this psychological work doesn't suit your approach, there's always the scalpel! But that approach has an edge.

Nip It, Tuck It, Take It Away

Cosmetic surgery offers a surgical solution to bodies that are behaving in ways we don't want them to. The number of procedures being conducted on a yearly basis is skyrocketing (see box below). How does all of this surgery affect women's self-esteem and body esteem? Does the surgical approach provide a shortcut to the contentedness that women otherwise attain through hard psychological work? It seems that cosmetic surgery does lead to women feeling better about the specific body part that was sculpted, but the good feeling seems to stop there. The body-esteem boost remains body-part specific. The improved feeling does not generalize to global body esteem or self-esteem. In short, you might feel better about your nose or your eyelids or your tummy, but that is not a ticket to greater overall body satisfaction.[3] In fact, for many that initial surgery is like a gateway drug for subsequent surgeries. It frees you up to focus on yet another flaw that you decide also needs to be corrected surgically.

One type of surgery gaining widespread popularity is bariatric surgery for the treatment of obesity. According to the American Society for Metabolic and Bariatric Surgery, the number of operations increased from about sixteen thousand in the early 1990s to more than 103,000 in 2003. Over 220,000 people in the United States were estimated to have had bariatric surgery in 2008.[4]

2008 TOP FIVE SURGICAL COSMETIC PROCEDURES

These are the top five surgical procedures performed in the United States in 2008. In parentheses is approximately how many surgeries are performed per year, followed by the average cost of the procedure. Cosmetic surgery is big business, but like other businesses it rises and falls with the economy.

1. Breast augmentation (307,000) ($3,500)
2. Nose reshape (rhinoplasty) (279,000) ($4,300)
3. Liposuction (245,000) ($3,000)

4. Eyelid surgery (blepharoplasty) (221,000) ($3,000)
5. Tummy tuck (abdominoplasty) (122,000) ($5,300)

As reported in the *New York Times*, in 2009 spending on plastic surgery in the United States fell 20 percent to $10.5 billion, down from the $13.2 billion spent in 2007, according to the latest statistics from the American Society for Aesthetic Plastic Surgery. Since 2007 the number of surgical procedures dropped by 30 percent, and nonsurgical treatments like wrinkle injections, chemical peels, and laser hair removal fell by 13 percent.[5]

Self-Esteem in the Sandwich Generation

During their forties and fifties, women are often still working outside the home, still busy with careers and/or families, still involved with communities, and still striving toward achieving life goals. Although time is catching up, women are basically on the treadmill, and many are running faster than ever. The fortunate ones are developing more respectful and accepting inner dialogue about their bodies, but women at this age continue to utter disparaging and disrespectful comments about themselves that undermine their goals and diminish their achievements.

If you are working at this age, chances are good that you are embedded in a male-dominated environment. The structure, culture, and norms were developed long ago when women were still in the home. Just like on an elementary school playground, the ground rules are set by the boys. Decades later you may still be experiencing that sense of not fitting in or of your work environment not really being a place where you can be yourself and thrive in a way that is congruent with your sex.

Etta Pisano, M.D., dean of the College of Medicine at the Medical University of South Carolina, has devoted a considerable portion of her career to promoting women in the medical school setting. In medical schools across the country, you see a similar pattern: There are more female medical students than male, but as you go up the ranks of faculty through assistant professor, to associate professor, and on to full professor, the percentage of women drops precipitously[6]—from 38 percent at the assistant professor level to 27 percent at the associate professor level and all the way down to 15 percent at the full professor level! Only 11 percent of chairs and 10 percent of deans are women. The higher up you go, the fewer women there are. Medicine is just one example, but this pattern holds in many fields. Although women comprise over 50 percent of the population, of those 435 public servants who represent us in the U.S. House of Representatives, only seventy-six are female—a whopping 17 percent. Finally, between 1901 and 2009, only forty-one Nobel Prizes have been awarded to women—and 765 to men. (With some individuals honored more than once, the actual total is forty females and 762 males.)

There are myriad reasons that women don't make it to the top or choose not to strive for the top. Some of the barriers require broad social change, but some of them are under our control. Women are not as skilled at or comfortable with self-promotion as men. Over the years, Dean Pisano noticed that whenever she encouraged or nominated women for powerful positions, often their responses were in the vein of "I'm not ready," "I'm not qualified," or "I don't know enough about management, finances, et cetera." This was in stark contrast to male nominees who, if anything, overestimated their own qualifications. She counseled women to take a risk, grab these positions, and learn as they go, yet many still hesitated. Her advice dovetails perfectly with career advice given by a wise colleague in Portugal who says that if you want to move up the ladder and someone offers you something, "Don't think, just say yes and panic later."

Not to advocate developing a completely male approach to self-promotion, but our inability to do so is wrapped up in our wavering self-esteem. Women can be mindful of and rewrite their internal scripts in order to self-promote more effectively and still stay within their comfort zone. Jane, for example, was treading water in her job, earning about sixty-eight cents for every dollar her male colleagues were earning even though she believed she was more conscientious and put in more hours than they did. She and a junior male colleague were being considered for a position that would entail a promotion, a $15,000 raise, and responsibility for ten additional staff. She had three years more experience and a stronger educational background. He was a good negotiator and self-promoted effectively. Her boss asked directly why he should support her application for the position above her colleague's. When asked, her inner dialogue was, "Wait, he doesn't really want me, he wants Josh, this is just an equal-opportunity interview. I'm not really qualified anyhow—I should be an assistant coordinator for a few years first and learn on the job." When pressed for an answer, all she could say was, "Well, I do have stronger management training on paper." She wanted the position, she knew she deserved the position, and she wanted equal pay for equal work, but she talked herself out of it by saying she wasn't prepared. She mollified herself by saying she should just be happy that she had a job in these difficult times. In reality, she was disappointed in herself and outraged that behind the scenes she was probably going to be telling Josh how to do his new job—while he would be getting paid to do it.

Josh had no internal struggle: He just responded to his boss's inquiry by saying, "Well, there's no question that I'm the man for the job. Jane has good qualifications on paper, but I'm more of a people person, a natural leader, and if there's anything I don't know, I'll waste no time getting up to speed before I take over." He assured the boss that he could be relied on to achieve all of the goals expected and more, and managed to negotiate for a $25,000 raise if he were offered the position.

Jane talked her way out of a promotion that she deserved and wanted. Her inner dialogue was plagued by self-doubt. She could not and did not feel comfortable selling herself. She was seething inside at the thought of having to work under Josh, but she could not trust herself enough to self-promote. What held her back? Like so many women her age, fears and doubts about her ability to succeed led her to put on the brakes. Most loud was the inner voice that feared that she might fail. A hundred "what ifs" went through her mind, causing her to doubt that she had the capacity to lead even though she knew she was more qualified. This complicated inner dialogue created a mental traffic jam that she could not get past to be able to say, "I can do that and I can do it better. You'd be wise to choose me." Instead she felt the burn of injustice even though, in part, her failure to be promoted was her own doing. Convoluted and self-doubting inner dialogue holds women down well into the adult years.

I'm Sorry

Guilt is a plague. Women seem to be able to feel guilty about just about anything: Guilt is like fertilizer for low self-esteem. It is also an emotion that festers and casts a broad shadow over other emotions and thoughts. Women's predilection for guilt is wrapped up in an overinflated sense of responsibility and fears that if they don't take responsibility and perform perfectly, they'll be judged harshly by the external eye.

"I should have seen that coming, I should have predicted that outcome; I should have been able to be in two places at once." Women experience guilt even when there is no earthly possibility that they could have done something about what they are apologizing for. The inner dialogue is, "If I were a better person, then I would have been able to do that." Many women wallow in guilt, and at times it appears that they almost seek it out. There are fundamentally two different types of guilt. Genuine guilt is when you mess up and should feel guilty. You run over a squirrel and hear that dreadful thunk in your wheel bed. You forget to pick your child up at school and drive up to find him sitting alone and forlorn with that "My mommy forgot me!" look on his face.

You have an affair and hurt the people around you deeply. Go ahead, feel the guilt, take responsibility for your actions, own the guilt and deal with it.

But then there's this second type of guilt that women manufacture that is distinct from genuine guilt. It is to this type of manufactured guilt that women seem to be pathologically attracted. For example, you have three children and they all need to be driven somewhere on Saturday at one P.M. Your husband is out of town and there are no car-pool options. Barring shelling out about a hundred dollars for taxis, you confess to the kids that there is simply no way you can physically get them to where they all need to be. Sophie's choice. You spend the whole weekend feeling guilty because you had to prioritize one child's needs over the others. You feel guilty because if you *were* a better mother, you would have been perfectly capable of driving three cars simultaneously to three different destinations! You positively swim in two full days of "I'm a bad mother." This manufactured guilt is less about the incident and more about a global responsibility for making the world of others a happier place. "If I were better, if I did more, if I sacrificed more, my kids' world would be better, my husband's world would be better, my boss would be happier." Women seem to find a contorted comfort and respite in this manufactured guilt. The feeling is familiar and it is safe. So what do women gain from this manufactured guilt?

On one hand, this type of guilt sends a message that you care and you tried. "Really, kids, Mom loves you and she tried driving three cars at once, but she's just not clever enough to pull it off." By expressing this kind of guilt, you communicate, "I care about your needs, but I am inadequate to fulfill them." We don't seem to be able to opt for the emotionless and honest, "Sorry, kids, let's think this through together—I don't see any solution. We need to come up with Plan B." It *hurts* not to be able to fulfill their needs. You *want* to be the perfect mom and not disappoint any of the children. Your shield of guilt is a self-defense against the harsh reality that you are not perfect and you are not Supermom. It is also a defensive shield against their anger and disappointment. It is easier to feel guilt from yourself than anger from your children. They'll be less likely to attack you if you are already attacking yourself.

This guilt fuels women's preemptive utterance of the over-used phrase "I'm sorry." Take a day and just listen to how often women say, "I'm sorry." For a real eye-opener, contrast that with how often men say it.

I had arranged to take four junior colleagues out to dinner to celebrate their recent accomplishments. We were meeting at the restaurant at six. When I arrived, Colleague #1 was already seated at the table. When I went to sit down, the floor around my seat was so sticky you could hear my shoes peeling themselves from the floor as I moved around. I said, "Wow, sticky floor." Colleague #1 said, "I'm sorry, yeah, that's really weird." Was she the one who put glue on the floor? Spilled a beer? Was it really her fault the floor was sticky? I'm her boss—should she have noticed it, called the manager or the hazmat team immediately, and had the floor sanitized before I arrived? Colleague #2 arrives (now 6:03) and spews an "I'm sorry" because she couldn't find a parking space. Colleague #3 arrives and I was pleased that there was no immediate "I'm sorry" that emerged . . . but that didn't last for long. Colleague #4 arrives at 6:05 and says, "I'm really sorry, I was doing an evaluation and it went overtime." So at least three of them were feeling sorry by 6:05. I was wondering what was wrong with Colleague #3: Wasn't she sorry about anything? Alas, when she ordered her dinner, out came the "I'm sorry." She was due to deliver a baby in two weeks, so she said to the waiter when ordering, "I normally love spicy food, but I'm so sorry, under the current circumstances [points to her belly], I need something a little milder. Can you do that?" So there she was apologizing to the waiter for the fact that this baby had basically squished her stomach up under her boobs. They were there for a celebration and they were all sorry!

We resolved this by deciding that after the next "I'm sorry" we heard, we would all say, "You should be!" When Colleague #2 apologized to the waiter because she was still working on her dinner when he tried to clear her plate, we all declared, "You should be!" at which point it became clear that apologizing for still eating in a restaurant was patently absurd!

"Sorry" is a preemptive defense. Saying sorry allows women to point out their flaws and shortcomings before anyone else has the chance to do so. It arms the external eye with criticisms that you are already aware of to keep you from being on the receiving end of an unsolicited critique that you are not prepared for.

The sandwich generation is prone to a particular kind of guilt. If you're spending time with your children, you worry that you're neglecting your parents. If you are spending time with your parents, you worry that you are shortchanging your children. Perhaps most common is that if you are spending time with or on yourself, you feel doubly guilty because you aren't attending to either of them. Caregiver stress is real.

Women in the sandwich generation do an enormous amount to care for their children and their parents. Even though they do it willingly and with love, over time it takes a toll on their stress levels and their physical health. Only through self-care can women provide the care that others need from them. But the guilt monster stands in the doorway when we think about getting a facial or a massage: "Shouldn't you be taking care of your mother, your father, your children, your husband, the third world first?" What the monster doesn't understand is that if you're not on top of your game, you are worthless to others. Self-care doesn't have to mean taking a week and flying to Aruba for cocktails and massages, but it can be more bite-sized self-care moments—talking a walk, going to the botanical gardens, regular exercise, lunch with a friend, talking with a therapist, a counselor, or a pastor—any guiltless endeavor that allows you to refresh yourself so that you can be of more value to those who need you.

Exercises

For this stage of life—whether you are in it or have already gone through it—catalog any situations when you have held back, stayed in the background, and watched someone else get credit for your ideas or work, or actively talked yourself out of advancement. We're still building a library of experiences as a foundation for the interventions that we will develop in Part Two.

Second, do an I'm-sorry inventory. Keep track of the number of times and situations in which you utter an automatic "I'm sorry" over the next few days. Don't hold back because you are keeping track: Let them roll as usual, just monitor them and start to think about what you are preemptively defending against.

SORRY INVENTORY

To whom	About what
Husband	Pouring my coffee first.
Person in elevator	Pushing a floor below. They would need to stop on my floor before they wanted to get off.

Print your own table online at www.womaninthemirrorbook.com.

CHAPTER 6

The AARP Years

"Our faces are lies and our necks are the truth."
—Nora Ephron, *I Feel Bad About My Neck: And Other Thoughts on Being a Woman*[1]

Lydia had just had her seventy-fifth birthday. She was always impeccably dressed—would never go out of the house without her nails done, every hair in place, and dressed to the nines. At a lunch with the ladies some time ago, she ordered a salad but asked them to hold the croutons and put the dressing on the side. At seventy-five, Lydia believed you had earned the right to say anything you were thinking, so she said to her friends, "You know I have rheumatism, arthritis, and osteoporosis. I'm in pain every day from the minute I wake up until the minute I go to sleep. But even though I'm in this old lady's body, I'm just like everyone else: Till the day I die, all I'll really care about is being skinny."

A few weeks later she found out she had cancer. When the treatment options were described to her, the thought went through her head, "Well, at least with chemo, I'll lose weight!" Her illness progressed and her prognosis was grim. She needed to get her affairs in order and started discussing funeral plans with her daughter who would be taking care of the arrangements. They went through casket selection, plots, headstones, and all of the unpleasant but practical details that Lydia wanted taken care of before she died. Even though she was dying, the negative internal self-talk was still going strong. At seventy-six years old and weighing as many pounds as she was years old, she made her daughter promise not to let them lay her out in her blue dress because "it makes me look fat."

When does it end? Whatever happened to the well-padded

grandma who cooked wonderful feasts for the family and had the best lap in town for story reading or falling asleep on? Was that grandma happy with her body? Was she resigned to the fact that at her age, this is what her body was made for? Or after the family went home and the grandchildren were in bed, did she take off her clothes, look in the mirror, and cry about what she saw? Did anyone ever wonder whether Grandma had body-image issues, or did we just assume that she was too old to care?

Body esteem during the perimenopausal years and beyond is a difficult topic and one that is gaining in importance as our society grays. The world doesn't want to think about older women, but our world is soon going to be heavily populated with women over fifty. Since women outlive men by an average of five years, they're a substantial social force. But there's a paradox. On the one hand, the world doesn't want to deal with older women. The world doesn't want to see their bodies because they foretell inevitable decline. The world doesn't want to think about them as sexual beings because younger people think it's "gross"—these old ladies should somehow have grown out of any sexual desires. We pay money to watch Hollywood glamorize winter-spring relationships between older men and younger women, (e.g., Richard Gere and Winona Ryder in *Autumn in New York*), but feel disgusted with relationships in which the woman is substantially older than the man. Cougars don't garner the same envy that men with trophy wives do. The world wonders what a younger man could possibly see in an older woman. Yet on the other hand, the world declares that seventy is the new fifty. The comfortable grandma role is eliminated and the modern grandma is expected to be slim, fit, reconstructed, and reconstituted—that is, as long as she doesn't show too much cleavage, bare arms, and, God forbid, her neck! Women over fifty are in the midst of an identity crisis, and their niche in the world is being redefined.

What we do know is that society has a "double standard on aging."[2] Older women are definitely judged more harshly than older men. While men become stately, distinguished, and dapper as they age, women become shrunken, wrinkly, and saggy. It is permissible for women of all ages to find older males from the age range of George Clooney to Sean Connery attractive. But if a young man declares a seventy-something woman attractive, eyebrows rise: The world thinks there is something downright unnatural about a younger man finding an older woman attractive. Men are permitted to continue to act and feel young as they age. It seems as if all women are expected to "act their age" and bury any youthful feelings or desires they may have. Men can have trophy wives and become grandpa daddies, but women, lacking the prerequisite eggs, rarely become grandma mommies, and when they do, the tabloids roll off the presses.

Middle- and late-adult women experience the discrepancy between their felt age (how they feel on the inside) and their chronological age (how old they actually are biologically).[3] If you are old enough to remember *The Thorn Birds,* an epic TV mini-series from 1983 about a sheep station in Australia run by the rich and powerful Mary Carson (played by Barbara Stanwyck), you'll recall that Mrs. Carson develops what we would now call a cougar crush on younger, not-so-priestly Father Ralph de Bricassart (played by Richard Chamberlain). When Father Ralph rebuffs her advances, she passionately exclaims, "Let me tell you something, Cardinal de Bricassart, about old age and about that God of yours. That vengeful God who ruins our bodies and leaves us with only enough wit for regret. Inside this stupid body, I am still young! I still feel! I still want! I still dream! And I still love you!" Mary Carson was gutsy in revealing her inner thoughts and feelings, but the rest of us should keep them under wraps because older women aren't supposed to have *those* kinds of feelings!

But what *are* women over fifty thinking and feeling? We know strikingly little about body esteem and self-esteem in older women precisely because no one asks them. Maybe the world assumes that they've matured out of the petty body preoccupation that younger women experience. Or maybe the world just doesn't want to know because we might find out that these women still harbor active dreams and desires, and that sits uncomfortably.

Many older women talk about becoming invisible as they age. Women who were used to being noticed because of their looks find themselves ignored at counters, having doors closed in their faces, and not being approached by sales associates in clothing stores. This is particularly ironic because often these women have much more to spend than the younger shoppers.

What little research there is suggests that how women perceive their bodies does transform in the AARP years. This does not mean that basic appearance concerns become any less important, but new ones come on the scene. Appearance concerns are amplified by concerns about competence (the physical sensations of aging, including feelings of agility, endurance, and power) as well as the experience of physical health and disease (including pain and weakness). On the appearance side, women contend with the long-term effects of gravity and the absence of estrogen: sagging and wrinkling of skin, further dropping of the breasts, reduction in height, and redistribution of fat from the arms and legs to the midsection.[4] In terms of competence, they experience a loss of muscle strength and aerobic capacity and, as one woman in her seventies said, "Basically, honey, all body systems pack in." The women who deal best with their aging bodies are those who actively engage in activities that offset the effects of aging.

Tackling Aging

Women approach aging in different ways. Two dominant patterns of incorporating aging into your identity and esteem are identity assimilation and identity accommodation.[5] Identity assimilation means that you continue to view yourself as *you*, even as the effects of aging become more visible. You say to yourself, I might be sagging and I might have wrinkles, but I'm still the same ol' me. In the show *Mamma Mia!* upon seeing Donna for the first time in years, old beau Bill says, "Age does not wither her," to which Harry, old beau number two, replies, "I was expecting a rather stout matron," and finally Sam, old beau number three, sums it up: "No, she's still Donna!" Donna is a wonderful example of identity assimilation. She's aging, her body is changing, but her view of herself still accommodates the image of fluorescent space suits and platform shoes, singing ABBA songs, and being able to fall in love again.

Identity accommodation is when the changes associated with aging become overwhelming and lead to a redefinition of who you are. This results when the negative self-talk about aging wins and erases older, more vibrant images of who you are. You say to yourself, I'm not the same Judy I used to be: Now I'm just an old person.

Of those two processes, identity assimilation is clearly the healthier option. Self-esteem and body esteem are most preserved in those women who acknowledge changes associated with aging but don't dwell on their impact or their psychological meaning. The key to maintaining (or developing) self-esteem at this age is allowing yourself to incorporate your aging body into your self-concept without allowing it to change your fundamental perception of who you are as a person.

Said more plainly by a woman approaching eighty, "Aging is crap, we all know it's crap, you wake up to a new surprise every morning—a new spot, a new creak, a new pain—but what the hell, at least you wake up. So when I hear women wasting their time bellyaching, I say to myself, The clock is marching on, sister, get off your duff and do something!" Anita Sinicrope-Maier, founder and director of the Pennsylvania Educational Network for Eating Disorders, commented as she approached sixty-five, "I can say I am so glad to have legitimately entered the wise-woman years. I see things so much clearer without the distractions of the beauty myth. I color my hair and wear makeup because it is *fun* . . . not because I need to be prettier. I like fancy. I am an old theater person, after all. As long as my body continues to move— despite the pain—it is my ally. Each day is a gift. Having men take me seriously as a person is so much sweeter than being an object. All in all, these are the golden years with a bit of rust in some places!"

Contrast this attitude with the legions of women who opt to erase any trace of their journey through any means possible. The silver screen provides examples of women who are dragged through the aging process kicking and screaming. Joan Rivers, an outspoken and witty comedian and actress in her late seventies, is a surgeon's dream, flaunting regular Botox injections as well as creative work done on her lips, breasts, nose, stomach, eyes, and arms.[6] She wholeheartedly encourages other women to have as many plastic-surgery procedures as they can afford. Rivers claims that her procedures have helped her look younger and feel happier. More power to her. This is your personal choice, but we can't all afford this approach to aging, nor do we all want to take it.

The problem comes when these high-profile women and surgeons turn this approach into yet another "should." Driving through the retirement-village mecca of central Florida reveals a new trend. Previously, the highway billboards advertised two things—ophthalmologists and urologists—both in high demand in retirement communities. But a new trend has emerged—cosmetic-surgery advertising. The images are a combination of young models and older models, obviously conveying the message that just because you are old doesn't mean you have to look old. The advertisements work, as baby boomers who are now retiring aren't taking the aging process lying down. The rates of cosmetic surgery are increasing in retirement communities, much to the dismay of many inhabitants. One retirement-village resident commented, "It used to be a fairly even playing field. Everyone here was varying degrees of old, and we didn't have to compete with all of these younger plastic women. Now we have this new crop of retirees turning retirement into a beauty pageant. I don't want to have to think about this anymore. But when I see one of them all nipped, tucked, and tidy, then I look at myself in the mirror, I start to wonder whether I 'should' get something done too. They've infected me!"

Since our knowledge about women in this age group is so limited, we developed an Internet survey about body esteem and self-esteem and circulated it to over two thousand women between the ages of fifty and ninety. We aimed to give women over fifty a platform to discuss topics about body esteem and self-esteem that were on their minds. The women had a lot to say. Five recurrent themes emerged to the question "What would you like for people to understand about women in your age bracket and their thoughts and feelings about their bodies and themselves?"

1. The mirror does not reflect my mind!

By far the most frequent response to this question was the complete disconnect between what these women saw in the mirror and how they felt inside. Just like Mary Carson, most of them reported getting a shock every time they looked in the mirror and asking, "Who is that old woman?" Women expressed that their mind doesn't recognize that they're older, that their body ages but their personality doesn't, that their brain doesn't match what their body says. Telling quotes: "Despite physical changes as one ages, inside is still a twelve-year-old girl. I am sometimes surprised to remember I am sixty-two." Similarly, "What you see on the outside is not what I feel on the inside. You see five foot three and 181 pounds. But inside I'm twenty-five, five foot four, and 130. My feelings about who I am don't age. They mature, but they don't age." And finally, "I feel like I am still thirty to thirty-five, in my thoughts—I may not feel, move, or look like it though!" All of these women described moments in which they were completely unaware of their actual chronological age when they were engaged in tasks, working, playing, dancing—and then a glance in the mirror highlighted the discrepancy between what they felt and what they saw.

2. We're not dead yet!

The sheer number of women who were compelled to remind others that they weren't dead yet was disheartening. This theme rang loud from the surveys and merged with the sense of invisibility that women over fifty felt in the world. Many commented on how our youth- and beauty-oriented culture leads to a fundamental disrespect or dismissal of maturity. Dovetailing with the discrepancy between one's feelings and the mirror, one respondent declared that she wished people understood "that most of us are as vital and youthful mentally and have had the added benefit of gaining some wisdom through a life lived. We still have our humor and our desires and passions." Women wanted others to realize that they are not irrelevant and that they have passions and energies and intelligence to offer to the world even if their bodies do not match the "youthful" ideal. Repeated chants were: We are not nonentities! We are not invisible! We still like to have fun! Don't dismiss us! Don't write us off! One particular response declared, "Just because a woman is over fifty, heavy, has gone through menopause, and is mateless and/or childless does NOT mean that she is DEAD. Women in their fifties and over have as much capacity for sex, emotions, activities, and togetherness as anyone younger and/or slimmer. Don't be a bigot—everyone is human inside." And another cautioned, "As we are, so will you be—if you live." Embedded in these warnings were some intriguing kernels of self-esteem. A clear sense that women over fifty have something to offer to the world permeated these cries for visibility. For example, "We have vast knowledge, experience, and the ability to teach many things if you would listen." And underscoring the clarity and maturity of perspective, "We are not invisible. The perimenopausal/menopausal woman is a largely untapped energy source. She is fascinating and fascinated, not much interested in bullshit, and ready for adventure. Not a good time to dismiss her as 'spent' but rather to stay close and enjoy the ride."

Women over fifty noted becoming invisible to men. Many of the women missed being flirted with, noticed, and paid attention to by men, but one in particular had a few choice words for the men around her on the topic of invisibility: "Well, the saying goes that women over fifty are invisible to men. I would be happy if some of the men I see were invisible. Overall, I think we take better care of ourselves than do our male counterparts."

3. *Who stole my waist?*
Another uniting theme was the incredulity associated with changes in their bodies. Women felt ill prepared for all of the things that happened to them around menopause and varied tremendously in how they processed and dealt with these extreme bodily changes. The loss of the waist and the gain of flabby bingo arms were the most bemoaned changes. Creative terms for the loss of the youthful waist included postmenopausal belly, inner-tube middle, beer belly, love handles, and middle-age muffin. No matter what they called it, they missed their waists and acknowledged that all of the approaches to weight and shape control that worked for them prior to menopause seemed to have lost their effectiveness after they crossed the menopausal divide. For some, the transformation was painful: "As I've aged, I've gained weight around my belly. It has become the litmus test of how my day will go. When I wake up, I lift up my pajama top to see if there's more, turning side to side. I grab the fat there, squishing it and trying to figure how much is there. Five pounds? Ten pounds? If I wear certain types of jeans, the waistband cuts into it and I feel fat the whole day. I've become obsessed with it, not only for the way it looks but its health implications." Other women relied on humor and friendship to deal with the changes. "I don't know how the majority of women feel," one respondent wrote, "but I do know about my friends my age. When we get together we all bitch about how fat we are, our spare tire in the middle, the veins on our legs and growing hair in strange places. I must say we have a good time during those sessions."

4. *Doctors and designers, please take us seriously!*
In part, women felt that much of the agony they were experiencing was because neither doctors nor designers took their bodies

seriously. They felt abandoned by the medical profession and abused by fashion designers who insisted that they fit their bodies into clothes that are designed for the bodies of twenty- and thirty-year-olds! From the designers, women demanded both comfort and style. They want to look elegant; they would love to buy age-appropriate clothing and shoes and beauty products and hair products without someone telling them they needed to try to look like they were twenty-five years old. Some clear requests: "I wish that there were more fashion designers who would work on flattering styles for women over fifty. I don't envy youth, I don't want to be young, but I would like more choices when I shop." "My biggest peeve is clothing. It is so hard to find clothing that fits and is comfortable. Hip-high pants just do not fit as well, nor feel as comfortable on most older women, but it is all that is out there, so I wear them. Low-cut tops and short skirts/dresses do not look as good, and yet cuts for mature women are not out there. Many clothes are also cut so they fit tightly. I would really like to find nice-looking clothing that is suitable to my age." De-siring tasteful options, one woman requested, "We would like clothing styles that reflect the maturity and taste we have ac-quired." Clarifying the position of women over fifty, "I'm not a sports model, I'm a serviceable sedan." Not only the designers took flack, but also the salespeople: "Clerks in the store—the young ones are dismissive of you and sometimes downright RUDE." Women urged clerks to acknowledge who has the money to spend and to treat them with respect! Given that our society is aging rapidly, any designer looking to profit in the next decade would take these women's advice seriously!

Physicians were roundly criticized for being inadequate at talking about and dealing with issues related to menopause and weight gain over fifty. Women wanted more preparation, more information *before* they entered the perimenopausal years to help them understand how best to adjust their diet and exercise ahead of time—so that they could preempt the eventual metabolic changes. They also wanted not to be dismissed. Many women felt that doctors would write off their discomforts to menopause without offering any approaches to symptom relief, whether medical or alternative. They felt that their doctors were poorly trained and ill prepared to even have conversations about menopausal challenges. One insightful respondent pondered what sorts of resources would be available if men went through menopause. She suggested that the government would put much more money into research and that there would probably be a "National Institute of Menopause Studies" in order to stop the suffering of millions of older men across America!

5. We are still juicy, sensual beings: Pay us a compliment now and then, please.

A final common theme was related to sensuality, sexuality, and affection. Underscoring how different the aging process is for women, women really varied in their thoughts about sexuality. Some women excitedly reported that sex over sixty was still strong, whereas others felt as if their desire dwindled and dried up starting in their fifties, some even earlier. The take-home messages were that there are no "shoulds" about sex after fifty—as one woman said, "It is what it is." Even the women who weren't feeling sexual reminded us that they still had sexy thoughts: "We still think sexy thoughts even though we may not look 'hot.' We appreciate a well-toned older man. We think it is unfair that aging women are judged differently than aging men." Many women were compelled to discuss the importance of continuing to experience sensuality, affection, and intimacy even if they are no longer conventionally sexually active. "Women at sixty-three still are sensual beings who like to use their bodies, whatever they look like, to comfort others, for sex, for dancing. We are juicy people who have a lot to offer younger people and others our own age." And on the topic of trying to get spouses to understand the changes in sexuality that they are experiencing, "I think few spouses of women fifty and over understand the intense need many women have to have their desirability and attractiveness reaffirmed," and "I still want my husband to treat me like a beauty and say nice things about my appearance even if I no longer look like I used to. That includes romantic touching, or even buying sexy nightwear (though that would be new for him). Women (everyone) still need their skin touched, and not just for sex. Women are generally very sensitive to a downgrade in appearance, if even their partners and friends don't think it matters."

Wise Words from Women Over Fifty

Our respondents also took the survey as an opportunity to give some advice about how to gain perspective on the aging process. So many women cautioned that we all age differently—and urged their fellow women, partners, and doctors not to generalize from one person's experience to all other women's. Most women who felt they were dealing with aging fairly well given the magnitude of the challenge advised others to stay active, eat well, and enjoy sleep (when you can). Likewise, there was much to be said for sharing the experience with others going through it. Women urged other women not to go it alone, to seek out support, and to find others you can laugh with about the changes you are experiencing.

Exercises

If you have experienced this stage of life, use this opportunity to answer the question we asked women in the survey: What would you like other people to know about women in your age bracket?

If you have not entered this age yet, forget about writing something down. Go listen to an older woman, take her seriously, pay her a sincere compliment, or learn something from her experience. Do something that makes her feel like a valuable citizen of the world.

PART TWO

Intervention

CHAPTER 7

Awareness

As women, we endure a lifetime of challenges and a society that seems to spoon-feed us negative self-talk. As soon as we cross the great pubertal divide, we start doubting ourselves, second-guessing ourselves, and fearing that we are not living up to some standard that is impossible to uphold. Some women have forged a path and found peace with their thoughts, their body esteem, and their self-esteem, and we will use them as role models. There also are specific tools that you can learn, whether you are in your twenties or your nineties. Once you master them, you will be well positioned to spread the word and to help others whom you love develop healthier relationships with themselves.

Hopefully, you now have an eye-opening grasp of how hurtful and damaging negative self-talk can be. I am hoping that some of the stories in Part One and the exercises you completed will have increased your awareness of some of your own thoughts and the thoughts that women around you choose to share.

Unfortunately, it is easier to hold on to your negative self-talk and your negative self-evaluations than to change them. They are familiar, consonant with society's expectations and the path of least resistance. However, they also pave the way to low self-esteem and low body esteem and are easily passed on to the next generation.

So you have reached a choice point. You can take the familiar and comfortable path and remain imprisoned by these thoughts for the rest of your life. Or you can actively transform negative self-talk for good! With practice, you can even replace it with compassionate and respectful self-commentary.

Since there is not a one-size-fits-all solution, you need to be in charge of fine-tuning the tools to suit you. When you get your piano tuned, the tuner doesn't make one adjustment and voilà, everything's perfect. Tuning is a series of small experiments and adjustments until the right tones are achieved. The same principle applies here. Once I provide you with the tools, you can tweak them and experiment with them and ultimately find the best way to use them to transform hurtful thoughts, one by one, to start building lasting body esteem and self-esteem.

The single most important step in transforming your inner dialogue is awareness. Until you learn how to capture your own negative self-talk, you won't be able to develop a more supportive and loving internal dialogue. Thoughts are like butterflies. They flit around in your head and often elude capture by taking unexpected turns, traveling in groups, and luring you into paying attention to them almost hypnotically. You need a thought net so you can catch negative self-talk as it happens, examine it, and work toward replacing it with self-statements that build you up rather than tear you down.

At any given point in time, women have any number of thoughts going through their heads. Typically we listen to our thoughts without really paying attention to them. So, for example, you might walk past a mirror and think, "Oh, yuck, I'm so fat." You "listen" to the thought—in that it makes you feel miserable about yourself, makes you self-conscious when you go out to the grocery store, and propels a cascade of related thoughts about your overall worthlessness as a person. You "listened" insofar as the thought got to you and influenced your other thoughts, your feelings, and even your behaviors. It was powerful. But the listening was automatic. You didn't critically evaluate the thought. You didn't capture it and examine how true it was. You didn't stop it and say, *"Hey, don't dis yourself like that; it's mean."* You listened, but you weren't really paying attention. It's more like an automatic program. You hit play and it's off and running.

Catching Negative Thoughts as They Happen
In order to start paying attention to the thoughts that bring you down, you need to catch them in action. Basically, you need the equivalent of a voice-activated recorder in your head. The recorder doesn't have to capture all of your thoughts—you would run out of memory pretty fast. At first all it needs to do is capture your negative self-statements. Until you understand when they arise and what they say, you won't be able to devise an effective plan to transform them.

To begin this process, return to some of the exercises you completed in Part One. Many of the negative self-thoughts you experience now are likely to have their roots in some of those early comments that were made by others that wormed their way under your skin and into your own self-commentary library.

In order to tackle your negative self-thoughts, start with appearance-related thoughts. The rationale for this is twofold. First, since these are concrete thoughts and often occur in predictable places (e.g., in front of a mirror), it's easier to learn how to capture them. Second, the tools you use to capture appearance-related negative thoughts will generalize smoothly to other types of negative self-thoughts—for example, thoughts related to self-esteem that are less predictable and sometimes harder to catch. Basically, you'll learn how to play "Mary Had a Little Lamb" before taking on a Bach fugue.

Maureen is a forty-five-year-old mother of two who described herself as stressed, hassled, and constantly hating her body. Maureen's life was on fast-forward and she wasn't even able to articulate the types of negative thoughts she was having. Her thought reports were all more impressionistic, sort of like Play-Doh when you mix a bunch of colors together—there are some streaks of colors, but the rest becomes a mash of gray to the point where you can no longer distinguish among the individual colors. Her first challenge was to slow down the chatter in her head to get her to the point where she could start to identify individual thoughts that were contributing to this miserable, gray, self-loathing feeling. She started paying attention to her thoughts and was instructed to capture the first negative thought she uttered about herself in the morning. Maureen was surprised to report that the first negative thought happened before she even got out of bed. She was lying in bed, put her hand on her stomach, grabbed some flesh, and said to herself, "Oh, no, I can grab so much—today *has* to be a diet day." The very first thing she said about herself in the morning was critical and demeaning. And that single thought had far-reaching effects. When asked how that thought affected what she did next, she reported, "I felt dejected before I even put my feet on the ground. All I had for breakfast was black coffee with sweetener. When I sat down at breakfast, my robe opened up and I caught another thought that said, 'My thighs are so fat, I have to cover them up.' Then I went upstairs to brush my teeth and while looking in the mirror, I thought, 'Look at those wrinkles. And I have bags under my eyes. I look old.' So I covered my face with makeup, got dressed, looked in the mirror, and thought, 'I *can't* go out of the house with those pants on, I look *huge!*' So I got undressed and redressed two more times until I thought, 'Well, I guess that's the best I'm gonna do, plus I'm late.' The rest of the day sucked— every time I saw myself in a store window, or saw other younger, thinner women at work, or even stupid things like not liking the shape of my fingernails . . . all I heard was this barrage of negative self-talk. I had no idea how mean I was being to myself—all day long."

Once she started paying attention, Maureen was able to see immediately how much her thoughts were torturing her and how much they were keeping her from engaging in life. She had taken one of her daughters to ballet class and realized part of the way through the class that she was not paying attention to what her daughter was doing on the dance floor at all, but rather she was comparing her own shape to that of the other mothers. Awareness helped Maureen realize how much her own thoughts were her worst enemy.

Capturing Your Thoughts

Capturing thoughts is not always easy and it does require you to slow down the chatter in your mind. To do this you need to develop meta-awareness. Meta-awareness is rising above the moment and actually thinking about thinking. By getting that bird's-eye view, you will be able to become a critical observer of your own thinking and your own behavior. Without that view, you'll remain trapped in your negative self-talk.

Maureen was able to start capturing her thoughts by "thinking about thinking" while she was still lying in bed in the morning. While this worked for her schedule, if you're someone who is being woken up by dogs or alarm clocks, beepers or children, you might have to go from zero to sixty in a split second, so other approaches to catching thoughts are important.

Since the mirror tends to be a place where derogatory appearance thoughts surface, one way to start capturing them is by taking a little extra time when you typically find yourself in front of the mirror—brushing your teeth, drying your hair, putting on makeup. In the beginning, doing it privately is probably preferred over, say, the mirror in the gym—although you'll get to the point where you can capture your thoughts anywhere, anytime.

As you go through the motions of putting toothpaste on your brush, brushing your teeth, or drying your hair, simply monitor what kind of statements are crossing your mind as you evaluate what you see in the mirror. Ask yourself the following questions:

1. *Where am I looking?* What body parts do you tend to focus on when you are looking in the mirror? Do you look at what you consider to be your attractive parts, or do you tend to focus on body parts that you are dissatisfied with? Follow your gaze to monitor how you survey your own body in making self-appraisals.

2. What is the nature of the comments I make about myself? When you see yourself in the mirror, do you compliment yourself (e.g., nice teeth, pretty hair, lovely smile, not bad for your age), or do you make more disparaging comments (e.g., crooked nose, too many wrinkles, flabby, age spots)?

3. How do the comments make me feel? If you make positive comments, do you walk away feeling more confident, head held high, self-assured? If the comments are more negative, how do they affect how you feel? Other thoughts you have? Your behaviors?

4. Is this the best way to "send myself off" in the morning? The morning often sets the tone for the entire day. When we walk our children to the bus, drop them off at school, or send them out the door, we try to give them encouraging words to launch the day in a positive way. Do your comments about yourself help you launch your day positively? Or do they demoralize you? Are you doing unto yourself what you do unto others?

This mirror exercise is your first tool in capturing your negative self-thoughts. Continue to practice really paying attention when you are looking into the mirror and becoming aware of the impact that your thoughts have on you.

The next step is to take your meta-awareness skills into the field and start to monitor your thoughts throughout the day. There is no doubt that once you start paying attention, the negative self-statements are going to start jumping out at you. Granted, it is basically impossible to quantify people's thoughts accurately, but several studies have attempted to do so. There is so much lore about how frequently men think about sex, but in reality we have them beat when it comes to thinking about appearance. The Kinsey Report revealed that the majority of men think about sex once a day (54 percent) with 43 percent thinking about sex a few times a month and about 4 percent less than once a month.[1] In contrast, women spend two years of their lives thinking about food (granted, part of this is because we are still typically the shoppers and cooks). This equates to forty-four minutes a day, five hours and nine minutes each week, one day of every month, or one year and eleven months over the average adult lifetime. When we add in how much we think about appearance, a survey by *Grazia* magazine of five thousand women shows that the average woman thinks about her body every fifteen minutes.[2] It doesn't matter if you are visibly overweight or rail thin, appearance occupies significant brain time. When you add in negative-self-esteem thought time, it's a wonder women ever get anything accomplished.

Keep a small thought journal using whatever approach works for you. You can go the low-tech route and use a little notebook, or the high-tech approach and use the memo function on your phone or a password-protected file on your computer. Whatever approach suits your lifestyle, accurately capturing your thoughts means getting them out of your head and onto a device or piece of paper. You won't always have to write them down, but as you are becoming more proficient at catching them, making them concrete is important. Even though this sounds simple, it is not. It's easier to forgive yourself if these self-deprecating thoughts just remain fleeting. The act of recording them can be painful because it can illustrate just how disrespectful you have become to your body and yourself.

Some women feel as if they deserve this negative commentary or that they have somehow brought it on themselves. That is a dangerous trap. Take it one step at a time, capture and record your thoughts, and this will be the start to developing a more respectful and supportive stance toward yourself. The table on the following page is an example of what a thought journal might look like. It is the work of Lisa, age twenty-three, who was working as an intern with an advertising firm at the time she was recording.

This is a snapshot of her thoughts on a day when she had an important meeting with several colleagues followed by happy hour at an upscale bar. As you can see, all day long Lisa was distracted from her work and her socializing by intrusive thoughts about her appearance. These thoughts ranged from spontaneous self-criticisms to comparative thoughts about female colleagues

Time	Situation	Thought
7:30 A.M.	Brushing	My teeth look yellow. I need to get them whitened.
7:40	Dressing for meeting	This suit makes my butt look big.
9:00	In meeting with advertising team	I look so frumpy compared to her.
12:30 P.M.	In bathroom looking in mirror	My stomach looks so fat after lunch.
2:30	In conference room, remembering article about "cankles."	I have such fat ankles.
4:00	In meeting, comparing myself to sleek colleague	She has such pretty arms—I look like a farmer.
5:30	In bathroom at happy hour after the meeting	My hair has fallen, my makeup is a mess, I have bags under my eyes. I really should have stayed home.
6:00	In booth with colleagues at happy hour	How can she still look so fresh and perky?
7:30	Driving home	I am so never going to make it in this field.

Print your own table online at www.womaninthemirrorbook.com.

whom she viewed as more attractive. In the end, this barrage of negative thinking culminated in a completely negative thought about her self-worth and her future career prospects.

What is especially noteworthy about this thought record is that all of the negative thoughts throughout the day focused on physical appearance—her size, specific features, how well put together she was—not on her professional abilities. It wasn't until seven thirty in the evening that it became clear that all the negative appearance-related thoughts were really a smoke screen for her fears about not being a success at her chosen career. This type of thought displacement creates a vicious cycle. In the short-term, burying all her fears about not making it in the advertising business under concerns about her appearance

Time	Situation	Thought
7:30 A.M.	Brushing	My teeth look yellow. I need to get them whitened.
7:40	Dressing for meeting	This suit makes my butt look big.
9:00	In meeting with advertising team	Is this suit sending the right message?
12:30 P.M.	In bathroom, looking in mirror	My stomach looks so fat after lunch.
2:30	In conference room, pulling down her skirt	I hate my knees.
4:00	In meeting	I feel so fat—I just want to take off this suit, put on sweats, eat ice cream, and cry.
5:30	In bathroom at happy hour after the meeting	I have bags under my eyes—I really should have stayed home.
6:00	In booth with colleagues at happy hour	I'm not being funny enough—why can't I do small talk well?
7:30	Driving home	I am never going to get that promotion!

rendered her so self-absorbed that it was impossible to do her job. In the long run, her ongoing negative appearance-related thoughts led to a crisis of professional confidence. It's not her faded makeup or fallen hair that impeded her success, it is the way her thoughts were constantly putting her down that interfered with her ability to focus on her work.

Taking that bird's-eye view also reveals the thoughts of her perky colleague. From Lisa's perspective, this woman had everything going for her and was the perfect advertising executive. But that was on the outside. The table on page 145 shows what this woman was thinking during the day.

From our omniscient perspective, negative self-talk clearly doesn't discriminate. Just because someone looks all put together on the outside doesn't mean she isn't being tormented by her own thoughts. Despite the outward appearance of being toned, fashionably dressed, perky, and competent, this successful ad executive was tortured by self-chatter almost identical to Lisa's. Even supermodels and actresses who are billed as the most prized beauties on the planet struggle with the barrage of negative self-talk.

Where Do Your Negative Self-Thoughts Live?
To do a thought inventory, mentally walk through your house or place of work or school to find out which rooms seem to promote the most negative self-talk. This type of thought field trip is a clever way to figure out what some of your cues are. Some patterns emerge across women. You might find some similarities here with your experience, but there are likely to be other spots that are unique to your life and environment that influence your negative thoughts. Here is the hierarchy of high-risk rooms:

1. **Bathroom.** The bathroom is the hands-down winner for negative thoughts. Looking into the mirror, stepping on the scale, lying in the bathtub, standing in the shower, even sitting on the toilet all seem to be common times when

negative self-thoughts emerge. Like gremlins, they just hang out there waiting for you to come in, take off your clothes, and either start critically inspecting yourself or subjecting yourself to the dreaded number on the scale. In most cases, the bathroom elicits one critical thought after another.

2. **Kitchen.** The kitchen is the second most popular hangout. Typically, these thoughts pop up in the refrigerator, the pantry, and other places where you have food stored. These thoughts can be more taunting. They might try to lure you into eating unhealthy foods by reminding you how good they taste or how much you deserve them. Then, after you listen to them, they turn around and slap you in the face for having succumbed. Unlike those in the bathroom, kitchen thoughts tend to be more love-hate.

3. **TV room.** Wherever you have your TV is where comparative thoughts seem to lurk. These thoughts set you up for continuous comparisons with the plastic people you see on the screen. They constantly pit you against them in terms of your size, your hair, your shape, your perkiness, your life. It's a no-win. If you're sitting at home in your sweats watching TV, you're never going to be a match for Hollywood glam—nor should you think you have to be. But the thoughts that come out in the TV room tell us we should!

4. **The bedroom.** This one pops up most for people who have partners. Affection, intimacy, and sexuality are all experiences designed to make you feel good about your body and what it can do. But when these moments become a threesome, when negative body-image thoughts come between you and your partner, whatever closeness you had is shattered by preoccupation and self-consciousness. Not taking off your clothes, only being intimate with the lights off, constantly thinking about what your partner must be thinking about your rolls, thighs, wrinkles, flaws . . . these thoughts take you out of the moment, destroy your intimacy, and interfere with your ability to love. Negative self-talk in

the bedroom affects not only you but also your closest relationships.

Where Do Your Positive Self-Thoughts Live?
You can invert your negative-thought inventory and map out where your positive self-thoughts live. Chances are good that they live in different and more diverse places and emerge in different situations from the negative self-thoughts. It is also harder for women to access where these positive thoughts arise, but here are some of the responses that emerged.

1. **Place of worship.** Many women reported that going to a place of worship, singing in a choir, or engaging in any spiritual activity gave them a reprieve from focusing on their body or themself. Being fully engaged in spiritual activities, thoughts, and feelings seems to have the ability to lift some women above more earthly concerns with body esteem and self-esteem. Women felt that being in the spiritual realm gave them perspective on what was important and allowed them to be more compassionate with themselves.

2. **Gardening.** The garden seems to be another place where positive self-esteem lies and body esteem matters less. It's a place where women get dirty (almost hearkening back to childhood days of making mud pies) and fashion and body mass index aren't issues. Women felt proud of what they grew and could lose themselves in the process of creating life. Whether it is flowers or fruits and vegetables, just being close to the earth seemed to ground women more. Occasionally a competition with a fellow gardener would burst that bubble (e.g., her roses are nicer than mine), but more often than not the garden was a refuge from negative self-talk.

3. **Playing with children or grandchildren—or any children, for that matter.** It seems like children demand so much of women's time and attention that they have less brain space to focus on body and self-esteem. With the

exception of going to the pool, where comparisons with other women often intruded on their fun, playing with children seemed to be a great way to escape from negative self-talk. Grandmothers especially seemed able to completely escape self-focus while they were with their grandchildren. Plus, children are more likely to judge you on your cookies than on your waistline.

4. **Volunteering with people.** Women reported everything from working in a thrift shop to handing out food at a shelter to tutoring underprivileged children. These tasks seemed to be so all-absorbing that there was no room for negative self-talk. Also, many women reported that they felt that their concerns were "petty" in comparison to those of the people with whom they were volunteering. As long as those thoughts didn't transform into guilt, they seemed to be enough to fend off negative chatter for the time they were working with people and even afterward.

5. **Volunteering with animals.** Whether women were cleaning out cages, walking or grooming dogs or cats, or just making social calls, the animals seemed to elevate them above any negative self-talk. Whether it is the unconditional love or gratitude that the shelter animals give, or simply the act of caring for another living being in need of care and warmth, the time at the shelter was rarely intruded upon by negative thoughts.

6. **Walking.** There is clearly something healing about walking. Many women said the whole character of their thoughts changed when they went out for a solo walk. Similar to how women described feeling in church and while gardening, walking seems to put them temporarily into a more healthy brain space. They did not feel judged by others or themselves and could create a fairly impenetrable thought world—almost trancelike. In fact, some women did report that they got so deep in thought when they walked that an intrusion like a barking dog or an

unexpected car really made them jump. By and large, the thoughts were positive and not self-deprecatory.

7. **Sports.** This category came up, but it was a little more complicated. For some, and depending on the type of sport, it could make women experience more negative self-talk. But for others sports gave them a break from negative chatter. From softball to golf and at all ages, sports played a role in building their positive self-talk library.

8. **Music.** Comments about music came in two forms. The first came from women who played an instrument. Several women who played the piano said that they could simply play away negative self-talk. Whether they were playing classical, pop, or religious music, the sheer act of getting absorbed in playing could get them outside of their own negative self-thoughts. Women who did not play an instrument often spoke of the powerful influence of listening to car radios or CD players and iPods to help clear their minds of negative chatter.

9. **Yoga.** A whole category of situations that seemed to block out negative self-talk was yoga, tai chi, and other meditative or peaceful activities. These activities came up commonly as refuges from negative self-talk, with one humorous exception. One woman said, "My peace was completely ruined when some perfectly muscled yoga bunny plopped her mat down beside mine. Her positions, her body, her everything was perfect. They should have their own class." Point well taken. You need to be careful that you find a place that suits your needs so that you can maintain your peace.

Your Self-Talk Map
We live in our space but spend very little time examining how our thoughts and feelings about ourselves change as we move through our own personal territory. This is a very vivid way to begin to understand how your environment can affect your self-esteem and your body esteem and be a powerful cue for negative and

positive self-talk. Take an inventory of where your positive thoughts reside in your home, place of work, or school. Both in terms of situations, but also physically: In which rooms of the house do you tend to feel best about yourself and about your body? Since we are trying to separate self-esteem from body esteem, it is best to rate each location on both dimensions. Map out your self-esteem and body-esteem space, and use it to help change the balance between your negative and positive internal self-talk.

Draw a floor plan of your house, including the outside space and the garage or carport where your car is, if you have one. Then rate each space according to whether it is a red, yellow, or green zone—separately for self-esteem and for body esteem. Red means danger zone—a high-risk space for negative self-talk. Yellow is a neutral zone. Green is a positive self-talk zone. You can use whatever symbols or colors you want—the red-yellow-and-green scheme is just a suggestion.

Ginny's floor plan and inventory is revealing. Her home is quite variable in terms of her negative self-talk. Moreover, all rooms do not affect her self-esteem and body esteem the same way. The biggest red zones for her negative body-esteem thoughts are the kitchen and the master bathroom. The reddest zones for her self-esteem thoughts are the laundry and the dining room, where she does the bills. The best zones in the house for her— green zones for both body esteem and self-esteem—are her car, her patio, and the area around the fireplace in the living room.

When Ginny analyzed her floor plan at home, the various red zones were red for different reasons. The kitchen and pantry were red zones for body esteem because she often went there to drown her feelings with food—these were areas where she dealt with negative emotions and thoughts in her life indirectly through eating. At the same time, she valued her cooking skills, so in terms of self-esteem the kitchen was a green zone. The master bathroom was a red zone because it had a huge wall of mirrors and very bright lights. She felt as if she were in a naked mug shot every time she stepped out of the shower, rattling off a list of things she didn't like about her naked body. The power of that bathroom over her body esteem overran any possibilities that it could be anything better than neutral for self-esteem. The dining room was a red zone for self-esteem because it was where she paid her bills and dealt with all of the legal issues about custody of her daughter. She dreaded going in there, knowing every time it was going to be a hassle. Same as the bathroom: The impact on her self-esteem was so strong that her body esteem didn't stand a chance in that room.

The green zones were also quite varied in their nature. The patio was a green zone for self-esteem because she loved sitting there alone, drinking coffee, and listening to the sounds of nature. She felt peaceful there. She rarely worried about her body on the patio because she could sit there in her robe or sweats; no one could see her and she felt completely unjudged by nature around her. Her car was a green zone for both body and self-esteem because it was *her* space. She refused to answer her cell in the car and she loved listening to Broadway music CDs and singing (even if people in neighboring cars thought she was a nutcase). The area around the fireplace near her living room was also green for both self-esteem and body esteem because she has wonderful memories of curling up with a book in front of the fireplace in winter and forgetting everything else around her—an escape from negative self-talk.

The goal of this exercise is to figure out what makes each of these areas a red zone or a green zone for you and how to both make the red zones more yellow and to increase the number of double-green zones. You can do the same exercise for your place of work or school, by the way, to help understand their high-risk zones for negative self-talk.

The first step is awareness of why the zones are red or green. The second step is to analyze whether there are ways to take elements of the green zones into your red zones in order to neutralize them. For Ginny, her greenest zone included listening to show tunes, so an obvious question was whether she could enjoy the music she loved anywhere else besides her car in order to neutralize some red zones. She had never even considered listening to her favorite music in the master bathroom, so she took her iPod and speakers in there just to see if she could reduce the barrage of fat talk she usually heaped on herself when she stepped out of the shower. What was nice about this was she could get so lost in the music and singing that it did distract her while showering and dressing.

It wasn't a complete success, though, because as she was singing away (she simply could not listen to this music without singing), her daughter was less than thrilled with her mom singing slightly off key at the top of her lungs, which evoked a rather teenage "Oh, God, Mom, you're embarrassing me." This was a fairly interesting event because it highlighted a number of issues for Ginny. First, she realized why her car was such a green zone—she didn't have anyone telling her how to act or that she embarrassed them for one reason or another. Second, she realized that in much of her own space at home, she was not truly able to be herself. Whether it was her daughter being embarrassed of her singing, or dealing with the legal and financial aspects of custody, she could not let the inner Ginny come out without some fear of being judged. Her daughter had no qualms about dancing and singing around the house when she was in a good mood, so we worked out a way for her to have a conversation with her daughter and to come up with a compromise so that she too could be herself in her own space. Not only did this exercise give Ginny an option for transforming a red zone into at least a yellow and sometimes a green zone, but it also jump-started an analysis and solution to helping her feel less judged and restricted in her own world. She began to understand that she had a right to be who she was in her own space, and she didn't always have to constrain herself because of the judgments of others. She needed to make her home her world.

This exercise gives a whole new meaning to making your home green.

Ginny's Floor Plan

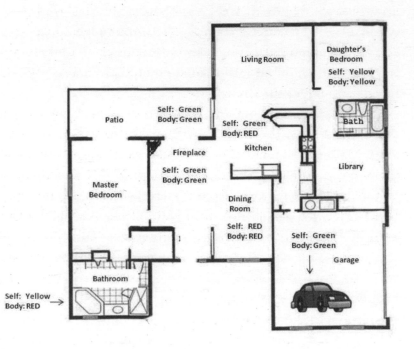

See this floor plan in color at www.womaninthemirrorbook.com.

Capturing Others' Thoughts

While you are working on capturing your own thoughts, use your skills to begin to pay attention to what other women and girls around you are saying about themselves. We have developed a culture of self-deprecation to the point where it is practically expected that we say negative things about ourselves. When was the last time that you went to work or a parent meeting or any gathering of women and heard someone say, "I really feel good about my body!" or "I am really proud of a breakthrough I had today"? More often, the expectation is that we share a flaw or a failure and somehow find community, compassion, and belonging in our shared misery. Even in school, boys are competing to see who is strongest, tallest, fastest, and developing more quickly, and girls are often bonding over whose flaws are worse—"I'm so fat, my legs are short, my arms are too hairy, I hate my curly hair, I hate my straight hair, I hate my freckles, I hate my dark skin, I hate my pale skin." If you admit satisfaction with your appearance, you are ostracized as stuck-up or conceited. The same unwritten rule holds for other self-esteem-related comments. Share your flaws; don't brag about your strengths.

The same way that you are recording your own negative thoughts, keep a record of what you are hearing from others. Whether they are real-life or television examples, jot them down along with the age of the speaker and other details about what you hear. Listen to girls, listen to older women, listen to any females that you encounter in any situation. As you build this chronicle, you will see just how polluted women's conversations are by negative self-talk. By clearly capturing your own thoughts and the thoughts of others, you are well on your way to defining the playing field so that you can take control of this negativity and transform your inner dialogue.

OVERHEARD COMMENTS

Situation	Age/Description	What I overheard
Walking past me in the mall	18–year–old girl, Latino	"I gained so much weight over the holidays."

Print your own table online at www.womaninthemirrorbook.com.

CHAPTER 8

Cues and Triggers— Recognizing Memes

"You bring me down, down, down, way down."
—Leona Lewis, "Bleeding Love"

After becoming proficient at identifying negative self-commentary, you need to identify the source. More often than not, negative self-talk doesn't come out of the blue. Typically, it is cued or triggered by something in the environment or something inside. Cues can arise from your mind ("I wish I were a size 8"), your body (feeling bloated), your emotions ("I'm feeling nervous today"), or the world around you (trying on clothes in a department store). A cue can occur in your head (a thought), or in your body (a bodily sensation), or in the world (situation), or it may be how you feel (emotion). A cue can be specific or vague.

Start by identifying cues that set off your negative thoughts— where do they live, when do they pop up, what are they associated with? Maybe every time you try on clothes at a certain store, or every time you meet with a certain person who rings your self-esteem bells, or every month when you're premenstrual, you can predict that the negative self-talk is going to escalate. You might think that your negative thoughts come out of the blue, but once you start paying attention you will start seeing patterns. Only after you can identify cues and start to predict them can you get power over them. Rather than just eliminating the cues from your world, you need to learn how to use them to your advantage. These cues will become calls to action rather than threats so that you can use them to get a head start on taking control of your inner dialogue. There are several types of cues.

People Cues

People cues are very common triggers for negative self-talk. They are not necessarily tied to just one particular person (although they can be), but can be related to any type of interpersonal situation or even the lack of interpersonal contact. For example, loneliness can be a powerful cue for self-deprecation. If you are feeling lonely or isolated, there is a tendency to try to figure out why or to attach some psychological meaning to it. A thought might surface like "I'm just boring, no one wants to be around me, that's why I'm alone," or "I'm so fat and disgusting, who would even think about dating me?" These thoughts stem from the *absence* of interpersonal contact—or nonpeople cues.

Another type of people cue can come from specific people who just know how to push your buttons. There is probably someone in your life who has a special talent for saying precisely the right thing to set off a torrent of negative self-statements. These folks have some finely tuned radar that allows them to hit the hurt bull's-eye, typically in an effort to boost how they feel about themselves. By planting a nasty seed in your head, they elevate their own self-esteem. This is classic mean-girl behavior, but it isn't limited to girls. The table on the following page holds examples from women of all different ages. It details the age of the "victim," the comment that was uttered, the effect it had on the victim's thoughts and feelings, and a guess about the effect it produced in the person who delivered the insult.

Sometimes these comments are delivered with a smile, and it isn't until later that you realize that they have infiltrated your self-esteem. Stay alert. Take notice when they fly your way and pay particular attention to how they make you feel. These people, and the barbs they deliver, are people cues for negative self-chatter.

Other people cues involve more overt unpleasant interactions—like arguments, relationship problems, tension, and direct conflict. Especially those people who prefer to avoid conflict can find that these sorts of interactions are potent cues for

Your age	Comment directed at you	What you think and feel	What she thinks and feels
10	"Where did your mom buy you that shirt, Walmart?"	I am so unstylish and ugly. All the other girls have nicer clothes.	Chic-er, richer, powerful.
17	"You got brochures from state schools? I'm sorry, I've been getting them from Ivy League schools mostly."	I am so stupid. I'm never going to get into a good college.	Smarter, one step ahead, falsely confident.
35	"*I* lost all my baby weight in two months."	Why can't I do that? Six months out and I still look like I'm in my second trimester. I should be able to do that.	Superior, attractive, builds self up to put you down.
55	"Some women just shouldn't wear sleeveless at our age."	Oh no, she sees my bingo arms. I need to lift more. This is embarrassing.	Justified in spending three hours a day in the gym, like she is defying aging, better than you.
70	"You must have spent many years in the sun."	You look like a prune, face it. Get a face-lift so you don't have to look at this in the mirror every day.	Preserved, prettier, less old than you.

Print your own table online at www.womaninthemirrorbook.com.

negative self-talk. Interestingly, cues don't just arise when the conflict is occurring, but often long afterward. Women tend to ruminate more *after* the conflict occurs. They can think and rethink arguments and conflicts, endlessly going over and over in their minds how they might have worded things differently, whether they might have hurt someone's feelings, whether they handled the situation properly.

Men handle these situations differently—not necessarily better—but definitely differently. I recall a meeting with three senior male researchers and a talented female trainee. These senior males started laying into each other—basically having in-your-face disagreements. None of their comments were prefaced with soft niceties like "I'm wondering whether" or "Perhaps we could consider," and there was not an "I'm sorry" to be heard! It was just plainspoken, direct conflict. The female trainee looked a little shell-shocked, and we both spent days afterward recovering from that meeting. I contacted one of the men a few days later with a quasi-apology that things had gotten so contentious. Astonishingly, he didn't even know what I was referring to! To him it was a faded memory. Once I reminded him what I was talking about, he replied that they always argue like that and told me they had played a very competitive round of nine holes afterward and all was obviously forgotten. So especially for women, conflict, argument, and the aftermath can be complicated cues for a wide range of unhealthy self-talk. I am not saying that women should convert to men's way of behaving—especially if it doesn't sit comfortably with who you are. Women could, however, benefit from some skin thickener. (Too bad Dove doesn't make that!)

People cues can also come in packs. Many people find that social gatherings, parties, dinner engagements, holidays, and speaking in public can all be potent cues for negative thoughts. Any situations in which you can imagine that "all eyes are on you" can trigger a parade of negative self-commentary.

To what extent are people cues an issue for your self-esteem or body esteem? Think carefully about both specific cues, in terms of individual people, and also general cues, in terms of types of interpersonal situations that have the tendency to make you think negatively about yourself or your appearance.

Thought and Feeling Cues

Cues don't always come from the outside. In fact, many cues for negative self-talk are completely internal. Two of the biggest internal cues are *thoughts* and *feelings*. Many people struggle telling the two apart. Learning how to distinguish thoughts from feelings will help define your task of identifying internal cues. On the most basic level, thoughts are the things that go on in your head. They may be little sentences or phrases that you say to yourself, or they may be pictures or visual images you see in your mind's eye. For example, seeing an image of yourself vacuuming the living room is a thought, as is hearing the sentence in your head, "I need to vacuum the living room." We all have different thinking styles: Some of us think more in pictures and others think more in words.

In contrast, feelings are emotions. They can't be identified by little sentences or images in our brains. Sometimes they are harder to wrap your head around because they can range in intensity from very subtle to quite intense. It can also become more complicated when they are paired—for example, you can feel excited and anxious at the same time. Typically, feelings can be reduced to *one word* that captures the underlying emotion. To identify them, you may need to sit quietly, turn your attention inward, and sense how you feel. In general, feelings are grouped into happy, sad, angry, confused, scared, weak, and strong types of feelings, but there are many variations and subtleties within each category.

It is important to learn how to distinguish between thoughts and feelings because we need to deal with them differently when they are acting as cues for negative self-talk. When Lisa says, "I *feel* like I really should be going to the gym today," she has confused a feeling with a thought. She might be *thinking* that she needs to go to the gym today—but that thought can't pass the "one word" test to identify a feeling. She might have feelings associated with her thoughts, but that statement is a thought, not a feeling.

Although both thoughts and feelings can be cues for negative thoughts, they are so deeply intertwined that we need to sort through them to understand the complex way in which they build on one another to contribute to low self-esteem and body esteem.

It seems fairly intuitive that feelings can be cues for negative self-talk, but it is slightly more challenging to understand how thoughts can serve as cues for other thoughts—as well as for feelings. Even though it might seem as if feelings come out of the blue, usually, if you pay close enough attention, you'll be able to trace them back to a thought.

Here's an example of how a thought can be a cue for negative self-talk. Leslie is sitting on the bus on her way to work, thinking about her next steps in life. Her fiancé, John has just been offered a job in another state, but she is perfectly happy where she is. She's afraid that she won't be able to find as good an opportunity in the state to which he wants to move. Those are the thought cues. What they lead to is related negative self-talk. Leslie thinks, "I'm a bad fiancée for not just shutting up and following him. His job is more important than mine because he'll earn more. It's selfish of me to even be thinking about this." That is her negative self-commentary. She doesn't even ask herself how she *feels* about the prospect of moving. She moves right into gut-wrenching conflict that comes from not acknowledging her own feelings. All of this negative chatter and guilt protects her from the uncomfortable emotions that she is *really* feeling. Deep down, she resents the fact that John even interviewed for this job without consulting her. He'd just assumed that she'd pack up and follow him wherever he went. But rather than dealing directly with him and with the issue, she swallowed her true feelings and her negative self-talk prevailed. Leslie gave up her job, moved to Oklahoma with John, got married, and could only find an unsatisfying job that did nothing to advance her career. She divorced him and moved back home after two years. Obviously, thought cues can be powerful things!

Body Cues

How our bodies feel physically can also be cues for uncompli-
mentary self-talk. Two common body cues are bloating and tiredness. Especially during the premenstrual period, if you tend to
retain water, this can be a major (and repeated) cue for negative
self-talk. The thought is that everyone on the outside can see your
change in size as much as you can feel it. You're bloated and all
you want to do is unbutton the top button of your pants (or better
yet, wear sweatpants or a muumuu to work all day). Inside your
head you think that everyone else can *see* how uncomfortable
you *feel*. In reality, we're talking about an inch or so around the
middle that no one could possibly detect. People just aren't that
good at detecting minuscule changes in other people's size. In
fact, we're not even that good at accurately estimating changes in
our own size. Bloating becomes a cue not only because we fear
others can see it, but because we misinterpret it as permanent
fat rather than temporary bloating. So we don't say to ourselves,
"I have temporary bloating related to my period, which will dis-
sipate in a few days as it has done for the past twenty years every
twenty-eight days." Instead, our self-talk reduces it all to "I'm so
fat!"—which makes it sound like a permanent condition and
completely misses the fact that this is a transient and predictable
symptom that you have watched come and go many times before.

A second common body cue for negative self-talk is tiredness. We all think less clearly when we are tired. Our thinking
is fuzzier and we simply don't have the energy to talk our way
out of mind traps. Tiredness is flypaper for negative self-chatter.
During the teenage years, my children might have seemed fine
after school, and then almost like clockwork at around nine
P.M., their faces transformed into sad looks and they started
spouting out all sorts of negative prognostications about tomorrow, this year, next year, college, and their future. It took me a
while to realize that they were just suffering from tired brain.
My kids are early risers, and by nine P.M., they were in no position to be thinking about big topics like their future. So we

made a rule: *No thinking after nine* P.M. I can recognize the look now and simply say, You need to stop thinking about that now because you are not capable of thinking clearly. We'll tackle that one with fresh brain tomorrow *before* the sun goes down.

Another body cue is a behavior that we don't talk about that often: body checking. You're probably aware that you check yourself out in the mirror or in windows, but you might be less aware of how often you touch yourself, pinch yourself, and measure yourself in an effort to gauge how big you are, how small you are, or how much you have changed from one moment to the next. Body checking is often completely unconscious. You might run your hand over your belly after a meal to see if it is "sticking out." The thought in your head might be, "Wow, my gut is really hanging out." But in reality, you just ate! The food has to go somewhere, and within minutes it will all be passing happily through your digestive system.

Jan became so preoccupied with whether she could feel fat on her waist that she got to the point where she was pinching her waist hundreds of times a day. Before she ate, after she ate, after she had a bowel movement, after she drank, before and after she exercised—she was looking for microscopic changes that would either reassure her that she was on target or badger her into sticking with her meal or exercise plan. Her body checking was accompanied by gendarme thoughts. Like Louis Gossett Jr. in *An Officer and a Gentleman*, if she felt a little flesh, her thoughts would command, "Drop and give me twenty" or "Don't eat that candy bar, Ma-yo-nnaise." Of course, the self-talk would never praise her when she didn't feel flesh. In those moments, the best she could hope for was escape from being yelled at by her own thoughts.

So monitor how and when you body check. What do you do to verify your size, to see if you have gotten bigger or smaller or shifted? And just in case you thought these were accurate measurements, they're not. These sorts of body checks are completely inaccurate. Our brains place so many filters on how we perceive ourselves that we can't trust our own perceptions.

BODY IMAGE FLUCTUATES WILDLY

We can't trust our evaluations of our own bodies. Why? Because so many factors influence our body image on almost an hour-by-hour basis. After ravenously obliterating a Big Mac Extra Value Meal, do you suddenly think that you need to start losing some weight? Whether you realize it or not, your perception of your own body size changes with the situation you are in. In particular, both mood and food play a crucial role in influencing your perception of your current size and your desired size.

In a small study, we presented women with bulimia nervosa and women without any eating disorders with a series of silhouettes and asked them to estimate which silhouette most closely resembled their current body size and which silhouette represented the size they would most like to be.[1] We wanted to see how mood and the thought of eating influenced estimations. Since it is unethical to really make people sad, we had a large group of people rate several pieces of music to select the saddest piece of music. We had two groups. One group listened to the sad music and the other group to neutral music. After listening to the sad music, even the women without eating disorders selected a smaller ideal body size. And, after we presented the participants with plates of their favorite food and asked them to imagine tasting it, the women with bulimia gave much larger estimates of their body size than when they were not presented with food. So both low mood and even just the thought of eating can influence how you estimate your size and what size you want to be.

Another study showed how powerful television can be in influencing our body-size estimations.[2] A team of researchers at Virginia Commonwealth University assigned some undergraduates to watch *The Swan*, a reality show about cosmetic surgery, and others to watch *Clean Sweep*, a reality show about home improvement. The ones who watched *The Swan* reported lower self-esteem that lasted for two weeks compared to the women who were assigned to watch *Clean Sweep*.

Maybe the next time you look at yourself and feel dissatisfied with your body or yourself, before jumping into an extreme diet, take a minute to consider the factors around you that may be influencing your body dissatisfaction. Perhaps you've had a tough week at work, or maybe you just finished watching a television show with an appearance focus. Or it might be that you just ate a double fudge brownie. Whatever the situation is, understand that your feelings about your body and yourself may be temporary and that having a laugh with a good sitcom could (at least temporarily) rescue you from your funk.

Magazine Cues

As we are checking out of the grocery store or sitting in the salon or the dentist's office, we grab dreaded women's magazines that bombard us with cues. How to lose ten pounds in a week. How celebrity X lost her postbaby weight in one month. How to be the best hostess you can possibly be, bake the richest, fluffiest chocolate cake in the world while having multiple orgasms, raising your children's IQ, keeping your man happy, and having a flat stomach—all at the same time! Magazines are the source of many of the "shoulds" that taunt women. You should be this, you should do that; everyone else in this magazine can do this, so you should too! These types of articles batter our self-esteem (see following box), yet we are pathologically drawn to them.

WHY DO WE KEEP BUYING THOSE MAGAZINES?

Waiting in the doctor's office or destressing after a long day at work, many women enjoy sitting down on a comfy couch and perusing a magazine. Whether it's the tidbits on the latest fashion trends, scandalous gossip about high-profile celebrities, or the eye-catching advertisements for new beauty products, it can be hard to resist the "guilty pleasure" of magazines. But these publications aren't exactly a harmless way to unwind, and they are not necessarily pleasureful. Reading fashion magazines actually makes women feel worse about themselves and their bodies.[3] In a fascinating study, forty-nine college women were randomly assigned (as by a flip of a coin) either to read fashion magazines, such as *Vogue* and *Allure*, or to read nonfashion magazines including *Newsweek*, *Time*, or *BusinessWeek*. After reading the magazines for thirteen minutes, the women who read the fashion magazines were less satisfied with their bodies, desired to weigh less, and were more preoccupied with being thin than the women who read the nonfashion magazines.

How exactly does reading fashion magazines lead women to feel less satisfied with their bodies? One theory is that when women read these magazines, they are seeking out information regarding what beauty is and how to achieve it.[4] Conscious or not, every time we pick up a fashion magazine, we are looking for guidelines to achieve attractiveness and happiness. When the magazine says we need to be five inches taller and twenty pounds lighter with poreless skin, we feel as if we don't measure up.

The most popular German women's magazine, *Brigitte* (readership 3.21 million), made a bold move in 2009 when it vowed no longer to use professional models. A glimpse through the magazine shows more healthy and diverse portraits of women from all facets of life. The myth that women won't buy magazines if they are not populated by skinny models was completely debunked as *Brigitte*'s sales continue to be brisk. Yes, women read *Brigitte* for the articles after all! Next time you are standing in the checkout line, before you grab a magazine, think carefully about what you are choosing and why. A crisp copy of *Field & Stream* might boost your mood more than your usual read!

Transforming Cues into Signals for Action

Some people err in thinking that once they identify their cues, the next step is to avoid them so that they don't have to encounter those internal or external situations that lead to negative self-talk. Avoidance only works in emergency situations and in the short term. Besides, it is virtually impossible to avoid those thoughts and feelings forever. Rather than avoiding cues, you need to harness them as signals for action. The beauty of identifying cues is that you can start to anticipate them. Once you can anticipate them, you have less of a chance of being blindsided and sent off on a negative-thought cascade that you were unprepared to deal with. You can even do some training and engage in planned exposure to your cues to see what happens when you control the impact they do or do not have on you.

Using External Cues as Signals for Action. Starting with external cues, imagine yourself checking out at the grocery store. This is typically a somewhat irritating and fairly mindless experience. As you wait in line, you casually pick up a magazine and look at the pictures. You might start having some thoughts like, "Wow, she got her pre pregnancy weight back faster than I did," or "I wish I had legs like that," or "I look like such a slob standing here in jeans and a T-shirt—she looks hot even when she's dressing down." If you're having reactions to the magazine, you're not in charge of your thoughts. You are reacting to the magazine cues and your brain isn't even engaged in the process. You are in basic stimulus-response mode—you see the pictures, bypass your rational and critical brain, and head straight into feeling miserable about yourself. You get into the car with your bags, find yourself opening up a chocolate bar, and have no idea how food shopping can so effectively wreck your self-esteem and body esteem.

The contrasting mindful experience is bracing yourself for the cues before you even get to the checkout line. You can prep yourself and start talking yourself out of being hijacked by the messages in the magazines. Coach yourself through the process and navigate the checkout gauntlet without letting those cues get under your skin. Here is some contrasting dialogue that Tammy has in her head when she is using the checkout cues as signals for action. Her last stop before checkout is the frozen-food section, and then she starts prepping for the checkout. "Okay, there are lines up there. I know those magazines are right there on the left side, and the candy and gum is on the right. I'll probably be standing in line for about five minutes. I can do this. I am going to read the headlines, focusing on the words only. I am not going to stare at the pictures and I am not going to pick up a magazine. I am not up for that today. Okay, headlines. Who's pregnant? Who got caught sleeping with another woman? Who tweeted raunchy pictures of themself? Do I really care about this stuff? Celebrity gossip is like flypaper, but I don't really care. I think I'll check my e-mail instead." She then checks her e-mail and notices that she is next in line. "My turn to check out—I did it! I am checking out. All clear."

Tammy was mindfully and actively processing her checkout experience. She knew those cues were going to be there, she anticipated them, and she developed a plan to deal with them. She didn't just avoid (although smartly she did avoid looking at the pictures). The coach in her head helped her use the high-risk cues as signals for positive action.

Now, on a day when she felt strong, she decided to take those cues into her own hands. Intellectually, she knew that everything she saw in those magazines was Photoshopped fantasy, but it still made her feel inadequate. The goal of her experiment was to read one of those magazines, including looking at the pictures, while fully engaging her brain. Instead of just being a passive recipient of the messages and images they were feeding her, she was going to confront the cues head-on. She wanted control over her cues. So the first thing she did to prepare herself was to sit down and watch the Dove evolution video. (See Dove Campaign for Real Beauty in the resources section.)

If you have never done this, do it now. Do it alone, do it with your daughters, do it with your partner, or do it with some friends so that you can all get a sense of just how unreal the images we are bombarded with are. Then Tammy got her magazine and page by page walked through it, asking herself questions like "What message are the writers trying to give me? How are they trying to make me feel about myself? Which products are they trying to get me to buy? What kind of comparisons am I making with myself, and what about them is not realistic?" She was able to attack that magazine from the top down with her brain engaged, rather than being victimized. The value of this exercise is that the next time she was in line at the grocery store, she remembered everything she did during that exercise and could engage her rational brain to protect herself from an onslaught of negative self-thoughts.

Using Internal Cues as Signals for Action. Tammy's experience is an example of how you can use external cues as signals for action. Internal cues can be more challenging. In part, this is because they can sneak up on you and their occurrence is unpredictable. Thoughts and feelings are constant and numerous. The National Science Foundation estimated that we think around fifty thousand thoughts per day.[5] Regardless of the accuracy of this estimate, even if reality is a fraction of that number, that's a lot of thoughts to sort through. Luckily, many of them are just passing phrases and images that are not of much consequence—right now we're focusing on only the thoughts that perpetuate negative self-esteem and body esteem.

Rebecca goes to use the public restroom before she goes into an important meeting with a client. She catches a glimpse of her profile in the full-length mirror as she is exiting. She turns to her side, sucks in, smooths down her hips, but the thought in her head is *I hate my body.* She has to go back out in public and perform, but that negative thought hitchhikes its way out of the restroom with her and joins her in that meeting, hanging over her head and sabotaging her. She is less crisp, less on top of her game, and her negotiations are less successful than she had hoped. The negative thought won.

Rewinding that clip and using Rebecca's thought as a signal for action, the outcome is completely different. In this take, Rebecca washes her hands, catches a glimpse of herself in the mirror and the same thought hits her: *I hate my body*. Rather than succumbing to the thought, Rebecca jumps on it and asks herself, "Why am I thinking that now? What's really going on?" Before heading back out, she takes a minute and asks herself what is truly driving that thought. Is there something else going on that's really bugging her, but it's just easier to project her feelings onto her body image? As it turns out, she's a little fearful about this meeting. She has heard the client is a tough negotiator, and there is considerable pressure on her to do well. "I hate my body" was just code for "I'm worried about this meeting." Once she figured that out, she could dump that original body thought and pull herself together. She took another minute, thought through her strategy for the meeting, looked at herself in the mirror, and said, "Game face on." She went into the meeting alone, no shadows of negative self-talk, and she nailed it. She used her negative self-thought as a signal for action. She drilled down and figured out what was really going on and took control of the situation.

If you can make your negative self-talk work for you by using it as a red flag for self-awareness, then it can help you plot a strong course of action.

The same procedure works for feelings. Sometimes it is crystal clear where our feelings come from. You get a bad performance review at work, you get notified that you are going to be audited by the IRS, someone cuts you off dangerously on the freeway, your child gets bullied at school—in these cases it is fairly easy to pinpoint why you are feeling angry, anxious, infuriated, or whatever other strong emotion emerges. The important piece of processing these feelings is keeping them tethered to the causal incident. In the first example, getting a bad performance review, the emotions you feel are disappointed (in your performance) and angry (because you don't think everything your boss said was completely fair or accurate). This is not a suite of positive emotions at all, but it is your appraisal of the situation. If you start to uncouple these feelings from the causal incident and say things like "I'm a bad person" or "I have no skills" or "I'm never going to make it in this world" or "If I were thinner and more attractive they would never have said things like this about me," then you have taken those feelings, run for a touchdown with them, and generalized far beyond the situation. This also means that you have robbed them of their ability to be signals to you for action.

When you get a bad performance review—it is just that—a "performance" review. It is a call to action. It is addressable. It is within your means to use that review, along with the feelings it generated, to make a change and rectify things. When you take that performance review and make it a global commentary on who you are as a person, what you look like, or what your prospects in life are, you can no longer use it as a call to action because you have generalized so far and wide that there's nothing left to do but wallow in self-pity. If you are going to learn how to use these negative feelings as calls to action, then you have to use your mental energy to keep them in perspective. By exaggerating them and turning them into global criticisms of your self-worth, you give yourself the comfort of self-pity—and you might get some comfort and pity from others who feel badly for you—but you can't use those feelings as signals for action, for taking the situation into your own hands, making it a teachable moment, and coming up with a game plan so that the next review of your *performance* will be better. Don't generalize from a specific situation to a global commentary on who you are or what you are worth. You lose valuable opportunities for growth, change, and problem solving.

It is considerably more challenging to transform what I call stealth emotions into calls to action. But it is doable. Stealth emotions refer to feelings that don't seem to be tethered to a specific event but seem to come out of the blue. These take a little more detective work to figure out. Sometimes you might wake up in the morning bathed in a feeling and you're not sure why. Maybe it was a dream. Sometimes a song on the radio can evoke a feeling. Sometimes feelings and moods might just come over you for no apparent reason. There probably is a reason, but you just can't access it. If we truly do have fifty thousand thoughts every day, we surely can't attend to all of them—but some of those fleeting thoughts affect our moods even if they don't make their way into our conscious awareness.

There are two things you can do with a stealth-feeling cue to turn it into a signal for action. Once you identify that it is there, you can do some feeling archaeology and try to figure out what the causal chain was that led to that feeling. Was it a dream? Was it a song? Was it a memory? If you can figure that out, then it ceases to be a stealth feeling: You can unpack its cause and use it as a signal for action. If you can't locate the source or choose not to try, sometimes it can serve a meaningful purpose just to allow yourself to feel the feeling. Often, trying to suppress or slide unpleasant feelings under the carpet can rob you of the opportunity to learn from them. This is especially true for negative emotions (except guilt, which women seem to revel in far too often). Learning how to navigate sadness or anger without burying them is a skill that can help whenever those emotions emerge. Experience the emotion and see what that experience brings.

Exercises: Cue Inventory
For the first part of these exercises, develop your own personal cue inventory. Make a list of cues that are known to affect your self-esteem and body esteem. Write down the type of cue and which esteem it tends to hit. (It might be both.)

Once you have established your cues for negative self- and body esteem, develop a powerful mental signal. The signal can be an image, a sound in your brain (like a bullhorn), or something

CUE INVENTORY

Cue	Type	Which esteem
Boss	Person	Self-esteem first, then it rolls into body esteem
Thinking about working out visitation with ex	Thought (and person, since my ex is a cue)	Self-esteem
Clothes shopping	Body	Body esteem, then it rolls into self-esteem

Print your own table online at www.womaninthemirrorbook.com.

external like a habit bracelet that you can snap onto your wrist. Anything will work provided you can activate it and it screams out "Cue alert!" Once that signal is activated, use it as a call to action. Rather than responding mindlessly and passively to a cue, engage your brain in the situation and harness your thoughts, your reactions, and your feelings to transform your responses to the cue. Use your meta-awareness to think in the moment and gain the upper hand.

CHAPTER 9

Establishing a Fat-Talk-Free Zone

Fat talk is a plague. It is insidious and ubiquitous. We barely know that it's coming out of our mouths, yet it is all around us. Fat talk destroys women and girls. Once you eliminate fat talk from your brain, you will start having less general negative self- and other talk as well. Eliminating fat talk is a worthwhile goal. You need to make your brain a fat-talk-free zone.

Fat talk is not just the comments we frequently say to ourselves like "Does this make me look fat?" or "My butt is too fat." It is much broader and sometimes more subtle and insidious. I have tried to develop categories of fat talk to help you figure out what types of fat talk you and those around you engage in. You might not even recognize some of them as fat talk. Chevese Turner, founder and CEO of the Binge Eating Disorder Association (BEDA), is a champion of destigmatization and has been on the receiving end of many of these sorts of comments herself. On the topic of fat talk, Chevese says, "After a lifetime of negative focus on the size of my body by myself and others, I now choose to accept and embrace it exactly where it is on any given day. It is not easy to avoid internal and external fat talk, but it is a matter of life and death. There are some basic techniques we can use in our efforts to destigmatize size, and they must include a look at the language we use and the assumptions we make."

Fat talk comes in many shapes and sizes.

Generic Fat Talk

This, the most common type of fat talk, gets down on you for your size no matter what your actual size is. These comments just roll off of your tongue. Spend a morning with a group of women, go clothes shopping, listen in at a high school reunion, and these comments permeate the airspace. It is practically required that we utter these phrases, or at least that we don't admit to their opposite thoughts. How often do you hear women ask, "Do I look too thin in this?" or "I love my hips" or "My figure is really way too awesome to wear a one-piece bathing suit." Such positive body esteem is rare. In fact, if you heard someone else saying it, you would probably label her a "skinny bitch."

Examples of generic fat talk

Do I look fat in this?
I'm so fat.
I hate my [insert body part here].
I need to lose ten pounds.
I'm too fat to wear this swimsuit.

Compliment-Fishing Fat Talk

This type of fat talk is designed to get someone to negate what you are saying and to give you a "but you're not fat" compliment. Everyone fishes for compliments now and again. Even if you are riddled with self-doubt about your size and shape, having someone else reassure you for a brief moment that you're not fat feels good. Not that you believe it, but you fish for it nonetheless. With this kind of fat talk, you put an extreme statement out there so that someone else can contradict it and make you temporarily feel better about yourself.

Examples of compliment-fishing fat talk

I look like a whale in this dress.
My thighs are ungodly ugly.
I don't deserve to be seen in public.

Comparative Fat Talk
This is the misery-likes-miserable-company form of fat talk. The goal of this type of fat talk is another form of one-upwomanship. The thought process behind this type of fat talk is "How dare you complain, I have it so much worse—my fat is worse than your fat!"

Examples of comparative fat talk

You think you're fat? Look at me!
You can shop in that department? Lucky you! I have to go to Women's World.

Can't-Take-a-Compliment Fat Talk
This is the fat talk that emerges when someone gives you a bona fide compliment and you completely undo it, saying that it can't possibly be true because you are clearly too fat to deserve it. This is the opposite of compliment-fishing fat talk. The difference is that when you are fishing for compliments, you are in control and asking for the compliment (or at least the negation of a negative self-statement). In this situation, someone else flings you a compliment and you are unable to take it. Women can be fairly abysmal at taking compliments, so they have to deflect it somehow. One reason that women are terrible at taking compliments is that they conflict with the negative self-talk that is going on in their heads about their bodies. If your internal tape loop is saying you look fat, you look gross, you look old—even if there is a small voice inside saying, "Not bad for your age"—when someone compliments you and contradicts your internal dialogue, you feel like you need to swat it away before you actually succumb to believing it. Zap, away it goes. Or you assume that they don't really mean it and are just being polite, so by negating the compliment you save them from being in the awkward position of watching you accept a compliment that they didn't really mean. This has the natural outcome of that person not giving you any more compliments (Who wants to compliment someone if they

get swatted away every time they do?), which then puts you in the position of resorting to more compliment-fishing fat-talk statements! It's psychological quicksand. This little badminton game involves quite a bit of mind reading and assumptions.

Examples of can't-take-a-compliment fat talk

Someone says, "You look great in that dress." You say, "I would look a lot better if I weighed ten pounds less."

Someone says, "That's a great outfit." You say, "Yeah, would have been better ten years and twenty pounds ago."

Someone says, "You look absolutely stunning tonight." You say, "Thank God for Spanx!"

Competitive Fat Talk

This type of fat talk can be quite off-putting. People who engage in this kind of fat talk talk incessantly about what they ate, how many calories they consumed, or how often or long they exercised. This kind of talk typically comes out when people are overtly or covertly competing with each other about body size.

Examples of competitive fat talk

All I have for lunch every day is a salad with dressing on the side.

I exercise seven days a week.

I never snack between meals.

Silent Fat Talk

This is the silent film of fat talk, the delicate dance that happens when a bunch of women have a meal together. Everyone in the group will be basing their choices on what others are ordering, rather than their own desires or nutritional needs. It can lead to eating less than you actually need in order to appear as though you have superior control around food. If this is what happens in public, then you are likely to go home and binge!

Joking Fat Talk

Joking fat talk is supposedly meant to be humorous. It's when the basis of the joke is rooted in someone's size. This type of fat talk can be about others, but many overweight people also use it as a defense against people's thoughts about their own size. This type of fat talk also gets extended to television and movies when the fat boy or girl is cast as the "clown" or awkward loner.

Examples of joking fat talk

> They better not stick me in the window-exit aisle, or else none of us will ever get out of this plane alive.
>
> Where does an elephant sit?
>
> She could smuggle drugs into the country under those rolls!

Stealth Fat Talk

This is fat talk in sheep's clothes. These can be compliments that suggest that there is something better about you now because you have shed some pounds—which implies there was something wrong about you back when you owned those pounds. Sometimes people are trying to be supportive when they say things like this and really aren't trying to engage in fat talk. This is a situation in which gentle education is advised: Many people really don't realize it's offensive. Evaluate the situation to determine whether it is a teachable moment. If it doesn't feel right, it might be best to let it slide and try to educate next time.

Examples of stealth fat talk

> You look great! Have you lost weight? (Translation: You looked bad before.)
>
> You must be spending lots of time at the gym. (Translation: You looked really out of shape before.)

Fat-Stigmatization Fat Talk

This type of fat talk is generalized and not directed at one person but at "fat people" in general. It includes "shoulds," and "should nots," and all of the deep-seated prejudices that we hold toward individuals of size. It also includes all of the assumptions we make about people's capabilities based on their size. For example, not asking a large friend to be a bridesmaid because she would ruin the image of the wedding!

Examples of fat-stigmatization fat talk

Fat people really shouldn't be allowed in here.

They should have to pay more for ice cream.

I don't want to have to pay for the extra material it takes to manufacture clothes in their size.

Someone like that would not make a very good first impression for the company.

You can't have *her* as a bridesmaid!

Fat-Is-Ugly Fat Talk

This type of fat talk perpetuates the myth that you cannot be attractive if you are fat.

Examples of fat-is-ugly fat-talk

Such a shame she is so big—she has such a pretty face.

That *could be* such a nice outfit.

She could be quite stunning.

Personalized, Disrespectful Fat Talk

This is targeted, personal, petty fat talk directed at a specific person about specific aspects of her or his appearance. If you listen to yourself and the people around you, it is astonishing how often people comment on the size of large people's bodies or what they are doing or how they look. In part it just might be that humans are programmed to notice things that stand out from average height and weight—we also comment on very tall people, very short people, and very underweight people. Noticing is one thing, but uttering mean and hurtful comments about people who inhabit those extremes is another. Some people believe they have the right to say these things even directly to overweight people—possibly because they think their comment might somehow make a difference.

Examples of personalized, disrespectful fat talk

She shouldn't wear that tight shirt!

My, that skirt is not flattering at all.

Who dressed her this morning?

Someone forgot to call the fashion police.

Do you really need that ice cream? (*Witnessed in a checkout line at a supermarket when a thin person commented directly to a large woman on the contents of her shopping cart!*)

How can she go out in public looking like that?

Bullying Fat Talk

This is the king of fat talk—the worst of the categories. Bullying fat talk goes beyond disrespectful and crosses the line to purposeful, hurtful, and power seeking. Bullying fat talk starts in children and persists long into adulthood. Grown-ups hurl these insults as well, sometimes to the people they are closest to. Bullying fat talk is like tattoo ink: It cuts deep and gets under the skin. It's difficult to forgive and forget.

Examples of bullying fat talk

You're a fat pig and I don't want you on my team.

I wouldn't be caught dead on a date with a fat girl like you.

You disgust me.

I can hardly stand being in the same room with you anymore. How could you have let yourself go so much?

To varying degrees, these types of fat talk are all around us. Depending on your own life story, you may be more or less aware of and sensitive to them. But there are many people in the world for whom all of these variations on fat talk can be extremely damaging. Large people retreat more and more from the external eye by not going out in public (or only going out during times when they are unlikely to be seen by others) or not engaging in healthy behaviors like exercise for fear of being the brunt of fat talk. This signals that our world is unsafe for people of size.

We don't have a blueprint for healthy ways of discussing size, but there are some models. One I learned on an airplane. I usually sit in an aisle seat because I hate crawling over people (of any size) to go to the lavatory. On this particular flight, my travel agent had me in the window seat of a bank of three seats. Everyone scans passengers as they board, wondering who their seatmate is going to be—the one with the loud music on the earphones, the crying baby, the loud gum chewer, the large person? On this flight, a very large woman occupied the seat next to me, and she was clearly physically uncomfortable. She simply did not fit into the seat. I was pretty uncomfortable, too, because her body took up her seat and a good part of mine; I had to sit on my right butt cheek in order to fit in the remaining space. A large man came walking down the aisle, and she said to me, "Good Lord, don't let him sit here with us!" At first I was a little surprised to hear her say that. She must have seen my surprise, because it started an interesting conversation. She acknowledged how hard it was for her to be stuck in the middle seat, and she just said, "Look, I know I'm one to talk, but if he were to sit here too, then you would basically have to sit on the wing, honey." For me it was refreshing to be able to talk about her situation and her discomfort and have her acknowledge mine. We had a dialogue about airlines cramming more and more people into smaller and smaller spaces and how difficult that is for people who are large (both in width and height). We had an open discussion about how to handle the next few hours. I was able to empathize with how difficult it must be for her, and I was able to share my general hesitancy to say "Excuse me" and crawl over people of any size! Even though she had to couch her conversation behind some joking fat talk about herself and the other man, we were at least able to have a conversation and work out a plan to deal with the situation in an open way.

Another flight was not so enlightening. This was one of those little Embraer planes with one seat on the left and two on the right. Often flight attendants will have to reseat people to balance the aircraft. A large woman was seated in seat 3A. I can only surmise that she selected that seat to make her journey more pleasant. The flight attendant made an announcement that she was going to have to move people around to balance the plane. She then walked down the aisle, stopped at this woman, and in a loud voice said, "Ma'am, the plane is unbalanced—I need you to move to the back and on the right!" The poor passenger was mortified. All eyes were on her. She must have just wanted to melt into oblivion. I ached inside as I watched her gather her belongings and struggle to the back of the plane. It was one of the most profound demonstrations of insensitivity I have experienced.

Eliminating Fat Talk

There are two tasks. The first is establishing a fat-talk-free zone in your head, and the second is establishing a fat-talk-free zone in your environment.

My mother told me a story that shows how you can change how you think and talk at any age. She always complained about her "stubby legs." I remember her making complimentary and even envious comments about other women's legs that she found more attractive than hers. She was also quick to point out other legs that she was not impressed with: She had a friend who she said had "bird legs." My mother is short; she doesn't have a lot of leg room, and her legs were clearly not her favorite body part. When she started having trouble with a knee, conventional medicine wasn't giving her any relief so she decided to see an acupuncturist. Somehow during the treatment she blurted out something like, "I've always hated my legs." As she retells the incident, this fifty-something Chinese man seemed almost personally wounded by her self-disrespectful comment. He looked at her in disbelief and asked how she could possibly say something so disrespectful about her own body. Had not her legs allowed her to walk many places around the world for over seventy years? Had not her legs provided her with the foundation for her body? Were not her legs an integral part of who she was as a person and all that she has accomplished? How can she possibly isolate a body part and distance herself from it by saying she hated it? "Ma'am," he said, "you must treat all of your body parts with equal respect. They work hard for you, and you must show them gratitude in return." This experience was a defining moment for my mother's body esteem. I have not heard her complain about her legs since, and this new perspective has helped her rise above the trap of the Western body ideal. Perhaps aging has played a role too, but I see her now as someone much more grateful for what her body allows her to do rather than as someone who is concerned about how it looks.

Sometimes it takes this type of paradigmatic shift to eradicate fat talk and develop respectful body talk in your head. Tools exist to help you focus on health, not weight or size.

Establishing a Fat-Talk-Free Zone in Your Head
With that enlightened stance as your goal, how do you get there? There are several steps you can take to lay the groundwork for a fat-talk-free zone in your head.

Identification. The first step in remedying a problem is to understand it. The goal is to increase your awareness of how often fat talk happens in your head and what type of fat talk it is. You can't change your behavior if you don't know what you need to change. No doctor would prescribe a treatment without a diagnosis. The same principle applies here. Frances knew she had some internal fat talk but was oblivious to the fat talk she directed at others in her head. See a table of her fat-talk monitoring on the following page.

Frances was actually quite upset with herself when she captured these thoughts on paper. Her first thought was that if

FAT-TALK LOG

Time	Situation	Comment	Type
7:00 A.M.	Bathroom mirror alone	I look bloated today.	Generic
8:00	Watching a morning show about the U.S. education system	That is not a flattering outfit. It really makes her bottom look fat.	Personalized disrespectful
10:00	Sitting at desk	My thighs are so wide when I sit down—man, do they spread.	Generic
12:00 P.M.	Lunchroom with friend	Told Dana that her dress was flattering to her figure.	OMG, that was a stealth fat comment. I really meant it made her look thinner.
2:00	Walking down hall behind two large people	They should make them walk single file.	Fat stigmatizing

Print your own table online at www.womaninthemirrorbook.com.

their recipients had heard her, she would have been ashamed—even her compliment to her friend was really just a personalized, disrespectful fat comment in sheep's clothes. She realized that even though she too was a large woman, she was prejudiced against and dismissive of other large people.

Undoing. Every time you identify a fat-talk comment in your head, note it and pair it with a respectful one. The goal of this "undoing" is to start to neutralize fat talk and to get you more accustomed to focusing on positive aspects of people and situations rather than searching for flaws. This holds both for comments about yourself and comments about others. Preferably, the paired comments will not be focused on appearance or trivial issues like what someone is wearing. Frances could have made the following pairings. "I look bloated today" could have been paired with "I am awake and alert and mentally prepared to engage in the day." "That outfit is not flattering" could have been paired with "Her point is really well taken: The U.S. education system really does need a major overhaul, and she articulated that very clearly." "My thighs are so wide when I sit down—man, do they spread" could be paired with "My legs are my workhorses and I am grateful for what they allow me to do." This might seem like a simplistic intervention, but its simplicity is elegant. You're basically forcing more positive thoughts into your brain space to take over real estate that had previously been occupied by fat talk. You're changing the character of your thought neighborhood—gentrifying your thought space with positive and more respectful reflections.

Spontaneous positive body talk. Positive comments don't just have to be paired with negatives. Start paying yourself random compliments. Like my mother's acupuncturist intimated, we don't do this often enough. "My gardenia had a second bloom today. One lone flower decided just to unravel right in the middle of the bush. My nose let me experience the unexpected late-summer redolence that a single gardenia blossom produced. There are people who have no sense of smell. My nose let me smell that flower today—nice nose!" "I wanted to say hi to a friend I haven't seen in ages who lives far away. I typed her an e-mail. My fingers allowed me to type a very long note and get back in contact with someone whom I care about very much. I have hands that work; others aren't so fortunate. Thanks, fingers!" We can't take our bodies for granted and constantly get down on them because they don't match up to some unattainable visual ideal that we think is worth striving for. Body gratitude is a good feeling and one worth cultivating.

If you do follow these steps for a few weeks, you are going to notice subtle changes in your outlook. Your own mind will become a kinder, gentler place, and you will feel more resilient to perceived judgments of those around you. It will become second nature to pair disparaging comments with respectful ones. So if someone on the outside slings an insult your way, you will be in a much better position to neutralize it with a positive self-statement rather than have it send you into a tailspin.

As with any new skill, you have to practice. Remember, fat talk is the default option in our society and it is always easier to go with the flow. It takes activation energy to approach the world differently. It takes practice and persistence, but the result is most definitely feeling more comfortable and welcome in your own shoes.

Establishing a Fat-Talk-Free Zone in Your Environment

Here are five steps to making your environment a fat-talk-free-zone. The first step is realizing that you can do only so much. It is a lot easier to do this work inside your own head than to try to change everyone around you. You can take a stab at it, especially with the younger generation and people who care enough about you to try, but there will be incorrigibles out there. Then the best you can do is change *your* internal response to them.

Identification. The same approach applies to establishing a fat-talk-free environment as with inside your own head. The first step is to identify who is doing it and when the fat talk is happening around you. Returning home to your family for visits or holidays can often be enlightening and might feel like a fat-talk festival because every bodily change comes under scrutiny when people haven't seen you for a while. Spend a few days listening to the people around you and keep an actual or mental log of who is doling out what kind of fat talk and when.

Awareness. Choose the people with whom you want to have frank conversations about reducing and ultimately eliminating fat talk. If you know someone is going to be a hopeless case, it is perhaps better not to joust with windmills. But if your partner or your children are falling prey to fat talk, making them aware of what they are doing is worth the effort. Just pointing out the behavior and reframing it can be a powerful motivator. Especially with fat talk directed toward others, it is good to ask how they think the recipient would feel if they heard them say the comment out loud. It can engage empathy and get people to think twice before engaging in personalized or stigmatizing fat talk.

Education. Tell the people you choose to engage in this process about the different types of fat talk. Point it out when it happens. Do it gently and in a manner they can learn from, not in an "A-ha! Gotcha!" manner that will just put them on the defensive or send their thoughts underground. Start the conversation and keep the dialogue going. Help them understand that it is no different from other kinds of prejudice or injustice, and encourage them to monitor their own thoughts in the same way you did.

Do not reinforce. If you want a child to stop engaging in a behavior, the best approach is to ignore it. Don't join in, don't rise to the bait, just move on to another topic. If you give it attention, you'll be reinforcing it and increasing the likelihood that it will happen again. Use the same approach that is effective with temper tantrums. Ignoring them is the best approach to sniffing out the behavior. If you ignore fat-talk comments enough, they will extinguish. You are giving a quiet signal that "this is not a conversation that I want to engage in with you."

Modeling fat-free talk. Especially the younger people around you are much more influenced by what you do than what you say. If you are talking up a fat-talk-free game, but they hear you complaining about your body or commenting on large people that you see, your attempts at education will fall on deaf ears. So be a fat-talk-free model for your children. Model respectful comments and help them develop a more positive relationship with their bodies that is not just focused on appearance.

CHAPTER 10

Your Inner Coach

In order to develop and maintain a healthy internal dialogue, you need a coach. Don't necessarily go hire one (although you could). Even if you did hire someone to jump-start this work, the ultimate goal would be for you to do it yourself: You can't carry your coach around with you all the time.

To succeed at self-coaching, you have to be willing to talk to yourself. You can do it silently, but occasionally you may need to cross that border and talk to yourself out loud in order to get your point across. The secret to successful self-coaching is that the words and phrases that you speak to yourself be planned motivational sentences. These phrases have to be more powerful than passive thoughts that pass through your head; they will influence your behavior in response to cues. They must give you focus, clarity, and purpose. This is not Pollyanna self-talk, nor is it meant to bully you into thinking or behaving a certain way. It's the kind of talk that a really superb coach gives at halftime when the team goes into the locker room. It motivates, it gives direction, and it inspires.

One way to begin to think about the effect of self-coaching thoughts is by considering a basic signal-to-noise problem in your brain. Imagine that your brain is a radar screen. The fifty thousand thoughts you have per day are like static—they are small blips all over the screen. Some of them yield bigger signals than others, and those are the ones that you typically pay attention to. The coaching thoughts are designed to be even stronger than those. Coaching thoughts are designed to light up your radar screen, focus you, and lead you to an action plan. Their strength outshines the rest of the static.

Self-coaching promotes mindfulness, and mindfulness is a critical component to refurbishing your brain and its negative self-thought library. Mindfulness refers to being completely in touch with and aware of the present moment. For example, when I shower in the morning I am typically not mindful. I am thinking about the thousands of things I have to do that day—answering questions from my kids, thinking about what to make for dinner, thinking about what I am going to wear—and I have some combination of sleep fog and caffeine in my brain. For a while, I kept getting out of the shower and not remembering if I had rinsed the conditioner out of my hair. I would feel my hair, ruminate whether I had rinsed it or not, then finally I would end up getting back into the shower, rinsing it definitively, and then carrying on with my day. Eergh! This little ritual took time; time that I didn't have to spare in the morning. So I decided to become more mindful in my showers—focusing on what I was doing, doing things in order, and talking myself through each step. I uttered to myself, "I am putting the *shampoo* bottle down now. I am picking up the *conditioner*. I am rinsing the *conditioner* out of my hair." When I was mindful, I was able to step out of the shower with confidence and move on to blow-drying without having to revisit the shower in the morning. I went from being mindless to mindful.

If we go back to the checkout line in the grocery store, you have a fairly weak-signaled negative self-thought when you look at the magazines at the checkout. The thought was, "I look like such a slob standing here in jeans and a T-shirt—she looks hot even when she's dressing down." It may be powerful so far as it affects your feelings, but in reality it was just a fly-by thought—brain static. The coach inside your head has to get into the locker room of your thoughts and overpower that weak-signaled although influential thought with a stronger, motivated, action-oriented thought. Your inner coach could bellow in her most encouraging and supportive tone, "You can make it through this checkout without feeling bad about yourself. Think! How is the editor of that magazine trying to make you feel? What is that editor trying to make you buy? Engage your brain! Get through this situation actively and take control rather than letting the checkout take control over you." Then, like any good coach, when you make it through the checkout line, your inner coach needs to pat you on the back: "Woo-hoo! You did it! You made it through without getting sucked into the magazine trap. Attagirl!"

The more you can have a dialogue with yourself in your head and coach yourself through tricky situations, the more successful you will be at silencing the self-insults. The art of self-coaching is grounded in two worlds. The first is athletics, and the second is cognitive-behavioral therapy. On the athletics side, if you have athletes who are anxious or having performance challenges, you work on their self-talk and visualization. Sometimes when you watch sports—anything from gymnastics to soccer—you can see how much athletes use self-talk to prepare themselves for events. Downhill skiers visualize the course before they head down. They have memorized every turn and bump and they take themselves down that course not by imagining crashes and errors, but by using positive imagery and self-talk. And the brain signal for the successful imagery has to be stronger than any negative, defeatist signals.

Occasionally you can practically see and feel when an athlete gets out of the zone and starts "thinking." These aren't good self-coaching thoughts but rather self-doubting thoughts that interfere with performance. "I can't do it. I'm going to flub it. This doesn't feel right." The negative-talk signals become more salient than the positive self-coaching signals; as you watch them, you cringe because you can feel it coming. In the classic sports movie *Bull Durham*, the experienced catcher "Crash" Davis, played by Kevin Costner, counsels hotshot rookie "Nuke" LaLoosh, played by Tim Robbins. Every time Nuke starts to think, his pitches go wild. Crash wants Nuke to focus on the pitch he calls and rid his mind of other chatter. Crash walks to the mound, hands him the ball, and says, "Don't think—it can only hurt the ballclub." The message was to rely on the coaching you received and not to let your own second-guessing undo the power of your coaching. Eventually Crash's wise voice works its way into Nuke's head and he becomes his own coach. The same principle applies to you when it comes to boosting your self-esteem and body esteem.

This precise approach forms the cornerstone of one of the most effective forms of psychotherapy to come around in decades. Cognitive-behavioral therapy (CBT) focuses on thoughts that you have that trip you up in one way or another—that make you depressed, anxious, eat too much, get anxious in social situations—and it helps you identify them and replace them with healthier alternatives. The approach is somewhat more refined than Crash Davis's, but the CBT therapist helps you identify the thoughts that trip you up, use them as signals for action, and replace them with carefully considered and health-promoting thoughts.

One of the most publicized strategies was Tyra Banks's "kiss my fat ass"—aka the best defense is a good offense—approach when tabloid photographers captured cellulite on a swimsuit shot. When a number of photos of Banks wearing a bathing suit appeared sporting headlines such as THIGH-RA BANKS, AMERICA'S NEXT TOP WADDLE, and TYRA PORKCHOPS, Banks fought back. As reported in E! Online,[1] in a tearful discussion of the experience, she said, "If I had lower self-esteem, I would probably be starving myself right now. That's exactly what is happening to other women all over this country." To the people who were criticizing her for weight gain, her inner coach produced a spicy retort: "I have one thing to say to you: Kiss my fat ass!" You don't always have to be that spicy (except when deserved), but her response created a Teflon shield that kept those hurtful headlines out, separated her self-esteem from her body esteem, and preserved her sense of self-worth—independent of her size.

You need to rely on internal strength, but you must also call on those who really care about your well-being for support. A great blueprint for defining who is on your sideline comes from Jess Weiner, who serves as Dove's Global Ambassador for Self-Esteem. Jess travels the world speaking and hosting workshops on self-confidence. She brings her own wisdom to bear in her work, which was also chronicled in her first book, *A Very Hungry Girl*, about struggles during her teen years with body image, eating disorders, and depression. In *Life Doesn't Begin Five Pounds from Now*, she further explores how low self-image controls the way women think about their health, wealth, family, career, and relationships. She recommends identifying your "esteem team." This is the core group of people in your life who lift you up, listen to you, laugh with you, and know your foibles. According to Jess, "Your esteem team is definitely not made up of the kind of people who throw you backhanded compliments or pretend to be joking when they've said something that hurt your feelings. You'll know you have the right 'esteem team' around you when you feel safe, heard, and unafraid to be your full self. Keep in mind, no one is perfect. And it's possible that you'll find conflict or tension with people who are on your team, but a key factor in trusting and building a strong 'esteem team' is that when conflict arises it's dealt with in a healthy and productive way and not by eliciting shame, blame, or abusive actions. Trust your gut on who you allow to stand close to you. Our gut never lies."

Establishing Your Inner-Coach Voice

An effective inner coach has distance and perspective. Whereas your self-denigrating thoughts are lost in the moment and automatic, your inner coach is able to step back from the situation and guide you through it mindfully. Establishing and nurturing this voice is a powerful intervention because, once established, you can call on it in almost any situation. The inner coach can help with anything from body-esteem thoughts to prepping you for a performance at Carnegie Hall. To be effective, it has to be authoritative and trustworthy. Your inner coach has several roles, each of which needs to be cultivated. Five important ones are coaching you in the moment, understanding the opposition, providing stock motivational phrases, rewarding you for a job well done, and processing effectively when things turn out less than optimally.

It's never too late to develop an inner coach. Your self-esteem and body esteem *can* recover at midlife and beyond. Just because you're down at halftime doesn't mean you can't come back and take control of the second half. Anson Dorrance, the UNC women's soccer coach and perhaps the greatest motivator of female athletes of all time, knows how to turn the tides at halftime. Your inner coach can learn from him. Coach Dorrance believes that the critical factor to motivating women at halftime is tone. As explained in his biography, a coach doesn't have to come in pacing, kicking, and screaming if a women's team is down at halftime, because women can tell just by looking at your face that you are upset. Dorrance knows that women need no help with self-flagellation. So instead all he does is calmly impart some wisdom or strategy to apply in the second half.[2] That is how he gets the best performance out of his players—not by yelling or criticizing or threatening. Dorrance explains, "You haven't criticized them at all, you've just reconstructed them a bit, and now when the halftime talk ends they are willing to die for you because all you've done is support them." That is what the coach in your head is for—not to beat you down, but to build you up, muster your strengths, and motivate you for the second half.

Coaching You in the Moment

An effective way to develop this feature of your inner coach is to think back about a teacher, parent, or coach who has been effective in teaching you something in the past. Chances are that person was able to break the task into manageable chunks, was able to provide concrete and easy-to-follow guidance on how to accomplish the various steps of the task, most likely used a calm and steady voice, and was probably patient. If there were other qualities that he or she had that made learning and developing a new skill easy, then be sure to incorporate them into the development of your inner-coach voice. Also related to this is who you want on the sidelines rooting for you. This can be the mental representation of your "esteem team" or other people you know would be rooting for you. Your sidelines should not be populated just by cheerleaders, but by representations of people who genuinely care about your success and who will support you in your endeavors.

In developing my inner-coach voice, my role model was my father when he taught me how to drive. I remember vividly. He got me situated in the car and had me adjust my seat and mirrors and check to make sure everything was comfortable and appropriate for my dimensions. He had me articulate out loud what I was going to do next before I did it, gently correcting me if I skipped a step. Then he would say, Okay, start the car. In the beginning, he would then have me verbalize what I was seeing and what I was doing. For example, "Okay, that car's slowing down but they don't have their turn signal on. I bet they are going to turn—I better slow down." We would end our lesson, he would say well done, and then we would calmly discuss anything that needed improvement or that I missed. He understood mindful self-coaching long before it was ever developed as a therapeutic tool.

My sidelines are populated by people I don't even know. As the first person in my family to go to college, and hailing from a working-class background, I populate my sideline with my ancestors—people who would be proud of what I accomplished even decades after they left the earth. Many people find having their family, their children, and even their personal god on their sideline to be highly motivating. Think carefully through your choices to ensure that your sideline will be there for you. You have complete control of who is there!

Complete the following table to help mold the nature of your inner-coach voice and your sideline support team. Included are some examples to get you started:

CHARACTERISTICS OF YOUR INNER COACH AND SIDELINE SUPPORT

Inner Coach	Sideline Support Team
Definitive	Love me
Calm	Are proud of me no matter what
Trustworthy	Respect me at all times

Print your own table online at www.womaninthemirrorbook.com.

Once you have established the qualities of your inner coach, have her start walking you through a few simple exercises. Like the example above when my inner coach walked me through the shower, allow yours to walk you through something low-risk and simple just to get some practice with self-coaching. Starting with simple situations is important in order to hone the skill and develop trust in your inner-coach voice. Without that foundation, it will be much harder to rely on that voice in challenging situations.

Understanding the Opposition

Good coaches watch opposing teams, either on tape or from the stands, to learn about their tactics, strengths, and weaknesses before they send their own team out to play them. Your inner coach can play this role for you. When she is fully engaged and mindful of what is happening, she can talk you through what any opponent might be trying to accomplish. This can be especially valuable when other people could be motivated by less-than-gracious agendas that might include putting you down, destabilizing you, or just taking potshots at how you look or who you are. When you are in the midst of an emotional situation with another person, the world can start blurring around you and you can lose that bird's-eye view that is necessary for clear processing of the situation. This whirlpool engages your emotional brain rather than your rational brain, so it becomes easier for you to become destabilized. This is also a time when insults more easily find their way under your skin—so you need your inner coach's help to keep perspective and maintain your watermelon skin (rather than your soft, bruisable banana skin).

For example: You're going into a meeting where several of you are presenting alternative ideas for an ad campaign. Before you enter the room, a catty coworker says, "Wow, on some people that dress would look very yesterday, but you manage to pull it off." Your head starts spinning off the comment immediately, "What did she mean by that? Do I look sloppy? What does she mean by 'manage to'? Oh, God, do I look fat." She has completely thought-jacked you. Your brain is supposed to be focused on your presentation, but her strategic placement of a catty remark got you exactly where she wanted you. Without your coach, you would go into that meeting thinking about your thighs, your dress, your weight—completely off your game. But your inner coach knows this opponent and warned you before you even headed up to the conference room to be on your guard for the blitz! Out comes her little remark, but before you can be thoughtjacked, your coach says, "Head in the game—she's trying to destabilize you, shields up!" So you stay focused, deflect her comment, keep your boundaries closed to any comment that would affect either your self-esteem or body esteem, and you go in there and get the job done. Your coach kept you mindful and even allowed you to peer into the mind of your opponent to keep a clear view of the playing field.

Stock Motivational Phrases

Win one for the Gipper. When the going gets tough, the tough get going. All for one and one for all! Knute Rockne, Joe Kennedy, and D'Artagnan might not have the right inspirational tone for you, but they provide good examples of stock phrases that can be pulled out at any moment to create a success space in your brain. They are motivational, engage sideline support, and convey positive feeling and a belief in yourself that you can accomplish what you are setting out to accomplish. You don't want to have too many, because then you get paralyzed by decision making when your inner coach is grabbing for a stock phrase. You only need one or two that really speak to you, motivate you, and support you. A phrase can be as simple as "You can do this." When paired with a deep breath, that might be all you need to jump off the diving board, step into the boardroom, enter the bakery, walk up to the microphone. These are your launch phrases—the final words before you engage in the task. They are also your "turn around the situation" phrases—if negative thoughts start worming their way into your head, you can utter one of these instantly to get your inner coach back on track. Try a few out to see what captures your needs best and provides the most motivation and support. Then use them—first for less challenging tasks and then for harder ones. The more you use them and the more they become paired with successes, the stronger they will become as motivators. Test a few below and then hone your list to the two most highly effective phrases that will be the backbone of your coach's motivational repertoire.

Stock Motivational Phrases to Rely On

1. You can do this.
2.
3.

Print your own list at www.womaninthemirrorbook.com.

Rewarding You for a Job Well Done

Even if you hate sports, turn on the TV or go to a game or a match just to watch the interactions between the coach and the players. When a player does something well, the good coaches reward them immediately—with a smile, a nod, a pat on the back, a butt slap, a fist bump. Their teammates do the same— chest bumps, teammates piled on top of them, clapping, hugs. When your dog learns a new trick or repeats an old one, you reward her or him. When your children get a good report card or help you around the house without being prompted, you praise them. Instinctively, you know these basic behavioral principles. If you want someone to do more of a good thing, you reward her or him for it. Yet you fail to reward yourself. This is where your inner coach comes in. Even if you tend to be one of those people who "undoes" every success you have by talking yourself out of feeling good about it, your coach can never do that. Your inner coach has to be the voice of reason who applies the same basic behavioral principles to you as you apply to everyone else. The next time you do something well, or even if you just do it better than you did before—even if you are not yet up to your ideal performance—your inner coach has to get in there before your negative thoughts do to say, "Well done—you did that better than you ever have before." Or, if you have truly done a superb job navigating a sticky situation, your coach will give you a pat on the back and say, "Take a moment, be proud, you did well." Good coaches don't divide their attention when they give praise. They also don't add in any "buts." "Well done, but . . ." is not praise at all because you focus more on the "but" than on the praise. For that reason, the praise needs to be genuine, clear, not cluttered by any qualifications, and you need to take a moment to feel it—not just do a drive-by, but really savor the praise. This allows your inner coach to do her work to help you build your self-esteem and body esteem. Ultimately, that is the inner coach's job. She will help you navigate sticky waters in a way that preserves both esteems and keeps them separate.

Ashley had to give a talk to a packed auditorium at her daughter's high school. She had always been terrified of public speaking and really wanted to avoid having to do this, but she felt passionate about engaging more parents in an anti-bullying campaign that she thought the school could benefit from. She was worried about whether parents would take her seriously because she was overweight, and she was terrified that she was going to flub when she saw all the people in the auditorium. Before she went on stage, she engaged her inner coach and walked herself through what she was going to do, step by step. Right after her name was called, she took a deep breath, said, "You can do this!" and went to the mike to make her plea to the parents. She had a few misspeaks, but her passion and belief in the program came across. As she walked off the stage, her inner coach said in a clear voice, "You did it! Well done." This helped her not to focus on the few words that she tripped over but to get some distance, focus on the big picture, and recognize that she had mobilized hundreds of parents to join her and support the anti-bullying campaign. Her kids and husband on her imaginary sidelines were jumping and cheering—and her real husband in the audience hugged her and said, "Well done, honey," when she returned to her seat. She realized afterward that she never thought about her weight once while she was onstage—she was completely engaged in the moment. Your inner coach can help you not feel alone when you're engaged in challenging tasks.

When Things Go Wrong

Teams don't always win, so coaches also have to be prepared to help the team work through what went wrong and then remotivate them for the next challenge. Your inner coach needs to be able to play this role as well. We all flub. You might do everything right in the buildup and you might have your inner coach engaged and your stock phrases ready, but something might happen that just leads to a less than optimal outcome. In the sports world, coaches don't just throw in the towel, walk off the field, and abandon their team. They figure out a way to learn from the experience by understanding it and then using that information to improve performance the next go-around. The only thing worse than messing up is not learning from it. Thinking back to school, I would wager that you remember the answers to questions that you got wrong more than you remember the answers to questions you got right. On my fifth-grade state-capitals test, I missed Cheyenne, Wyoming. Since then, I have never forgotten that Cheyenne is the capital of Wyoming—but I always forget Dover, Frankfort, and Salem, and I got those right!

What this means is that every time you do execute something less well than you'd hoped, or if your body esteem or self-esteem take a beating, rather than beating yourself up about it, turn it into a teachable moment. Walk through the experience in your mind with your inner coach and dissect where things went sour. Rather than wallowing in self-pity, take an active approach and problem-solve. Ask, What could I have done differently (and what can I do differently in the future) to ensure a better outcome? Also take this time to ensure that you have not crossed the divide between self-esteem and body esteem, letting a hit to one bleed over to a hit to the other.

Imagine that Ashley's presentation to the PTA assembly had gone differently. She made it to the stage, looked out at the audience, panicked at the number of people in the room, and started thinking about all of the parents there who were more qualified to give this presentation. She started to shake and noticed that her voice was quivering. At one point she lost her place and had difficulty pinpointing where she was on her note cards. She saw a thin, toned mom smirking in the front row, and she got embarrassed that she had on stretch cords and a blouse that made her look a little pregnant. She finished her plea for participation, but all she could think about was getting off that stage. She was devastated and thought there was no way she could have convinced a single parent in the room with that performance. Without an effective inner coach, Ashley might vow

PERFORMANCE REFLECTION WORKSHEET

Choice point	What I did	What I could have done differently
Panic about people in the room	I started comparing myself to everyone and thought about how much smarter, more educated, more qualified they were—made me doubt myself.	• I could have looked at all of the people before I took the stage and reminded myself that I was doing this because I was passionate about anti-bullying. Any smart, educated parent would agree that bullying was a bad thing—they were on my side, not competition or opponents. • I could have engaged my sideline and reminded myself who I was doing this for. • I could have used one of my stock motivational phrases before I went out onstage to get my courage up.
My hands were shaking	I kept holding my note cards, and everyone could see them shaking.	I could have put my cards down on the lectern so that people didn't see them shaking.
Quivering voice	I just kept talking, and I think I started talking even faster and messed things up more.	• I could have slowed down instead of speeding up. • I could have taken some deep breaths and concentrated on my breathing while I was speaking
Lost my place in the notecards	I made them using 12-point font! That was not so smart.	I should definitely have used a larger and bolder font. Next time I will do that for sure.
Thought about my clothes and being overweight	I got completely derailed by the smirking skinny woman.	• Get appearance out of my head. • This is about bullying. Appearance bullying is part of the problem—I have to live what I am promoting!

Give up and not follow up	I was afraid to call parents and follow up because I was so embarrassed.	• I could call them up and just lay it out there—"Hi, this is Ashley Cook from school, I wanted to make another attempt at telling you why I think this program is so important for our children." • I could print a flyer for kids to take home from school and try to reach the parents again that way. • I can have a second chance!

Print your own table online at www.womaninthemirrorbook.com.

never to speak out about something she feels passionate about again, thinking she'll just leave that up to some other parent. She might also even give up the fight this time and not follow through with phone calls because she doesn't want to remind other parents that she was the pathetic one who was too nervous to even ask for their help on an anti-bullying campaign. But luckily, she had developed her inner coach to help her work through the situation. Once she left the auditorium, she found a quiet place outside where she could walk through everything that happened. She made a table (starting on page 201) to help her figure out how else she could have handled the situation.

Ashley worked through these different approaches and outcomes, and as she did she found that her panic and her embarrassment reduced dramatically. She felt like she had the courage to do telephone follow-ups with parents and continue to push for a program she believed in. Notice in Ashley's recording of the event that she was paying careful attention to as many "choice points" as she could. With every event, there are so many little decisions and behaviors that can influence the outcome. The more choice points you can identify, the more flexible your behavior becomes. She also brainstormed more than one option for several of the choice points. This helps to underscore that there are many ways to change the momentum of a situation: There isn't just one right approach, but several options for small alterations you can make along the way that will influence the outcome in your favor. This part of inner coaching helps you learn from your slipups and gives you a solid repertoire for improving in the future.

Revisiting Comments from Your Past with Your Inner Coach on Your Shoulder

Your inner coach can not only help you with thoughts and events that are under your control, but she can also be useful when someone flings a real or imagined insult about your body or yourself that gets right under your skin. In Part One, you kept a running log of things that people said or situations that affected your self-esteem or body esteem negatively since childhood. Return to that log now and put your inner coach to work on reprocessing some of those negative comments that populate your thought library.

The trusted voice of your inner coach and the techniques you have learned up to now will help you revisit these old insults and discard or repackage them in ways that no longer perpetuate long-standing wounds or self-denigration. With those early insults, you still had a child's brain. Your emotions were more raw and your brain was not developed enough to work through the comments critically. But now, together with your inner coach, you can revisit them and try to neutralize their effects. You won't necessarily forget them, but you can deprioritize them and strip them of their ability to rob you of self-esteem or body esteem.

An important life goal for any woman is to reach the point where she can convincingly separate her self-esteem from her body esteem. A wise woman who had worked through this illustrated the progression in her mind:

When I was young, I endured teasing and people thinking I was dumb and ugly, so I thought, "I'm fat, so I'm a bad person." As I got older, after hundreds of diets (all of which failed) and some life experience including some career success and some good friendships (with people who didn't care how much I weighed), I resigned myself to my size, and in the same vein as people who say, "She's pretty for a big girl," in my head I was able to say, "I'm a good person for a fat person." Then as I got even wiser (and older) and cared less about what other people thought about me, after fifty years I finally realized who I was—both a good person *and* fat, I was finally able to say, "I'm a good person and I'm a fat person." They are, after all, not related. It took me fifty years, but I finally figured out that I can be both things and they are completely unrelated to each other. It's the same as saying, "I am a woman and I have brown hair!"

Pull out the tables you completed after each of the chapters in Part One and revisit the comments and the events that have stuck in your craw for so many years—only this time with your coach engaged. Allow your inner coach to read through the library of comments and experiences with you mindfully and put them to the test as Ashley did. Reexamine these comments and events using your knowledge of the opposition. What was the speaker trying to accomplish? Why were they trying to get under your skin? Think about how else you could respond if you ever encountered something like that again, and deeply evaluate the thoughts and feelings that arose from each comment, paying special attention to how they might have blurred the division between body esteem and self-esteem.

To illustrate how this is done, recall in the middle school chapter exercises how the skinny chain-smoking aunt told the mother within earshot of her daughter, "She's really developed quite the pear shape, hasn't she?" The girl was twelve when she overheard that comment—far too young to gain perspective on this particular aunt and what her agenda might have been. The comment launched a lifelong preoccupation with her hips and an indelible memory of that skinny aunt making that biting comment. After thirty years, with her inner coach engaged, Susan revisits that comment. Her first thought is "What a bitch!"—completely fair. But when she engages her inner coach to try to understand her opponent, what she realizes is that the comment probably wasn't about her at all. This aunt was incredibly competitive with her mother and would lord her thin physique over Susan's mom all the time to establish her moral superiority. In reality her mom had completed her education, was married, had two children, and was happy. This aunt had dropped out of college to get married, been divorced twice, and had difficulty holding down a steady job. The only realm where she could "win" in her mind was that she weighed less than Susan's mom. So this comment hadn't really been about Susan and her hips at all. It was really just another chapter in the competitive battle between Susan's aunt and mother.

This realization didn't erase all the effects of her aunt's historical comment, but it helped fade the memory from a blinking neon sign that dictated her behavior and affected her body esteem to a more gray memory that was categorized under the heading of her aunt's pathology rather than her own body esteem.

At the end of the college and life-transition chapter, Tara recalled being rejected by a sorority when her friend Beth got in. She still had flashbacks to that rejection experience whenever she drove by the sorority. She revisited that memory with her inner coach engaged and approached it as a failure experience, wondering what she could do differently the next time. As she reviewed the process, she realized that there really wasn't anything that she would have done differently. She portrayed herself authentically in the interviews, was friendly and gracious to the other girls, and honestly appraised her strengths and weaknesses. Her honest responses were completely in line with her values. What her inner coach pointed out to her was the fake sweet smile that the sorority sister had on her face when she broke the news to Tara that she would not be invited to be a member. It was the incongruity and utter falseness of that smile that had stuck with her all of those years. Her inner coach helped her realize that she did not possess the same false niceness that the other girls in that sorority had, and in fact it would not have been a good fit for her. She soon would have felt out of place there, and where she did end up was in fact a much better fit for her personality.

Use this approach to recatalog all of the events and comments that you included in your tables throughout the first part of the book. Take your time, allow these memories to be reshelved, and evaluate whether this process can diffuse some of the destructive power they had previously held over your self-esteem and body esteem.

CHAPTER 11

Protecting the Next Generation

"Every time a woman passes a mirror and criticizes herself, there's a girl watching . . ."

—Gloria Steinem

You want to protect your daughters from having to go through what you have gone through, battling negative self-talk. However, you can only do so much: You are but one of many factors that will influence her developing self-concept. Although your maternal instinct would love to be able to, you simply cannot protect your daughters from everything. This does not mean you are powerless. In fact, you can be a powerful role model and help your daughter and other girls around you defend themselves from the lure of negative self-talk.

Parents and Daughters
What do your daughters see when they watch you? How do your thoughts and words become the building blocks for their own identities? Children seem to be able to hear your innermost thoughts. Your daughter sees everything. If you skip a meal, cut down on your portion size, get Botox or a facelift, have breast implants, go on sequential diets, or say disrespectful things about your own body or yourself, your daughter is watching, listening, and absorbing. She watches your face when you look in the mirror. She watches how you respond to your successes and how you take compliments. Even if you consistently praise her for who she is and the skills and gifts she brings to the world, if she continually hears you appraising yourself based on your dissatisfaction with your own appearance, that's what she'll

remember. The single best gift you can give your daughter is also a gift to yourself, and that is taking stock in your own self-esteem and body esteem. If you can find peace with yourself and your body, that is the most powerful message you can pass on to her.

You observe your daughter. Your face, your eyes, your words (and those of your husband, partner, friends, and family members) reflect information back to her that she constantly filters and incorporates into her own identity and self-concept. Your comments about her appearance—both positive and negative—all get processed and cataloged in her brain. You *will* make mistakes and you *will* say the wrong things. Every mother does. Perfect mothering does not exist. But it is far better to make mistakes and be aware of them than to be oblivious to the impact of your commentary on your daughter—at least then you have a chance to implement damage control.

When your daughter uses your eyes as a mirror, what does she see? Does she see a loving mother who appreciates and respects her for who she is and what she has accomplished? Or does she see a reflection of her flaws—"You could lose a few pounds, get a better haircut, dress more neatly, improve those grades"? This is the tightrope of parenting. You want to help your children become all they can be without criticizing them for who they are. One of the essential ingredients to succeeding at this parenting task is to recognize that your daughters are not you. You are you and your daughter is your daughter.

This can be a difficult interpersonal line to draw for any parent. If physical appearance is an important component of your identity, you might worry that people will judge you or your parenting ability based on the appearance of your daughter. If academic success is important to you and your daughter brings home Cs, you might worry the world will pass judgment on your parenting style. Indeed, there are people out there who might do just that. Many people will judge the parents if the child is overweight or underweight, does poorly in math, or has pink hair.

You can't control their judgments of you, but you can control your reaction to their judgments.

A young woman from the Deep South broke family tradition and went to college out of state in the North. At the end of each school year she would go on crash diets, get her hair highlighted and cut, try to get in shape, and buy new clothes because she would get letters from her family—starting months before summer break—that said things along the lines of "Now, my dear, don't forget, we want you to make a good impression when you come home." There would be parties when she came back home that all would attend, and she would be on display for friends and family to see just how well she had been keeping herself. For this poor girl, her desperate attempts to "show well" for her family drove her right into bulimia. Now her family in no way caused this eating disorder. This was a clash of cultures and expectations that was so powerful across generations that it resulted in extreme behavior. They loved one another dearly, but the social expectations of their appearance-oriented society were deeply entrenched and powerful.

Culture may also play a role. In *Hijas Americanas*, Rosie Molinary highlights that many Latina women feel that the way they dress and present themselves is a reflection on the family. The pressure to be properly presented is deeply rooted in the parents' concerns about what others might think and say.[1]

In extreme cases, parents try to live out their own unfulfilled hopes and dreams through their daughters. Pageant moms who never wore a crown themselves might live vicariously through their daughters' successes—long after their daughters have ceased enjoying pageant life. The injured parent athlete might push a daughter to achieve the Olympic dreams never attained. The subtle subtext is "I love you for becoming what I was never able to become." Breaking away from these symbiotic ties is one of the most difficult steps toward independence children can make—but not breaking away puts them at risk of being smothered and never developing their own identities.

Helping Your Child Develop Body Esteem and Self-Esteem

Developing healthy boundaries between yourself and your child starts the moment the child is born. Especially with all of the focus on child obesity and child BMI, parents are becoming ever more preoccupied with their children's weight. As children grow, others are bound to make comments about their shape and weight and developmental progress, and often these comments are comparative. At five months, my first born was positively roly-poly. We called him the Michelin Man (now I would consider that to be fat talk), but we would literally find food in his fat rolls at bath time. This was completely natural. He was a fully breast-fed baby and he was not yet mobile. As soon as he started crawling like a madman, he shed his rolls. But comments from outsiders were intrusive. A well-meaning relative who was wary of breast-feeding said, "Maybe you should stop breast-feeding—you can't tell how much he is getting that way." Not only was it a bad health recommendation, but it was a suggestion that I was incompetent to feed my child properly and included an embedded comment that he was too fat for his age. Then later when he went through the lanky-toddler phase, the same relative asked, "Are you feeding him enough? He looks like a rail." Well, indeed he does, he's *supposed* to be lanky at this age. People feel compelled to talk about size—especially when it comes in extremes. In neither of these situations, however, was my baby a reflection of me. My baby was a reflection of himself and of normal child development and his eating and activity patterns at the time. But these outsiders tried to make him a reflection of me and my competence as a parent. I had to draw the boundary not only in my own head but in communicating with them. I thanked them for their concern, indicated that I would take their suggestion under advisement, and then proceeded to ignore everything they said.

Once your children become cognizant of what people are saying and doing around them, your measures to protect them have to become more active. When others make inappropriate comments, you may experience it as judgment and it may be judgmental, but it could also be motivated by the best of intentions or by sheer ignorance. How you respond may vary from culture to culture and depend on who the person is and what role he or she plays in your child's life, but in most cases it is acceptable to simply say, "Thanks for your concern," and not feel that you have to justify yourself or your child. We know, however, that these comments may still get under your skin and make you start to doubt yourself. What can you do to help these comments have less of an impact on you and your child?

Let's return to the example of my junior colleague whose father-in-law always comments on her daughter's appearance and her son's personality. She has developed both active and reactive ways to protect her daughter from these comments: First, she tries to beat her father-in-law to it by being the first one to talk, detailing all of the wonderful non-appearance-related things her daughter has been up to. The first thing her daughter hears is that her mother wants to tell relatives about things other than her appearance. If, however, her father-in-law beats her to it, then she just says thank you and adds all of the other wonderful things about her daughter she wants to convey. That way her daughter still hears what is important to her mother and not just the father-in-law's appearance-focused compliments.

This year her daughter asked, "Why does Grandpa always just talk about how I look?" When they are old enough to provide their own commentary, you have to decide at what level to answer your child. My friend just said, "Grandpa has always been interested in how people look, but we value all sorts of things about people like their brains, their sense of humor, and how loving they are." It became a teachable moment when mother and daughter could have a frank discussion about values and relationships. Her very clever daughter responded, "I know appearances aren't important, Mom!" validating all of the buffering work she had done for so many years.

Although it is valuable to think deeply about the complex

and intertwined psychology of parents and daughters, what most parents (of all ages) want and need are more practical and here-and-now solutions for protecting their daughters. This box provides some frank guidelines for talking with your daughters about these delicate topics.

The following list, written by Karen Springen for iVillage and culled from the advice of eating disorder experts, provides some frank guidelines for talking with your daughters about weight, shape, eating, and physical activity.[2]

TEN TIPS TO TEACH YOUR DAUGHTER ABOUT A HEALTHY RELATIONSHIP WITH FOOD

1. **Ditch the diet discussions.** "It should all be about healthy eating, not weight loss," says Elizabeth Alderman, M.D. a pediatrician at Montefiore Medical Center. Convey the importance of "inner beauty, not just how you look [on the outside]."

2. **Send the right message.** Keep the focus on being healthy, says Delia Aldridge, M.D., service director of the eating disorders and self-injury program at Alexian Brothers Behavioral Health Hospital in Hoffman Estates, Ill. At family dinners, serve and consume moderate portions. Take a healthy attitude toward food and physical activity. Incorporate some physical activity into your regular routine. After a meal, take a walk together.

3. **Don't disparage your body—or anyone else's.** Don't tell fat jokes. And nix questions like "Do these pants make my butt look fat?" says Edward Abramson, Ph.D., psychology professor and author of *Emotional Eating.* Though comments like "you're just a little above the average weight" won't *cause* an eating disorder, it could trigger its onset, according to the American Academy of Pediatrics.

4. **Listen for, and address, unusual body-related comments.** When your daughters complain about being fat or ugly, instead of saying, "don't be silly," ask, "You're talking about this a lot. What are the things that you're worried about?" says psychologist Stephanie Zerwas, Ph.D., associate research director in the eating-disorders program at the University of North Carolina. She suggests a further response: "Honey, you know I think you're beautiful, and I'm not just saying it because I'm your mother. But I want you to know that beautiful people come in all shapes and sizes . . . I think you're beautiful on the inside and out. Can you think about another way to evaluate yourself than the number you see on a scale?" Avoid critiquing your children's appearance, and instead reassure them about all their strengths, says Rebecka Peebles, M.D.: "I'd prefer that parents aren't judging kids for their weight." And remember that kids who gripe about being fat may be imitating their moms.

5. **Watch for strange or restrictive eating habits.** If your daughter insists on making all her own food, something could be going on. "Anything with the word *fat* in it, I didn't want to eat," says Kristin Kaye, now twenty-one, who developed anorexia at fifteen. "I prepared myself very plain stuff. I was very afraid that if someone else prepared the food for me, they would sneak something else in it." What to do? Cheerlead for cooking together! Encourage parents and children to work together in the kitchen. June Alexander, a fifty-nine-year-old grandmother who struggled with anorexia and subsequently bulimia from ages eleven to fifty-five, says she often shunned food until after six P.M. The coauthor of *My Kid Is Back: Empowering Parents to Beat Anorexia Nervosa* worried that if she ate earlier in the day she would be unable to control herself and would eat too much.

6. **Foster a healthy, realistic body image.** Help your daughter understand that many of the photos she sees in magazines are airbrushed. Show her real images. Help her develop a sense of what is normal. "Kids don't know these have been retouched," says Peebles, who recommends Dianne Neumark-Sztainer's book *I'm, Like, So Fat!: Helping Your Teen Make Healthy Choices About Eating and Exercise in a Weight-Obsessed World.* Britney Spears just released unretouched photos of her Candie's ads, which reveal larger thighs and (gasp!) cellulite. Talk to your daughter about all the imperfections (moles and the like) that are removed rather than just discussing thinness. "Focus on everything that is duping you into believing that perfection exists," says [director of the eating disorders program at the University of North Carolina, Cynthia] Bulik.

7. **Don't outlaw certain foods.** "The minute you start throwing taboo labels on things, they become more desirable," says Bulik. Encourage moderation instead of deprivation. Enjoy birthday-party cake and summer nights getting ice cream without guilt, says Bulik. "It's best not to say, 'We'll have cake tonight, then cut back tomorrow,' or 'Today treats, tomorrow diet.'" But dish out appropriate amounts of these sweets—and model eating moderate (not supersize!) portions yourself. "Be a healthy eating model," says Peebles. "Have lots of healthy food available in the house. Prepare fresh food." Don't condemn brownies as "the devil's food," says Peebles. But don't keep a plate of them around every day. What's most important: Show your child that you are active and you eat well, says Peebles.

8. **Look at your kids' Web browsing history.** A 2006 Stanford University study found that 96 percent of girls who already had eating disorders and visited pro-anorexia sites said they learned new weight-loss techniques there. "I don't know that you can block all of those Web sites,

because new ones crop up every day," says Peebles, the lead author of that study. "[But] I think you need to really discuss the Internet and monitor it." Talk to your kids about how some information on the Internet is "not true and not useful," says Peebles. "I would advocate open dialogue."

9. **Act on your suspicions to nip eating disorders in the bud.** Early detection and early, complete treatment is the key. Parents should not wait and think that she's just going through a phase or a fad. Don't wait. There is no shame in asking questions, raising concerns, calibrating your worries with a professional. When a 14-year-old shows up weighing 60 pounds—or 220 pounds—the road to recovery is more difficult.

10. **Don't worry too much.** "To develop anorexia nervosa is like a very complicated recipe for a cake you try to bake," says psychologist Daniel Le Grange, Ph.D., director of the eating disorders program at the University of Chicago. "Every single ingredient has to be there, in a certain amount of time and in a certain order." You can try to prevent that perfect recipe. Remember that anorexia is surprisingly rare. Less than 1 percent of adolescent girls suffer from anorexia. And happy endings do occur: studies show that 30 percent to 70 percent of anorexics recover completely.

Read more: Visit iVillage.com and search for "Dying to Be Thin."

Throughout our life, development is a gradual process, yet at several points, it happens in rapid bursts. In the first trimester of pregnancy, for example, although the baby weighs only about one ounce, an amazing amount of development occurs, including development of the circulatory system; appearance of facial features and the umbilical cord; growth of the baby's head, reproductive organs, and other internal organs; development of fingernails and toenails and external genitalia; and production of neurons in the baby's brain, with up to 250,000 new neurons produced every minute of the day.[3]

Puberty is also a growth rush. Girls gain on average 50 percent of their ideal adult body weight and 3.54 inches per year, practically transforming them overnight.[4] The first year of college shows the same type of developmental acceleration, although less physically and more psychologically and socially. Without preparation and a good sense of humor, the first homecoming can be pretty dramatic for the family. At the same time, this is the first time your daughter is presenting the new her on the old stage. If parents are expecting the same little high school girl to come home, often they get quite the surprise. This example contrasts dramatically from our southern college student who felt pressure to conform.

Ten pounds heavier, ten pounds lighter, dreads, pink hair, no hair, pierced cartilage, pierced tongue, pierced other unmentionable areas, hidden tats, not so hidden tats, new clothes, different food likes and dislikes, new styles, new words, new friends, new ideas, newfound sexuality. The first homecoming after going away from college can be a shock to every family member.

After four months away, the phone calls and e-mails have gotten less frequent, but Mom figures it's because her baby's just so busy with college. Mom is looking forward to sitting around the breakfast table over coffee talking about college, new friends, classes, and activities. She's stocked up on all of her daughter's favorite foods and planned her favorite pot-roast dinner. Waiting at the bottom of the escalator at the airport, she sees someone who vaguely resembles her daughter. She recognizes the pink(ish) low tops, but wow, those are very low riders. Is that a spiked leather belt? Hm, there's a good amount of flesh showing in that middle section. Is that a thong? Mom's heartbeat is escalating.

Then she sees the pink spiked hair. Trying her best not to look shocked, she thinks, "What happened to my baby?" Mom smiles. They hug, and Mom sees the unicorn tattoo on her daughter's shoulder. She thinks, "Oh, my God, I made that skin, and look what she did to it!" Then she hears the lisp, and Mom thinks, "Oh, boy, it's a tongue piercing!" And she remembers what a friend of hers said when her son's girlfriend got her tongue pierced: "You know there's only one reason to pierce a tongue!" Mom sends Dad a text from the baggage claim that just says, "Brace yourself!" There are no talks over coffee about college, and her (old) favorite foods that mom took care to buy never get eaten (the daughter is vegan now). The daughter basically locks herself in her bedroom and sleeps through most of the break.

The first homecoming is not always that dramatic, but as a mom you never know who is going to get off that plane after the first semester at college. As a daughter, you also never know how your mom is going to react to your new identity—no matter how subtle or flamboyant.

In this scenario, the inner dialogues of both mother and daughter shed light on what is really happening. The daughter just wants to be left alone. She is tired. Starting college has been an exhausting transformation, and there is nothing more that she wants to do than to retreat to the comfort and safety of her old room—stuffed animals and all. She's wondering how her parents are going to react to all of her changes and she's poised to fight, but if they don't react, there's nothing to push back against. Mom's plagued with self-doubt. "Where did I go wrong?" she asks. Quite possibly nowhere. After all, her daughter did choose to come home for break, even if she did just hibernate the whole time.

Parents have to be patient and take the long view. Accepting new identities can lead to interesting shifts in relationships. Accepting does not apply to major concerns like eating disorders or substance abuse or depression—then you need to take immediate action and get your child help. But if it is just a matter of pushing the identity boundaries, then the new relationships can even be a little fun.

Your children are trying on and sorting through identities just as they do with clothes in the dressing room. Over time they stabilize, and parents regain some status in their eyes. When they're in elementary school, they still think you're smart. Once they're in middle school and high school, you steadily lose IQ points in their eyes. "Mom, you are so dumb." "You have no idea what it's like." "Maybe it was like that back in the day when the dinosaurs roamed the earth." So you learn that regardless of how many degrees and the life experience you have, to your children, basically you know nothing. Then that first phone call comes, or they sit down to ask your advice. Or hell freezes over and they say something like, "Hm, that was a good idea, Mom," and you're in shock. After all those years, they've returned a few IQ points to you.

Thorny Issues for Parents

Some challenging questions are posed again and again by parents when it comes to raising daughters in the current world. For many of these questions there are no perfect answers, and the specifics may differ depending on the nature and situation of your child. A panel of experts weighs in on these common questions to help parents find the best approaches.

What do I do if my child is actually overweight or obese? How do I talk about it with her?

Pediatrician Eliana Perrin, M.D., M.P.H., suggests, "First I would make sure she is actually overweight or obese. Schools are doing BMI screening and some are conducting this screening correctly, but it is best if you follow up with your pediatrician or family physician. If your primary care provider has let you or your child know that she is overweight or obese, I would focus your conversation on health and partnership. Tell her that the reason the doctor is concerned is that it may mean she is less healthy over time. Tell her that it's a great time for the whole family to work on being healthy—to drink water instead of sugar-sweetened beverages, have less screen time, less fast food, and be more active. Even if others in the family are not overweight, these key behaviors establish healthy habits for everyone. Assure her that the whole family will work on these goals so everyone can have healthy, strong bodies. Do not encourage dieting, as this is usually a pathway to other unhealthy eating. Remember, your job is to support her emotionally and make your home and lifestyle a healthy one."

What should I do if I suspect my daughter is binge eating?

Suzanne Mazzeo, Ph.D., who studies binge eating in adolescence, says, "Talk to her. Wait until a time when you are both calm, and not arguing about another topic." She recommends thinking about her behavior in general and whether there have been any other trends—does she seem more guarded and noncommunicative in general? Withdrawn? Moody? You could start the conversation by talking about your overall concern. For example, you could say, "I've noticed you seem to really be keeping to yourself these days."

Chances are, food is not the primary problem—and she will be less defensive when you get to the food question if you bring up these other issues first. When you move into the food area, it is best not to be accusatory but to be compassionate and calmly mention what you have noticed: candy wrappers in her room, or eating late at night alone, for example. Remember that the conversation is about your concerns about her physical and psychological well-being. You can talk about your concern that she feels a need to sneak these foods or feels some sense of shame about eating them. Explain that your concern is not what she's eating, but that she feels a need to sneak around to do it.

You can also indicate that you understand that sometimes

people feel as if their eating can get out of their control and wonder whether that has ever been her experience. Try to get a sense of how often this might be happening to her. Sometimes these eating habits can just happen when zoning out after a stressful day or if she is worrying about something. If, at the end of this conversation, you think she might be binge eating, talk about your specific concerns. Always keep the focus on health, mental and physical well-being, and *not* on weight. Suggest a visit with a dietitian or a mental-health practitioner if she feels as if her eating is out of control or if you think an external opinion would be valuable. Stay on her side. Emphasize that you understand she may feel ashamed about this behavior, but that you don't think any less of her for binging and want to help her so she doesn't feel a need to sneak or use food in a negative way.

What do I do when my child is teased or insulted or on the receiving end of mean-girl behavior?

Teasing is mean, cliques are damaging, and insults can leave perpetual psychological wounds. All can contribute to the development of eating, mood, and anxiety disorders in girls. The reality of middle and high school is that they are hotbeds for these behaviors. Even though schools often develop programs to curb teasing, teasing events need to be processed at home as well. The intense social pressure that results in teasing can lead your daughter down paths of behavior that you would never have imagined possible. Unfortunately, the shame of being teased can lead girls to go underground and not share their humiliation with their parents.

Dr. Perrin adds that it hurts when your child is teased or insulted. She encourages moms to remain friendly listeners. Help bolster your daughter's self-esteem and remind her of her specialness and worth. We often use the analogy of teaching her to have "watermelon skin," which doesn't bruise or affect the delicious fruit within, instead of "banana skin," which does.

It's important to help your daughter to recognize that meanness often comes from the deliverer's own insecurity. You can teach your daughter some of the skills that you learned that allow you to develop more of that watermelon skin. One of the hardest things to learn and execute is that ignoring the behavior rather than reacting to it is still the best way to get it to stop. At the same time, work with your daughter's school. If it does not yet have effective anti-bullying policies, encourage its administrators to put them in place.

Equally disturbing is if your daughter is the mean girl. It is difficult for parents to hear reports that their daughter is the one who is tormenting someone else. In this case, work with your daughter to develop empathy for the girls she is teasing. Do whatever you can to help her take the perspective of other people in order to reduce this kind of behavior. Develop a zero-tolerance policy for teasing and model respectful dialogue toward others.

Would my decision to have cosmetic surgery send the wrong message to my daughter?

Ultimately, having cosmetic surgery is your personal choice. It is your body, after all. But if you have decided or are deciding to undergo a procedure to change your body in some way, it is wise to think through the impact that this might have on your daughter and on her perception of you. The first step is to make sure that you have come to terms with your own values that led to your decision to have cosmetic surgery. If there are health reasons for your surgery, then you can emphasize that dimension. If it is purely cosmetic, then it is wise to carefully consider what you are modeling to your daughter about the importance of physical appearance. Whatever you do, keep body esteem and self-esteem separate when you have the conversation. Do your best to avoid any implication that you expect that having cosmetic surgery will improve your self-esteem. It might make you feel better about your nose or your breasts or your bottom, but it will not improve your self-esteem. They have not invented a surgical procedure for that yet!

If I used to have an eating disorder, is that something I should share with my daughter? Will I be able to help her separate her self-esteem from her body esteem?

If you have an eating-disorder history, you may be less comfortable trusting your own perceptions of your daughter's health and development than someone who never had an eating disorder. For that reason, it is especially important to seek out the advice of a trusted health-care provider.

In terms of sharing your history with your daughter, there are several things to consider. First, any reasons you would not share might be related to stigma that you perceive about the eating disorder—that it is somehow shameful to have gone through it. We tell our children if we have histories of breast cancer or cardiovascular disease or asthma—so that they can take appropriate measures and be aware and take preventive action. The same should hold for eating disorders. Stigma is a barrier to effective prevention. Dr. Perrin adds that it is important to wait to tell your daughter until she is old enough to understand, which is typically around adolescence. It is wise also to share ways you have helped your own recovery and your hopes that because of all the hard work you did, you can help her to avoid the same path.

What do I do if I have negative thoughts about my child's body shape or weight?

One of the things that's sometimes hard to talk about is your inner thoughts and feelings about your own children. It's hard to acknowledge that sometimes your own internal critical voice might be the one making comments about your child's appearance. But it's important to be aware that this critical voice can exist, because it might affect how you relate to your child. There are a few components to this. One is to better understand what is causing these negative thoughts. Is your child dealing with something that you never had to deal with, like acne or weight problems? In these cases it is important to do your best to focus on what your child is experiencing and help her or him navigate the waters rather than focusing on yourself and your own thoughts about the issue. Take great care that you are not imposing perfectionistic ideals on your child. None of us has the perfect child!

Dr. Perrin adds that it is important for you to think each day about your child's wonderful attributes that have nothing to do with appearance and only to do with inner light—how their laughter helps the family enjoy dinner, how their memory astonishes you, how they treat their friends. Do your best to concentrate on health and healthy behaviors and remove your focus from shape and weight.

Positive Steps to Affirm Your Child's Self-Esteem

The vast majority of images we see in the media are false and unrealistic. Regardless of how enlightened you think you are about Photoshopping and other techniques, the media has a bigger influence on our minds than we realize.

In a program we conducted with dads of middle school and high school girls, their number-one unanimous fear about their daughters' lives was the Internet and media in general. The fathers explained that in the past, parents used to know their children's friends as well as which television shows and movies their daughters watched. Parents never needed to worry about Internet sites that encourage starvation, self-harm, suicide, or sexuality. Now it seems that if you put your finger in one hole in the electronic dike, there are just hundreds of more dangers and traps that your daughter can fall into. When you let your daughter have free and private access to the Internet, text messaging, and television, you could be inadvertently exposing her to dangers.

Between sexualized music videos, YouTube, Facebook, and sexting we are facing new parenting challenges. Our parenting playbook has not caught up with the technology. You have to remain empowered as parents to impose limits when necessary in order to adequately protect your daughter.

Being aware and critical of media and advertising is the first step to developing immunity to the media's distorted messages. Fathers and mothers can engage in this conversation by doing several of the following.

Point out how unrealistic media images are. Use some of the resources in the back of this book to find videos and blogs that you can discuss together. Talk back to the TV (or magazine) when you see messages about beauty that are unrealistic or negative—or turn it off! Help your children distinguish between when a favorite character is being entertaining and when he or she is being used to try to sell something. Children just see their favorite character—they can't distinguish between when that character is on a show versus on a commercial. That is precisely why child-focused marketing is so effective! Start teaching your children that they have to become "advertising spies"—on the lookout for people trying to trick them into buying something they don't need. Finally, while we've already talked about the fact that media images are everywhere, it is still a good idea to minimize children's media exposure—both now and as they grow up.

Keep the discussion current. The approach you took to parenting with your daughter when she was three or seven is unlikely to be effective when she is twelve or sixteen. In fact, the approach that worked on Monday may no longer be effective on Friday. It is essential to adapt your parenting strategies to your maturing girl.

Take an un-diet stance. If your thirteen-year-old girl came home from school and said, "I'm going to have my first cigarette today," or "I'm going to have a beer with dinner," or "I'm going to have sex this weekend," you would immediately go on red-alert status. Yet when our daughters come home and say, "I'm going on a diet," it often goes unnoticed and may even be encouraged. We need to be alert to diet behaviors and help our daughters to develop an un-diet stance regardless of whether they are dealing with overweight or inappropriate restrictive eating. You can take the same balanced approach to address two other alarming trends in our society: adolescent obesity and adolescent eating disorders. The middle-of-the road stance that is marked by balanced healthy eating and regular physical activity is critical in the prevention of both obesity and eating disorders.

Eat breakfast and family meals. Eating breakfast is one of the most simple but effective health and mental-health interventions that you can do for your children and yourself. Breakfast eating is associated with better school performance, decreased delinquency, less experimentation with drugs and alcohol, and lower risk of eating disorders![5,6,7] Even if you have bleary-eyed teenagers around the table, make breakfast a priority. Touching base in the morning is also a valuable launch to the day. Having everyone gather in the kitchen or dining room at least once a day is a safety and health anchor for all family members. Sometimes with busy sports and activity schedules, it is more feasible to make breakfast the family meal than dinner. Even if you cannot all be there, getting a proper meal in your belly before work or school is a high-potency prevention tool.

Help her separate self-esteem from body esteem. We have covered many techniques in this book to help you separate your self-esteem from your body esteem. Every one of them is applicable to your daughter. Help her learn some of these techniques and help her to free her own mind space from thoughts about weight and shape and inadequacies toward a healthy respectful dialogue that frees her to accomplish anything she wants in this world.

Get Dad involved. New studies suggest that the father-daughter relationship is an important but undervalued influence for adolescent girls. Dads can communicate effectively with their daughters about media, perfectionism, and peer communication. In fact, their perspective as males can be very valuable to young girls. Bring the men in your family into these conversations. Have them watch the videos in the resources section. Help them understand the influence that the media and fashion world have on your world and that of your daughters.

Don't forget your sons. This book is mostly about women, but don't forget that your sons can get caught up in unhealthy body-esteem and self-esteem traps as well. If you hear unhealthy self-chatter coming from your sons, don't ignore it because you think it's a problem that only girls encounter. Boys are struggling with increasing BMI as well—overweight and obesity are rampant in children and adolescents, and boys, like girls, who are teased about their weight can develop negative body esteem. Simultaneously, we are seeing an increase in eating disorders among boys and men of all ages. Unrealistic media images are also permeating advertisements and publications aimed at boys and men espousing unrealistic body types that can only be achieved by unhealthy methods such as steroids. Obesity and eating disorders do not discriminate—don't be blinded by the sex of your child.

Another way you can help your sons is to teach them respect for body diversity in girls. Many young women date the onset of their low body esteem or even their eating disorders to obnoxious comments by boys. If you hear your sons making disparaging comments about girls and women based on their shape and weight, call them on it. Teach them about fat talk. Help them develop empathy and an appreciation for how damaging their offhand comments can be to the lives of girls. Help them become better friends and to look beneath shape and weight to appreciate the person within.

Accurate vigilance: seeking help early. It is not uncommon for a family to wait until their daughter has reached sixty pounds or two hundred before seeking help. What keeps parents from reaching out for help earlier? Sadly, stigmatization continues to be one of the biggest barriers to seeking treatment. After decades of bearing the blame for their children's problems, parents have become reluctant to seek treatment for fear the doctor's finger will point back to them as the cause. Parents therefore hope that whatever behaviors their daughter is experiencing will just be a passing phase or that she'll "grow out of it." But things escalate rather than remitting spontaneously as hoped. Finding sympathetic health-care providers who understand adolescence and support—rather than blame—parents is a critical step in getting the help and support you need.

In the end, you may not be able to reverse global warming for your children. Nor will you be able to turn the economy around or stop wars from happening. But with changes you make in yourself and with efforts you make to help your children separate their body esteem from their self-esteem, you may be able to help make them more comfortable in their own skin, value themselves for who they are and what they contribute to the world—not for their appearance—and pass this enlightened approach on to the next generation.

Coda: Imagine a World Where You Like and Respect Yourself

"I am woman, hear me roar."
—Helen Reddy, "I Am Woman"

What's left in your head when you take this horrible inner dialogue away? Is it just a void? Are there other, healthier thoughts that start to fill your consciousness? The empty space that remains after removing the self-insulting chatter is a canvas for your new life. You will be gifted with thought time, peace, esteem, and outward focus that will allow you to cast a new, positive light on your experience in the world. When you can look in the mirror and say, "I've earned those wrinkles," or "Every stretch mark reminds me of one of my wonderful children," or "They might have dropped, but I gave three children a great start in life," you will have conquered the tyranny of negative self-talk. Now you will have the freedom to put your brain space to better use, to remove the focus from your appearance and your perceived shortcomings, and become a full participant in the here and now.

Acknowledgments

I am grateful to the following people for the time, energy, and thought they contributed to the making of this book. To Richard Curtis for believing in my work and Jackie Johnson for bringing clarity to the project.

To the faculty and staff of the University of North Carolina Eating Disorders Program for their skill and patience. To Millie Maxwell, Ph.D., for her expertise with high school and college girls and to Stephanie Zerwas, Ph.D., for her social-media genius. Special thanks to all of the very helpful people (VHPs) in my lab who helped research and fact-check this book. Thanks to: Rui Cheng, Lauren Metzger, Tarrah Mitchell, Sara Hofmeier, Rebecca Dunn, Emily Bulik-Sullivan, Natalie Bulik-Sullivan, Katie Weinel, and Alaina Boyle.

Resources

GENERAL RESOURCES

National Institute of Mental Health (NIMH)

Offers a wide variety of information to help people better understand mental health, mental disorders, and behavioral problems. NIMH does not provide referrals or treatment.

www.nimh.nih.gov

6001 Executive Boulevard

Room 8184, MSC 9663

Bethesda, MD 20892

866-615-6464

On Facebook: National Institute of Mental Health and Twitter @NIMHgov

Dove Campaign for Real Beauty

Excellent resources for building self-esteem, appreciating real women, and gaining self-confidence.

www.dove.us/#/cfrb

On Facebook: DOVE campaign for Real Beauty and Twitter @Dove

Girls Inc.

Unique online activities that guide girls through the goal-setting process, interviews with accomplished women and girls, and education resources.

www.girlsinc.org

On Facebook: Girls Incorporated and Twitter @girls_inc

Creating a Nation of Confident Women and Girls
Web site devoted to promoting positive self-esteem in females of
all ages.
www.jessweiner.com
On Facebook: Jess Weiner and Twitter @JessWeiner

Wired Kids
This Web site provides effective tips for parents on how best to
manage and monitor their children's Internet use.
www.wiredkids.org

RESOURCES FOR MOMS

BabyCenter
Provides moms with trusted advice from experts, medical advisory
board–approved information, friendship with other moms, and
support at every stage of child development.
www.babycenter.com
On Facebook: BabyCenter and Twitter @BabyCenter

Babble
From Babble's Web site: "Babble tries to help parents navigate and
keep pace with the modern, ever-changing world of parenting
while building a community of like-minded parents."
www.babble.com
On Facebook: Babble.com and Twitter @BabbleEditors

CafeMom
CafeMom is a great social network for moms to get advice, feel
supported, or just relax.
www.cafemom.com
On Facebook: CafeMom and Twitter @cafemom

Motherlode
The *New York Times* Motherlode blog by Lisa Belkin explores
everything from parent-babysitter relations to the right amount of
praise for children.

parenting.blogs.nytimes.com
On Twitter @NYTMotherlode

EATING-DISORDER AND BODY-ESTEEM-RELATED RESOURCES

Academy for Eating Disorders (AED)

The Academy for Eating Disorders is a global, multidisciplinary
professional organization that provides cutting-edge
professional training and education and is the international
source for state-of-the-art information in the field of
eating disorders.
www.aedweb.org
111 Deer Lake Road, Suite 100
Deerfield, IL 60015
847-498-4274
On Facebook: Academy for Eating Disorders and Twitter
@aedweb

Eating Disorders Coalition (EDC)

The Eating Disorders Coalition lobbies on Capitol Hill to improve
funding for eating-disorder research, treatment, and education. It
is also working toward securing better insurance coverage for
individuals with eating disorders.
www.eatingdisorderscoalition.org
720 7th Street NW Suite 300
Washington, DC 20001
202-543-9570
manager@eatingdisorderscoalition.org
On Facebook: Eating Disorders Coalition

National Eating Disorders Association (NEDA)

NEDA is the largest not-for-profit organization in the United
States working to prevent eating disorders and to provide
treatment referrals to those suffering from anorexia, bulimia, and
binge eating disorder, as well as those concerned with body image
and weight issues. NEDA sponsors National Eating Disorders

Awareness Week, which takes place every year in February.
www.nationaleatingdisorders.org
165 West 46th St.
New York, NY 10036
212-575-6200
Toll-free information and referral helpline: 800-931-2237
On Facebook: National Eating Disorders Association and Twitter
@NEDAstaff

Binge Eating Disorder Association (BEDA)

From the BEDA Web site: "BEDA provides the individuals who
suffer from binge eating disorder the recognition and resources
they deserve to begin a safe journey toward a healthy recovery.
BEDA also serves as a resource for providers of all kinds to
prevent, diagnose, and treat the disorder.

"By establishing strong connections among members and sister
organizations, BEDA's goal is to give everyone access to the tools
they need to live with, treat, and, ultimately, prevent the disorder."
www.bedaonline.com
637 Emerson Place
Severna Park, MD 21146
855-855-BEDA (2332) Toll-free
On Facebook: Binge Eating Disorder Association and Twitter
@BEDAorg

Families Empowered And Supporting Treatment of Eating Disorders (F.E.A.S.T.)

F.E.A.S.T. is an international organization by and for parents and
caregivers to help loved ones recover from eating disorders by
providing information and mutual support, promoting evidence-
based treatment, and advocating for research and education.
www.feast-ed.org
P.O. Box 331
Warrenton, VA 20188
540-227-8518
info@FEAST-ED.org
On Facebook: F.E.A.S.T. and Twitter @FEASTtweets

Beating Eating Disorders (BEAT) (United Kingdom)

Provides help lines, online support and a network of UK-wide self-help groups to help adults and young people in the UK beat eating disorders.
http://www.b-eat.co.uk/
Wensum House
103 Prince of Wales Road
Norwich, Norfolk
NR1 1DW, United Kingdom
+44-0300-123-3355
On Facebook: beat and Twitter @beatED

The Butterfly Foundation (Australia)

Dedicated to bringing about change to the culture, policy, and practice in the prevention, treatment, and support of those affected by eating disorders and negative body image.
http://www.thebutterflyfoundation.org.au/
P.O. Box 453
Malvern, Victoria 3144
+61-03-9822-5771
103 Alexander Street
Crows Nest, New South Wales 2065
+61-02-9412-4499
On Facebook: The Butterfly Foundation and Twitter @Bfoundation

Eating Disorders Association of New Zealand (EDANZ)

Established in September 2007 to provide support and education for parents and caregivers of people with eating disorders.
www.ed.org.nz
+64-09-522-2679

Eating Difficulties Education Network (EDEN)
(Auckland, New Zealand)

A non-profit community agency based in Auckland, New Zealand. Their purpose is to promote body trust and satisfaction, size acceptance, and diversity on an individual and societal level.
www.eden.org.nz

395A Manukau Rd.
Epsom, Auckland, New Zealand
P.O. Box 26 713
Epsom 1023, Auckland, New Zealand
+64-09-378-9039
On Facebook: Eden Auckland and Twitter @EDENAuckland

Eating Awareness Team (EAT) (Christchurch, New Zealand)
Offers support, education, and early intervention for those
affected by eating disorders and disordered eating in the South
Island, New Zealand.
http://thepulse.org.nz/Me/My-Body/Image/EAT/
+64-03-366-7725
On Facebook: Eating Awareness Team (EAT)

National Eating Disorder Information Centre (NEDIC)
(Canada)
NEDIC is a Canadian nonprofit organization that provides
information and resources on eating disorders and weight preoccupation.
http://www.nedic.ca/
200 Elizabeth Street
Toronto, Ontario, Canada
416-340-4156
1-866-NEDIC-20 (633-4220) Toll-free
On Facebook: National Eating Disorder Information Centre
(NEDIC) and Twitter @nedic85

Notes

CHAPTER 1: FROM ELEMENTARY TO MIDDLE SCHOOL: LOSS OF IDENTITY

1   Walter B. Hoard, ed., *Anthology: Quotations and Sayings of People of Color* (R and E Research Associates, 1973), 36.

2   Linda Smolak, "Body Image Development in Children," in *Body Image*, eds. Thomas F. Cash and Thomas Pruzinsky (New York: Guilford Press, 2008), 65–73.

3   Ibid.

4   Alice Bah, Elisabeth Tarras-Wahlberg, and Paul Hansen, *Victoria, Victoria!* (Stockholm: Ekerlids, 2002).

5   Shelly Grabe and Janet S. Hyde, "Ethnicity and Body Dissatisfaction Among Women in the United States: A Meta-Analysis," *Psychological Bulletin* 132, no. 4 (2006): 622–40.

6   Scott A. Baldwin and John P. Hoffmann, "The Dynamics of Self-Esteem: A Growth-Curve Analysis," *Journal of Youth and Adolescence* 31 (2002): 101–13.

7   The American Association of University Women Educational Foundation, "The AAUW Report: How Schools Shortchange Girls." Wellesley College Center for Research on Women, 1992.

8   Charlotta Einarsson and Kjell Granström, "Gender-based Interaction in the Classroom: The Influence of Gender and Age in the Relationship between Teacher and Pupil," *Scandinavian Journal of Education Research* 46 (2002): 117–27.

9   Dan Kindlon and Michael Thompson, *Raising Cain: Protecting the Emotional Life of Boys.* (New York: Random House, 1999).

10   "Jessica's Daily Affirmation," www.youtube.com.

11   "Anorexi Bulimi Kontakt," www.youtube.com.

12   Florence R. Rosenberg, and Roberta G. Simmons, "Sex Differences in the Self-Concept in Adolescence," *Sex Roles* 1 (1975): 147–59.

13   Kim Rolland, Douglas Farnill, and Rosalyn A. Griffiths, "Body Figure Perceptions and Eating Attitudes among Australian Schoolchildren Aged 8 to 12 Years," *International Journal of Eating Disorders* 21, no. 3 (1997): 273–78.

14   Linda C. Andrist, "Media Images, Body Dissatisfaction, and Disordered Eating in Adolescent Women," *MCN: American Journal of Maternal and Child Nursing* 28, no. 2 (2003): 119–23.

15   Michael Levine and Linda Smolak, "Body Image Development in Adolescence," *Body Image*, eds. Thomas F. Cash and Thomas Pruzinsky (New York: Guilford Press, 2008) 74–82.

16   Christopher Bartlett, Richard Harris, Sara Smith, and Jennifer Bonds-Raacke, "Action Figures and Men," *Sex Roles* 53 (2005): 877–85.

17   Richard Leit, Harrison G. Pope Jr., and James J. Gray, "Cultural Expectations of Muscularity in Men: The Evolution of *Playgirl* Centerfolds," *Sex Roles* 29 (2001): 90–93.

18   Lina Ricciardelli and Marita McCabe, "Self-Esteem and Negative Affect as Moderators of Sociocultural Influences on Body Dissatisfaction, Strategies to Decrease Weight, and Strategies to Increase Muscles Among Adolescent Boys and Girls," *Sex Roles* 44 (2003): 189–207.

19   Ibid.

20   Courtney G. Pope, Harrison G. Pope, William Menard, Christina Fay, Roberto Olivardia, and Katherine A. Phillips, "Clinical Features of Muscle Dysmorphia among Males with Body Dysmorphic Disorder," *Body Image* 2, no. 4 (2005): 395–400.

21   Michael Quinion, "Some New Words from the Oxford Archives," World Wide Words, www.worldwidewords.org/articles/wordsof97.htm.

22   Dieter Wolke and Maria Sapouna, "Big Men Feeling Small: Childhood Bullying Experience, Muscle Dysmorphia and Other Mental Health Problems in Bodybuilders," *Psychology of Sport and Exercise* 9 (2008): 595–604.

23   Linda Smolak, Michael P. Levine, and J. Kevin Thompson, "The Use of the Sociocultural Attitudes Towards Appearance Questionnaire with Middle School Boys and Girls," *International Journal of Eating Disorders* 29, no. 2 (2001): 216–23.

24   Marika Tiggemann and Levina Clark, "Appearance Culture in Nine- to 12-Year Old Girls: Media and Peer Influences on Body Dissatisfaction," *Social Development* 15 (2006): 628–43.

25   Hemal Shroff and J. Kevin Thompson, "Peer Influences, Body-Image Dissatisfaction, Eating Dysfunction and Self-Esteem in Adolescent Girls," *Journal of Health Psychology* 11, no. 4 (2006): 533–51.

26   Delyse M. Hutchinson and Ronald M. Rapee, "Do Friends Share Similar Body Image and Eating Problems? The Role of Social Networks and Peer Influences in Early Adolescence," *Behavior Research and Therapy* 45 (2007): 1557–77.

27   Susan J. Paxton, Helena K. Schutz, Eleanor H. Wertheim, and Sharryn L. Muir, "Friendship Clique and Peer Influences on Body Image Concerns, Dietary Restraint, Extreme Weight-Loss Behaviors, and Binge Eating in Adolescent Girls," *Journal of Abnormal Psychology* 108, no. 2 (1999): 255–66.

28   Eliana M. Perrin, Julie C. Jacobson Vann, John T. Benjamin, Asheley Cockrell Skinner, Steven Wegner, and Alice S. Ammerman, "Use of a Pediatrician Toolkit to Address Parental Perception of Children's Weight Status, Nutrition, and Activity Behaviors," *Academic Pediatrics* 10 (2010): 274–81.

29   ABCNews.com, "First Lady Promotes Healthy Living," 2009, http://blogs.abcnews.com/politicalpunch/2009/10/first-lady-promotes-healthy-living.html.

CHAPTER 2: THE INS AND OUTS OF HIGH SCHOOL

1   National Institute of Mental Health, "Antidepressant Medications for Children and Adolescents: Information for Parents and Caregivers," http://www.nimh.nih.gov/health/topics/child-and-adolescent-mental-health/antidepressant-medications-for-children-and-adolescents-information-for-parents-and-caregivers.shtml.

2   Donald E. Greydanus, Flora Bacopoulou, and Emmanuel Tsalamanios, "Suicide in Adolescents: A Worldwide Preventable Tragedy," *Keio Journal of Medicine* 58, no. 2 (2009): 95–102.

3   Ibid.

4   Centers for Disease Control, "Increasing Prevalence of Parent-Reported Attention-Deficit/Hyperactivity Disorder Among Children: United States, 2003–2007," *Morbidity and Mortality Weekly Report* 59, no. 44 (2010): 1439–43.

5   Vicki Abeles and Jessica Congdon, *Race to Nowhere*, Real Link Films, 2010.

6   Marla E. Eisenberg and Dianne Neumark-Sztainer, "Friends' Dieting and Disordered Eating Behaviors Among Adolescents Five Years Later: Findings from Project Eat," *Journal of Adolescent Health* 47 (2010): 67–73.

7   "American Teen Girls Feel Pressure to Be Thin," Reuters, February 1, 2010.

8   Kathy Chu, "Extreme Dieting Spreads in Asia," *USA Today*, March 29, 2010.

9   Mae Lynn Reyes-Rodríguez, personal communication, 2011.

10   Rosie Molinary, *Hijas Americanas* (Emeryville, CA: Seal Press, 2007), 182.

11   Lisa Rubenstein, "Give Credit Where It's Due," *Raleigh News and Observer*, November 9, 2010.

12   Kirk R. Williams and Nancy G. Guerra, "Prevalence and Predictors of Internet Bullying," *Journal of Adolescent Health* 41, no. 6, Supplement 1 (2007): S14–21.

13   Centers for Disease Control, National Health and Nutrition Examination Survey, 2008, http://www.cdc.gov/nchs/data/hestat/obesity_child_07_08/obesity_child_07_08.htm#table2.

14   Eliana M. Perrin, Jane Boone-Heinonen, Alison E. Field, Tamera Coyne-Beasley, and Penny Gordon-Larsen, "Perception of Overweight and Self-Esteem During Adolescence," *International Journal of Eating Disorders* 43, no. 5 (2010): 447–54.

15   Gary S. Goldfield, Ceri Moore, Katherine Henderson, Annick Buchholz, Nicole Obeid, and Martine F. Flament, "Body Dissatisfaction, Dietary Restraint, Depression, and Weight Status in Adolescents," *Journal of School Health* 80, no. 4 (2010): 186–92.

16   Meg H. Zeller, Jennifer Reiter-Purtill, and Christina Ramey, "Negative Peer Perceptions of Obese Children in the Classroom Environment," *Obesity* (Silver Spring) 16, no. 4 (2008): 755–62.

17   Deborah R. Glasofer, Marian Tanofsky-Kraff, Kamryn T. Eddy, Susan Z. Yanovski, Kelly R. Theim, Margaret C. Mirch, Samereh Ghorbani, Lisa M. Ranzenhofer, David Haaga, and Jack A. Yanovski, "Binge Eating in Overweight Treatment-Seeking Adolescents," *Journal of Pediatric Psychology* 32, no. 1 (2007): 95–105.

18   Veerle Decaluwe and Caroline Braet, "Prevalence of Binge-Eating Disorder in Obese Children and Adolescents Seeking Weight-Loss Treatment," *International Journal of Obesity and Related Metabolic Disorders* 27, no. 3 (2003): 404–09.

19 Isnard Pascale, Gregory Michel, Marie-Laure Frelut, Gilbert Vila, Bruno Falissard, Wadih Naja, Jean Navarro, and Marie-Christine Mouren-Simeoni, "Binge Eating and Psychopathology in Severely Obese Adolescents," *International Journal of Eating Disorders* 34, no. 2 (2003): 235–43.

20 Steven L. Gortmaker, Aviva Must, James M. Perrin, Arthur M. Sobol, and William H. Dietz, "Social and Economic Consequences of Overweight in Adolescence and Young Adulthood," *New England Journal of Medicine* 329, no. 14 (1993): 1008–12.

21 Helen Canning and Jean Mayer, "Obesity—Its Possible Effect on College Acceptance," *New England Journal of Medicine* 275 (1966): 1172–74.

22 Robert Crosnoe, "Gender, Obesity, and Education," *Sociology of Education* 80 (2007): 241–60.

23 Charles A. Register and Donald R. Williams, "Wage Effects of Obesity Among Young Workers," *Social Science Quarterly* 71 (1990): 130–41.

24 Lesleyann Coker, "Jenny Kirk on Figure Skating's Eating Disorder Epidemic," Huffington Post, January 20, 2010.

25 Craig Johnson, Pauline S. Powers, and Randy Dick, "Athletes and Eating Disorders: The National Collegiate Athletic Association Study," *International Journal of Eating Disorders* 26, no. 2 (1999): 179–88.

26 Jill M. Holm-Denoma, Vanessa Scaringi, Kathryn H. Gordon, Kimberly A. Van Orden, and Thomas E. Joiner Jr, "Eating Disorder Symptoms Among Undergraduate Varsity Athletes, Club Athletes, Independent Exercisers, and Nonexercisers," *International Journal of Eating Disorders* 42, no. 1 (2009): 47–53.

27 Julie A. Hobart and Douglas R. Smucker, "The Female Athlete Triad," *American Family Physician* 61 (2000): 3357–64.

28 Ron A. Thompson and Roberta T. Sherman, *Eating Disorders in Sport* (New York: Routledge, 2010), 205.

CHAPTER 3: TRANSITION TO INDEPENDENCE

1 Pamela K. Keel, David J. Dorer, Kamryn T. Eddy, Debra L. Franko, Dana L. Charatan, and David B. Herzog, "Predictors of Mortality in Eating Disorders," *Archives of General Psychiatry* 60 (2003): 179–83.

2   National Institutes of Mental Health, "Anorexia Nervosa," http://www.nimh.nih.gov/health/publications/eating-disorders/anorexia-nervosa.shtml.

3   National Institutes of Mental Health, "Bulimia Nervosa," http://www.nimh.nih.gov/health/publications/eating-disorders/bulimia-nervosa.shtml.

4   American Psychiatric Association. *Diagnostic and Statistical Manual of Mental Disorders: Fourth Edition Text Revision* (Washington, DC: American Psychiatric Press, 2000).

5   James I. Hudson, Eva Hiripi, Harrison G. Pope Jr., and Ronald C. Kessler, "The Prevalence and Correlates of Eating Disorders in the National Comorbidity Survey Replication," *Biological Psychiatry* 61 (2007): 348–58.

6   Eric C. Stice, Nathan Marti, Heather Shaw, and Maryanne Jaconis, "An 8-Year Longitudinal Study of the Natural History of Threshold, Subthreshold, and Partial Eating Disorders from a Community Sample of Adolescents," *Journal of Abnormal Psychology* 118, no. 3 (2009): 587–97.

7   Kelly C. Berg, Patricia Frazier, and Laura Sherr, "Change in Eating Disorder Attitudes and Behavior in College Women: Prevalence and Predictors," *Eating Behaviors* 10, no. 3 (2009): 137–42.

8   Dean D. Krahn, Candace L. Kurth, Edith Gomberg, and Adam Drewnowski, "Pathological Dieting and Alcohol Use in College Women—a Continuum of Behaviors," *Eating Behaviors* 6, no. 1 (2005): 43–52.

9   Anne M. Prouty, Howard O. Protinsky, and Donna Canady, "College Women: Eating Behaviors and Help-Seeking Preferences," *Adolescence* 37, no. 146 (2002): 353–63.

10   Ruth H. Striegel-Moore and Cynthia M. Bulik, "Risk Factors for Eating Disorders," *American Psychologist* 62, no. 3 (2007): 181–98.

11   Suzanne E. Mazzeo and Cynthia M. Bulik, "Environmental and Genetic Risk Factors for Eating Disorders: What the Clinician Needs to Know," *Child and Adolescent Psychiatric Clinics of North America* 18 (2009): 67–82.

12   Sherrie Selwyn Delinsky and G. Terrence Wilson, "Weight Gain, Dietary Restraint, and Disordered Eating in the Freshman Year of College," *Eating Behaviors* 9, no. 1 (2008): 82–90.

13   Jill M. Holm-Denoma, Thomas E. Joiner, Kathleen D. Vohs, and Todd F. Heatherton, "The 'Freshman Fifteen' (The 'Freshman

Five' Actually): Predictors and Possible Explanations," *Health Psychology* 27, no. 1, Supplement (2008): S3–9.

14 James E. Gangwisch, Dolores Malaspina, Bernadette Boden-Albala, and Steven B. Heymsfield, "Inadequate Sleep as a Risk Factor for Obesity: Analysis of the NHANES I," *Sleep* 28, no. 10 (2005): 1289–96.

15 Ibid.

16 "Survey of College Alcohol Norms and Behavior," ed. Higher Education Center for Alcohol and Other Drug Prevention: National Institute on Alcohol Abuse and Alcoholism, http://www2.edc.org/snmrp/pr000908.html (2000).

17 Sarah Kershaw, "Starving Themselves, Cocktail in Hand," *New York Times*, March 2, 2008.

18 Mildred Maxwell, "Pathway to Awareness in College Eating (PACE)," http://www.pace.unc.edu/.

19 Frank Bruni, *Born Round: The Secret History of a Full Time Eater* (New York: Penguin Press, 2009), 89.

20 SM Strong, Donald A. Williamson, Richard G. Netemeyer, and James H. Geer, "Eating Disorder Symptoms and Concerns About Body Differ as a Function of Gender and Sexual Orientation," *Journal of Social and Clinical Psychology* 19 (2000): 240–55.

21 Christine Yelland and Marika Tiggemann, "Muscularity and the Gay Ideal: Body Dissatisfaction and Disordered Eating in Homosexual Men," *Eating Behaviors* 4, no. 2 (2003): 107–16.

22 Harm J. Hospers and Anita Jansen, "Why Homosexuality Is a Risk Factor for Eating Disorders in Males," *Journal of Social and Clinical Psychology* 24 (2005): 1188–1201.

23 Michael D. Siever, "Sexual Orientation and Gender as Factors in Socioculturally Acquired Vulnerability to Body Dissatisfaction and Eating Disorders," *Journal of Consulting and Clinical Psychology* 62, no. 2 (1994): 252–60.

24 Tamara L. Share and Laurie B. Mintz, "Differences between Lesbians and Heterosexual Women in Disordered Eating and Related Attitudes," *Journal of Homosexuality* 42, no. 4 (2002): 89–106.

25 Susan E. Beren, Helen A. Hayden, Denise E. Wilfley, and Carlos M. Grilo, "The Influence of Sexual Orientation on Body Dissatisfaction in Adult Men and Women," *International Journal of Eating Disorders* 20, no. 2 (1996): 135–41.

26   Lars Wichstrom, "Sexual Orientation as a Risk Factor for
     Bulimic Symptoms," *International Journal of Eating Disorders*
     39, no. 6 (2006): 448–53.
27   Matthew B. Feldman and Ilan H. Meyer, "Eating Disorders in
     Diverse Lesbian, Gay, and Bisexual Populations," *International
     Journal of Eating Disorders* 40, no. 3 (2007): 218–26.
28   Mae Lynn Reyes-Rodriguez, Margaret Sala, Ann Von Holle,
     Claudia Unikel, Cynthia M. Bulik, Luis Camara-Fuentes, and
     Alba Suarez-Torres, "A Description of Disordered Eating
     Behaviors in Latino Males," *Journal of American College Health*
     59, no. 4 (2011): 266–72.
29   Maxwell, "Pathway to Awareness in College Eating."
30   Delta Delta Delta, "Reflections Body Image Program," http://
     www.reflectionsprogram.org.

CHAPTER 4: MARRIAGE AND FAMILY . . . OR NOT!

 1   Ivanka Prichard and Marika Tiggemann, "Unveiled: Pre-
     Wedding Weight Concerns and Health and Beauty Plans of
     Australian Brides," *Journal of Health Psychology* 14, no. 7 (2009):
     1027–35.
 2   Susan L. Averett, Asia Sikora, and Laura M. Argys, "For Better
     or Worse: Relationship Status and Body Mass Index," *Economics
     and Human Biology* 6, no. 3 (2008): 330–49.
 3   Tobias Greitemeyer, "Stereotypes of Singles: Are Singles What
     We Think?" *European Journal of Social Psychology* 39, no. 3
     (2009): 368–83.
 4   Phillipa Hay, "The Epidemiology of Eating Disorder Behaviors:
     An Australian Community-Based Survey," *International Journal
     of Eating Disorders* 23, no. 4 (1998): 371–82.
 5   Pamela K. Keel, Mark G. Baxter, Todd F. Heatherton, and
     Thomas E. Joiner Jr., "A 20-Year Longitudinal Study of Body
     Weight, Dieting, and Eating Disorder Symptoms," *Journal of
     Abnormal Psychology* 116, no. 2 (2007): 422–32.
 6   Frank Stafford, "Exactly How Much Housework Does a Husband
     Create?" University of Michigan Institute for Social Research,
     http://ns.umich.edu/htdocs/releases/story.php?id=6452.
 7   National Heart Lung and Blood Institute, "BMI Calculator,"
     http://www.nhlbisupport.com/bmi/.

8   Institute of Medicine, "Weight Gain During Pregnancy: Reexamining the Guidelines," (Washington, DC: National Academies Press, 2009).

9   Cynthia M. Bulik, Ann Von Holle, Robert M. Hamer, Cecilie Knoph Berg, Leila Torgersen, Per Magnus, Camilla Stoltenberg, Anna-Maria Siega-Riz, Patrick Sullivan, and Ted Reichborn-Kjennerud, "Patterns of Remission, Continuation and Incidence of Broadly Defined Eating Disorders During Early Pregnancy in the Norwegian Mother and Child Cohort Study (Moba)," *Psychological Medicine* 37, no. 8 (2007): 1109–18.

10 Samantha Meltzer-Brody, Stephanie Zerwas, Jane Leserman, Ann Von Holle, Taylor Regis, and Cynthia M. Bulik, "Eating Disorders in Women with Perinatal Depression," *Journal of Women's Health* 20, no. 6 (2011): 863–70.

11 International Labour Organization, "Conditions of Work and Employment Programme," 2010, http://www.ilo.org/public/ english/protection/condtrav/family/reconcilwf/specialleave.htm.

12 United Nations Statistics Division, "Statistics and Indicators on Women and Men," 2010, http://unstats.un.org/unsd/demo- graphic/products/indwm/ww2005/tab5c.htm.

13 Kathryn A. Lee, Mary Ellen Zaffke, and Geoffrey McEnany, "Parity and Sleep Patterns During and after Pregnancy," *Obstetrics and Gynecology* 95, no. 1 (2000): 14–18.

14 Annette M. Swain, Michael W. O'Hara, Kathleen R. Starr, and Laura L. Gorman, "A Prospective Study of Sleep, Mood, and Cognitive Function in Postpartum and Nonpostpartum Women," *Obstetrics and Gynecology* 90, no. 3 (1997): 381–86.

15 Claire Mysko and Magali Amadei, *Does This Pregnancy Make Me Look Fat?* (Deerfield Beach, FL: Health Communications Inc., 2009).

16 Ruowei Li, Natalie Darling, Emmanuel Maurice, Lawrence Barker, and Laurence M. Grummer-Strawn, "Breastfeeding Rates in the United States by Characteristics of the Child, Mother, or Family: The 2002 National Immunization Survey," *Pediatrics* 115, no. 1 (2005): e31–7.

17 Britt Lande, Lene F. Andersen, Anne Baerug, Kerstin U. Trygg, K. Lund-Larsen, Marit B. Veierod, and Gunn-Elin Bjorneboe, "Infant Feeding Practices and Associated Factors in the First Six Months of Life: The Norwegian Infant Nutrition Survey," *Acta Paediatrica* 92, no. 2 (2003): 152–61.

18 Jennifer L. Baker, Michael Gamborg, Berit L. Heitmann, Lauren Lissner, Thorkild I. Sorensen, and Kathleen M. Rasmussen, "Breastfeeding Reduces Postpartum Weight Retention," *American Journal of Clinical Nutrition* 88, no. 6 (2008): 1543–51.

19 Louise Story, "Many Women at Elite Colleges Set Career Path to Motherhood," *New York Times*, September 20, 2005.

20 Belkin, Lisa. "The Opt-Out Revolution," *New York Times*, October 26, 2003, http://www.nytimes.com/200310/26/magazine/26WOMEN.html.

CHAPTER 5: THE SANDWICH GENERATION

1 Judith Rodin, Lisa Silberstein, and Ruth Striegel-Moore, "Women and Weight: A Normative Discontent," in *Psychology and Gender: Nebraska Symposium on Motivation*, ed. T.B. Sonderegger (Lincoln: University of Nebraska Press, 1985), 267–307.

2 Margaret A. McDowell, Cheryl D. Fryar, Cynthia L. Ogden, and Katherine M. Flegal, "Anthropometric Reference Data for Children and Adults: United States, 2003–2006," U.S. Department of Health and Human Services, Centers for Disease Control and Prevention, National Center for Health Statistics, 2008.

3 David B. Sarwer, Thomas A. Wadden, and Linton A. Whitaker, "An Investigation of Changes in Body Image Following Cosmetic Surgery," *Plastic and Reconstructive Surgery* 109, no. 1 (2002): 363–69; discussion 70–71.

4 National Institute of Diabetes and Digestive and Kidney Disease, "Longitudinal Assessment of Bariatric Surgery (Labs)," http://www.win.niddk.nih.gov/publications/labs.htm#howmany.

5 Tara Parker-Pope, "Spending Less on Plastic Surgery," *New York Times*, March 9, 2010.

6 Lynn Nonnemaker, "Women Physicians in Academic Medicine: New Insights from Cohort Studies," *New England Journal of Medicine* 342, no. 6 (2000): 399–405.

CHAPTER 6: THE AARP YEARS

1   Nora Ephron, *I Feel Bad About My Neck and Other Thoughts About Being a Woman* (New York: Knopf, 2006).

2   Sara Wilcox, "Age and Gender in Relation to Body Attitudes: Is There a Double Standard of Aging?" *Psychology of Women Quarterly* 21 (1997): 549–65.

3   Laura Hurd Clarke, "Older Women's Bodies and the Self: The Construction of Identity in Later Life," *Canadian Review of Sociology and Anthropology* 38 (2001): 441–64.

4   Susan Krauss Whitbourne and Karyn M. Skultety, "Body Image Development: Adulthood and Aging," in *Body Image*, eds. Thomas F. Cash and Thomas Pruzinsky (New York: Guilford Press, 2002), 83–90.

5   Marika Tiggemann, "Body Image Across the Adult Life Span: Stability and Change," *Body Image* 1, no. 1 (2004): 29–41.

6   John Cloud, "Joan Rivers' Cure: Will Plastic Surgery Make You Happier?" *Time*, January 30, 2009.

CHAPTER 7: AWARENESS

1   Alfred C. Kinsey, Wardell B. Pomeroy, and Clyde E. Martin, *Sexual Behavior in the Human Male* (Philadelphia: W. B. Saunders, 1948).

2   Rajeev Syal, "Women Fret About Their Bodies Every 15 Minutes," *Sunday Times*, April 11, 2006.

CHAPTER 8: CUES AND TRIGGERS: RECOGNIZING MEMES

1   Frances A. Carter, Cynthia M. Bulik, Rachel H. Lawson, Patrick F. Sullivan, and Jennifer S. Wilson, "Effect of Mood and Food Cues on Body Image in Women with Bulimia and Controls," *International Journal of Eating Disorders* 20, no. 1 (1996): 65–76.

2   Suzanne E. Mazzeo, Sara E. Trace, Karen S. Mitchell, and Rachel W. Gow, "Effects of a Reality TV Cosmetic Surgery Makeover Program on Eating Disordered Attitudes and Behaviors," *Eating Behaviors* 8, no. 3 (2007): 390–97.

3   Sherry L. Turner, Heather Hamilton, Meija Jacobs, Laurie M. Angood, and Deanne H. Dwyer, "The Influence of Fashion Magazines on the Body Image Satisfaction of College Women: An Exploratory Analysis," *Adolescence* 32, no. 127 (1997): 603–14.

4   Michael P. Levine and Linda Smolak, "Media as a Context for the Development of Disordered Eating," in *The Developmental Psychopathology of Eating Disorders: Implications for Research Prevention and Treatment*, eds. Linda Smolak, Michael P. Levine, and Ruth Striegel-Moore (Mahwah, NJ: Erlbaum, 1996), 235–57.

5   Charlie Greer, "What Are You Thinking? (Part Deux)," http://www.hvacprofitboosters.com/Tips/Tip_Archive/tip_archive7.html.

CHAPTER 10: YOUR INNER COACH

1   Sarah Hall, "Tyra Pounds Tabloids Over 'Fat' Photos," E! Online, http://www.eonline.com/uberblog/b54313_tyra_pounds_tabloids_over_fat_photos.html.

2   Tim Crothers, *The Man Watching* (Ann Arbor, MI: Sports Media Group, 2006), 77.

CHAPTER 11: PROTECTING THE NEXT GENERATION

1   Molinary, *Hijas Americanas*, p. 47.

2   Karen Springen, "10 Tips to Teach Your Daughter About a Healthy Relationship with Food," iVillage, http://www.ivillage.com/dying-be-thin/4-a-152420?p=2#ixzzow6kx9pLY.

3   Pregnancy Rx, "Fetal Development: Your First Trimester," http://pregnancyrx.com/fetal_development_first_trimester.php.

4   Palo Alto Medical Foundation, "Puberty Changes for Females," http://www.pamf.org/teen/health/puberty/girlschanges.html#Growing!

5   Mickey T. Trockel, Michael D. Barnes, and Dennis L. Egget, "Health-Related Variables and Academic Performance Among First-Year College Students: Implications for Sleep and Other Behaviors," *Journal of American College Health* 49, no. 3 (2000): 125–31.

6   David Benton and Pearl Y. Parker, "Breakfast, Blood Glucose, and Cognition," *American Journal of Clinical Nutrition* 67, no. 4 (1998): 772S–78S.

7   Anna Keski-Rahkonen, Jaakko Kaprio, Aila Rissanen, Matti Virkkunen, and Richard J. Rose, "Breakfast Skipping and Health-Compromising Behaviors in Adolescents and Adults," *European Journal of Clinical Nutrition* 57, no. 7 (2003): 842–53.

Index

A NOTE ON THE AUTHOR

Cynthia M. Bulik, Ph.D., F.A.E.D., is the Distinguished
Professor of Eating Disorders in the department of psychiatry
at the University of North Carolina at Chapel Hill, where she
is also professor of nutrition in the Gillings School of Global
Public Health and the director of the UNC Eating Disorders
Program.

A clinical psychologist by training, Dr. Bulik has been
conducting research and treating individuals with eating
disorders for more than two decades. She received her B.A.
from the University of Notre Dame and her M.A. and Ph.D.
from the University of California at Berkeley. She completed
internships and postdoctoral fellowships at Western Psychiatric
Institute and Clinic in Pittsburgh. She developed outpatient,
day-patient, and inpatient services for eating disorders both in
New Zealand and in the United States.

Her research has included treatment, laboratory, epidemio-
logical, twin, and molecular genetic studies of eating disorders
and body-weight regulation. She also develops innovative means
of integrating technology into treatment for eating disorders
and obesity. She has active research collaborations throughout
the United States and in nineteen countries around the world.

Dr. Bulik has written more than four hundred scientific
papers and chapters on eating disorders and is author of *Eating*

Disorders: Detection and Treatment (Dunmore), *Runaway Eating* (Rodale), *Crave: Why You Binge Eat and How to Stop* (Walker), and *Abnormal Psychology* (Prentice Hall).

She is a recipient of the Eating Disorders Coalition Research Award, the Academy for Eating Disorders Leadership Award for Research, the Price Family National Eating Disorders Association Research Award, the Women's Leadership Council Faculty-to-Faculty Mentorship Award, and the Academy for Eating Disorders Meehan-Hartley Advocacy Award. She is a past president of the Academy for Eating Disorders, past vice president of the Eating Disorders Coalition, and past associate editor of the International Journal of Eating Disorders. Dr. Bulik holds the first endowed professorship in eating disorders in the United States. She happily married with three children and is also a United States Figure Skating gold medalist in ice dancing.